THE BEGINNING OF

CHINA'S NATIONAL RENEWAL

www.royalcollins.com

THE BEGINNING OF CHINA'S NATIONAL RENEWAL

A Century of the Communist Party of China

SHAO WEIZHENG & LIU XIAOBAO

RC

Books Beyond Boundaries

ROYAL COLLINS

The Beginning of China's National Renewal:
A Century of the Communist Party of China

Shao Weizheng & Liu Xiaobao

First published in 2021 by Royal Collins Publishing Group Inc.
Groupe Publication Royal Collins Inc.
BKM Royalcollins Publishers Private Limited

Headquarters: 550-555 boul. René-Lévesque O Montréal (Québec) H2Z1B1 Canada
India office: 805 Hemkunt House, 8th Floor, Rajendra Place, New Delhi 110 008

ISBN: 978-1-4878-0888-4

To find out more about our publications, please visit www.royalcollins.com.

We are grateful for the financial assistance of B&R Book Program in the publication of this book.

Preface

THE WHEEL OF HISTORY KEEPS turning. As we move forward into 2021, socialist China is reaching a historic crossroads in its pursuit of the 'Two Centenary Goals.'

General Secretary Xi Jinping has repeatedly emphasized that even as we make progress towards the future, we must not forget the road we have walked. No matter how far we go, or how dazzling a future we reach, we must not forget the past, nor why we chose to set out in the first place. As we face the future and its challenges, the Party must not forget its initial goals, even as we move forward.

The founding of the Communist Party of China (CPC) was the beginning of a century of rejuvenation for the Chinese nation. Looking back on the history of the Party thus enables us to gain a better understanding of the present, which places the future within our grasp. It is for precisely this reason that when we study Party history, we firstly go back to the very start and learn about the history of the founding of the CPC. Only by doing this will we truly be able to understand why the Party was founded, and what its original intentions were. It is the only way to truly cherish the hard-won successes of today, and be more determined to move towards a future that is full of challenges.

In conceptualizing and writing this book, *The Beginning of China's National Renewal: A Century of the Communist Party of China*, our purpose was to travel back through time – through the 100 years since the Party's founding – to look at the very first steps that were taken. We sought to paint a concise, lively, and vivid portrait of the historical backdrop of a century ago, and to expound the details of the Party's founding. With an understanding of the initial aims and mission of the CPC, we can then forge forward into the future from a fresh historic starting point.

History is a reflection of the development process and objective laws of all things, but progress is often made via a series of twists and turns. Before we can truly understand the road that we have traveled, we need to become fully cognizant of the historical background, the harrowing struggles, the difficult choices made, and the hard work put in. The same is true for the CPC. After a long and difficult period of struggle and upheaval, it has finally become the choice of the people and of history. In this sense, the birth of the CPC was the inevitable result of the economic and political development of modern China. The revolutionary struggle of modern China objectively required its presence, and it is the product of Marxism-Leninism and the Chinese labor movement combined.

Much has already been written about the history of the founding of the CPC, and every book on the topic has its own merits. This one seeks to situate the founding of the CPC accurately within its historical context. It details the background of the Party, analyzes the key elements of its founding, and looks back on its activities, ultimately arriving at an integrated analysis of the gradual process of its founding. To this end, three fundamental concepts underpin the text.

The first is that history is a dynamic, developmental process. We wish to highlight that the founding of the Party was a process, not a product of happy chance. The CPC was a historical inevitability – the product of China's struggle, the call of the times, and the choices of the people. Its founding was not carried out independently by a few founding individuals, but rather was a result of the bold choices of a group of trailblazing progressive elements who made complex explorations, breakthroughs, and innovations. Establishing the Party was not accomplished in one go, by a general meeting or a resolution. Rather, the process involved allowing the initial intentions to sprout, namely seeking truth, debating key principles, choosing paths, adjusting strategies, and establishing goals. The supposed specific 'starting point' of the Party is simply a dividing line established by later historians for ease of understanding. The truth is that history is a dialectical process that moves from quantitative change to qualitative change.

The second grounding concept of this book is that the founding of the Party was a response to the call of the times – a requirement of national rejuvenation, and a necessity for historical progress. We wish to emphasize that the founding of the Party was a response to the contemporary needs of that period, and that it has a national and inevitable character. We take a broad view of the historical background, outlining the unique aspects of the CPC's founding from multiple perspectives, and diving deeply into the its historical inevitability.

The third concept is that the importance of history lies in the way it combs through, analyzes, and interprets the past and the present. We situate the founding of the CPC in the context of the wave of revolution that was sweeping the globe at the time, and interpret it in light of the century of rejuvenation that the Chinese nation is currently experiencing. We highlight the twisting path that our revolutionary ancestors followed as well as their fighting spirit in the difficult early days of exploration, and provide an in-depth exploration of their original mission. Finally, we comprehensively evaluate the critical importance of the CPC's founding to the noble cause of the rejuvenation of the Chinese nation.

From the macro perspective of the great cause of Chinese national rejuvenation and the 100th anniversary of the founding of the CPC, this book traces the arduous course of its founding 100 years ago. It lays out the historical context of the founding, analyzes and interprets its historical background and inevitability, and fully reveals its starring role in and far-reaching significance for the cause of Chinese national rejuvenation.

It is hard to know how difficult something is until one has done it. Bringing the reader back to that moment in history is even harder. The first difficulty lies in the fact that today, the standard statement is "only the CPC can save China," whereas at the time, people were still feeling about in the dark, searching for the right way forward. It required a difficult journey.

Secondly, people at the time were in the midst of a complex historical moment. They were restricted and controlled by both subjective and objective conditions, and various internal and external forces competed, compromised, and even colluded to affect the historical figures of the time. They faced a huge variety of tests and choices as to what to do and where to go. As the great Party historian Hu Sheng wrote, "It was not easy at the time for Chinese people to have a concrete, genuine understanding of the world around them as well as China's place within that world. It was not just a matter of acknowledging the truth of what had already happened, but of having the courage to break the mold and create a new situation. The latter was far harder."[1]

Thirdly, there was a need to maintain the right direction in practice, to constantly be on the lookout to correct mistakes, to perfect countermeasures, and to solve concrete problems. This was hardly plain sailing. Of course, we cannot return to the past to live through those simultaneously glorious and painful days firsthand. However, what we *can* do is painstakingly dig out the historical details, describe and reconstruct the historical environment, and analyze the causes and consequences of various events. In doing so, we bring readers closer to history and allow them to experience both the difficulties and the original mission of those founders.

Based on the above considerations, this book is centered on the four major modules set out by the Party, namely its historical background, how its foundation came about, the organization and preparation, and finally the improvement and enhancement. The book has eight parts and 34 subsections. The first and second parts focus on the historical background and societal basis of the emergence of the CPC. The third and fourth parts describe how the guiding ideology of the CPC was established, how the development of the labor movement formed the foundation of the Party, and how progressive elements bridged Marxism and the Chinese labor movement, creating a preliminary combination. The fifth and sixth parts reflect the organization and preparation that went into the founding of the Party, from the establishment of early regional organizations to the formal creation of the centralized national CPC. The seventh and eight parts consider the full-scale push of the actual revolutionary movement led by the Party, the formulation of the Party Constitution, the launch of the democratic revolutionary program, and the completion of the founding mission.

This book puts historical facts before argumentation, and combines academic theory with popular ideas. It is aimed at both Party members and ordinary people, and strives to combine history and theory. We hope to inspire

1. Hu, Sheng. *From the Opium War to the May Fourth Movement.* People's Publishing House, 2010, p. 3.

thinking, to strike a balance between depth and breadth, and to satisfy both elevated and popular tastes. Lastly, we hope that this book fully demonstrates how the Party's history can be used as a political and educational guide, and that readers will find its language interesting and readable.

On the occasion of the 100th anniversary of the founding of the CPC, it is not only our responsibility and mission as workers who study Party history to publish this book, but also a supreme honor. We hope that the pages that follow will provide an intellectual yet readable history of the Party, which will serve 'Four Histories' education. We hope that our readers will enjoy this 'birthday gift' to the Party.

Table of Contents

THE BEGINNING OF
CHINA'S NATIONAL RENEWAL

PART 1

The Fall of Chinese Civilization:

From an Independent Sovereignty to a Semi-Colonial and Semi-Feudal State

China is a major Eastern nation with a long and storied history. As an ancient civilization with an impressive past, it has made outstanding contributions to the development of mankind. However, after the first Opium War in 1840, China was shattered, and lives were lost due to the barbaric invasions of Western powers and the corruption of feudal rule. The Chinese people were beaten down and forced to bear great humiliation. The nation suffered in an unprecedented way, and society was gradually reduced to a semi-colonial, semi-feudal state.

1

A BROKEN EMPIRE

During the feudal era, especially in the Tang and Song Dynasties, China had a lot of contact with foreign countries. Trade was highly developed and reciprocal. For instance, there was the famous Silk Road in the Tang Dynasty, while Song Dynasty trading was centered in Guangzhou. China was a nation that set great store by ceremony and propriety, and it was both open and inclusive. There was a culture of hospitality and friendliness to merchants and people from all over the world, without ethnic prejudice. This aspect of its history is one that Chinese people still speak of with pride and pleasure today.

However, when we read modern history, a commonly agreed-upon point is that China's isolation led to regression, which in turn led to passivity in the face of external attack. Those defeats then led to the century of humiliation, and thence to democratic revolution. As such, it is clear that isolation, or cutting off the country from the outside world, was the logical starting point and the historical root of modern China's century of humiliation. So what made a vast and inclusive country into a self-isolated, 'closed' one?

If we consider internal reasons, the chief one is conservative ideology. Since Qin Shihuang – the first emperor, who united China – the emperors considered themselves masters of all under heaven. As the saying goes, "There is no land under the skies that does not belong to the emperor; there is no man on earth who is not his subject." China was the 'Kingdom of Heaven,' and the emperor was the 'Son of Heaven,' who held sole dominion over all. Therefore, the Emperor of China was the supreme ruler of all people, and no nation could have dealt with China on an equal footing. No individual could hope to be the equal of the Emperor.

This was the foundational belief of the tributary system under which Chinese feudal rulers handled their foreign relations. In the past, the imperial courts had no ministry of foreign affairs, let alone a specific department for foreign trade. Any official foreign exchanges or trade were handled by the Ministry of Rites, and were seen as a matter of a vassal state paying 'tribute' to the sovereign country.

From an objective point of view, this conservatism was related to the vastness of China's geography, its abundance of resources, and the resulting self-sufficiency. During the Ming Dynasty, Matteo Ricci pointed out in his *Reading Notes on China* that "within her boundaries are all that is necessary for Man's sustenance, and there are many other delightful things besides. China not only has no need to beg other countries for assistance: she has enough surplus to meet the needs of neighboring and faraway countries besides, and these countries have always hoped to visit and tour China." He also pointed out that "the Chinese prefer to be self-sufficient, rather than to rely on imports. Whatever is needed for sustenance they prefer to produce themselves."[1]

It is worth noting that Chinese people in the past seemed to have had a sort of self-contradictory psychological belief. On the one hand, they were arrogant, conservative, and inward-looking. They believed in China's overwhelming strength and dominance, but had no desire to conquer and occupy small neighboring countries. China believed that whether it actually sought to conquer another land or not, it would be a vassal state anyway. On the other hand, the Chinese people also felt that China's vast territory contained all that they needed, and hence had no desire to expand and grow its market. There was a sense that even if other lands did not pay tribute, the Chinese people would lead good lives anyway.

With regard to this, Matteo Ricci pointed out that "in such a country, with its practically infinite population, limitless territory, and exceedingly rich resources – not to mention its well-equipped army and navy – it would be easy to invade neighboring territories, but China's Emperor and people have never thought of starting a war of conquest. They are content with what they have, and have no ambitions of conquest. In this respect, they are very different from

1. Ricci, Matteo. *Matteo Ricci: Reading Notes on China (Vol. 1).* Translated by He Gaoji, Wang Zunzhong, and Li Shen. The Commercial Press, China Travel and Tourism Press, 2017, p. 6.

the Europeans, who are typically dissatisfied with their own government and seek what others possess."[1]

During the 300 years from the start of the Ming Dynasty to the Qing Dynasty, China mainly pursued an isolationist policy in its foreign trade. There was a policy that stated that Chinese nationals were not allowed to leave; China prohibited its own people from going to sea and trading with foreign nations. Furthermore, outsiders were kept out; China tightly restricted the entry of foreigners who were seeking to trade. These policies were unproblematic while China remained dominant, but it would soon become obvious that this was a strategic mistake, as the rest of the world was rapidly on the rise.

Unfortunately, in the 17th and 18th centuries, the global situation went through a number of revolutionary changes, including the emergence of disruptive new technologies. This caused an unprecedented shift in the balance of power between East and West.

In 1640 – the Year of the Dragon in the Chinese lunar calendar, and the 13th year of the reign of the Ming Emperor Chongzhen – the bourgeois revolution began in England. This broke the yoke of feudalism and replaced it with a capitalist system of production. In 1760 – also a Year of the Dragon, and the 25th year of the reign of the Qing Emperor Qianlong – Britain began its Industrial Revolution, transitioning from small-scale workshops based on manual labor to large-scale production powered by machines. Man's power over nature was further fueled by several developments: the application of chemistry to industry and agriculture, the boom in steamships, the development of railroads, the use of the telegraph, the navigation and connection of waterways, and the development of whole continents. Two hundred years after the British bourgeois revolution, Western capitalist nations were rapidly expanding their productive capacity through frenzied, rapacious plunder of foreign territories as well as a cruel, unfeeling accumulation of capital.

Even as the West set off on its campaign of overseas colonization, the emperors of the Qing Dynasty continued to bury their heads in the sand. They were unable to acknowledge the changes in the global situation, and thus not only refused to keep up with the changing tides, but also adopted even stricter

1. Ricci, Matteo. *Matteo Ricci: Reading Notes on China (Vol. 1)*. Translated by He Gaoji, Wang Zunzhong, and Li Shen. The Commercial Press, China Travel and Tourism Press, 2017, p. 93.

regulations on foreign trade. Although Emperor Kangxi had opened up the sea routes, permitted foreign trade, and tolerated Western missionaries – after pacifying Taiwan, no less – this changed under Emperor Yongzheng, who began strictly controlling foreign trade and forbidding missionaries who were not from the inner court from entering China.

By 1757, in the reign of Emperor Qianlong, the Qing imperial court announced that all trade ports along the coast would be closed save for a portion of Guangzhou, which would remain open to foreign trade. Furthermore, detailed and strict restrictions were imposed on trading activities there. For instance, when foreign tradespeople arrived in Guangzhou, their business activities had to be transacted through local Chinese merchants, called *yanghang* (literally 'ocean traders' or 'foreign traders') who had been pre-authorized by the Qing government. Their daily activities were similarly restricted by the *yanghang*. During their time in Guangzhou, they could only live in establishments purpose-built for them, called 'Yi Houses' (literally, hotels designated solely for foreigners). They were not allowed to leave the Yi Houses, other than being allowed to visit designated places of leisure on designated days every month. They were not permitted to spend the winter in Guangzhou (in other words, they were allowed to enter between May and June, and were required to leave between September and October every year). Foreign businessmen were not allowed to bring their wives and children with them. They were not permitted to ride in sedan chairs like Chinese officials and gentlemen. They were not allowed to employ Chinese people, and Chinese people were not allowed to borrow capital from them. Of course, as a sovereign state, the Qing government had every right to make binding regulations on foreign trade, but its conservative views of foreign relations and its backward preconceptions of foreigners resulted in it isolating itself from the world, and should be taken as a warning to China today.

That said, having considered the chief internal reason, let us consider the external ones. From this point of view, the main reason for China's change from an inclusive nation to a 'closed' one was the aggressive encroachment of capitalist colonialism.

As the Renaissance deepened and expanded, the nations of Western Europe entered a capitalist period of resource acquisition and accumulation, in which they set out to all corners of the Earth on a mission of plunder, killing, invading, and colonizing. Against this backdrop, Ming and Qing Dynasty China was not spared either. In his 1910 book, *A Sketch of the Relations Between China and the Western World*, the American writer Chester Holcombe – a former US envoy to China – described the actions of the Westerners who went to China in the 16th and 17th centuries thus:

> "They endlessly harassed China's southern coastline, pillaging, destroying villages, killing tens or even hundreds of innocent people and children, and then 'peacefully' sailed away. Otherwise, they went further into the mainland, forced the Chinese people to build them forts, carried off Chinese women in the most beastly manner, robbed them of their property, and violated all the rules of humanity and civilization."[1]

In the face of these unwelcome visitors, the Chinese naturally sought to put safeguards in place, to defend against them. According to John Foster, "[This] led the Chinese authorities to stringent measures in the 17th century, which resulted in the closing of all ports except that of Canton [Guangzhou], and even at that port foreign intercourse was conducted under very onerous conditions."[2]

Thus, it was the combination of conservative and backward thinking from Chinese feudal rulers as well as brutal piracy and plunder from Western powers that led to China's long-term policy of isolation during the Ming and Qing Dynastics.

Under the influence of this policy, Chinese merchants could not take the initiative to seek overseas markets, which led to the slow development of Chinese craftmanship. Cultural exchange between the East and the West was not smooth, and this hindered China's development of modern science and technology. With regard to this, even Marx, who was far away in the Western hemisphere at the time, regretfully remarked on observing China's situation that "an empire accounting for almost a third of the world's population has failed to consider the nature of the times, and is content to remain as she is: artificially isolated from the world, and therefore doing her utmost to deceive herself with the illusory notion that China is perfect."[3]

1. Holcombe, Chester. *A Sketch of the Relations Between China and the Western World.*
2. Foster, John W. *American Diplomacy in the Orient.* pp. 6–7.
3. *The Collected Works of Marx and Engels, Vol. 1.* People's Publishing House, 1995, p. 716.

The nation that had the lion's share of Guangzhou's trade was Britain, which had already established a firm foothold in India and was seeking further access to the huge Chinese market. Due to Guangzhou's hot climate, it was difficult for Britain to push its woolen textiles, but Chinese goods – such as tea, porcelain, and silk – were popular luxuries in Britain. However, these Chinese specialties had to travel long distances to reach Guangzhou, coming from the Yangtze River Basin or even from the north of China, over the Wuling Mountains. This was not only time-consuming and laborious, but also made the goods more expensive due to the increased transportation costs. This led to trade between China and Britain being more favorable to China, and the British very much wanted to change this situation. They felt that the solution was to open trading ports further north of Guangzhou, at the mouth of the Yangtze, or even along the coast at the Bohai Bay. This way, woolen textiles could not only be marketed to the vast areas of northern China, where the weather was colder, but goods such as porcelain and tea could also be bought at lower prices.

In 1793 – the 58th year of the reign of the Qing Emperor Qianlong – Britain sent George Macartney as an envoy to China, heading a vast delegation that numbered more than 700 people, including astronomers, physicists, engineers, military officials, and soldiers. They carried with them the cutting edge technological achievements that Britain had accrued after the Industrial Revolution, including globes, telescopes, steam engines, cotton-spinning machinery, mortars, and rifles. These were meant as gifts, to be presented to Emperor Qianlong on the occasion of his 83rd birthday. The British were hoping to formally establish diplomatic relations with China, and to open bilateral trade.

Unfortunately, the imperial court of the Qing Dynasty was ignorant of the general state of the rest of the world, and still regarded itself as the 'Kingdom of Heaven,' seeing other countries as 'barbarous.' They denigrated the advanced scientific and technological achievements of the West as merely cunning tricks, and refused to take them seriously.

The ideological differences between China and Britain also focused – quite theatrically so – on questions of etiquette. According to the rules of the Qing government, and in accordance with traditional Chinese etiquette, foreign envoys had to kneel thrice before the emperor and kowtow nine times. Macartney refused to do this on the grounds that it was not in accordance with

British manners, and offensive to the dignity of the British Empire besides. Eventually, the two sides managed to reach a compromise, in which Emperor Qianlong received Macartney the way he would receive a tribute, and Macartney, in line with British etiquette, went down on one knee to present his credentials as an envoy. However, it still came down to a question of protocol, which led Emperor Qianlong to reject all of the delegation's requests for bilateral trade. Later, Macartney commented that "[t]he empire of China is an old, crazy, first-rate man-of-war... which a fortunate succession of able and vigilant officers has contrived to keep afloat for these hundred and fifty years past."[1]

As such, by the start of the 19th century, Western capitalism was already surging forward rapidly, carrying out a large-scale colonial expansion. At that point in time, China was in the late stages of feudalism. This, combined with its isolationist policy, caused Chinese society to become ever more ossified and conservative.

Britain did not give up hope of expanding bilateral trade. In 1816, it sent another delegation to China, headed this time by William Amherst. Emperor Jiaqing, like his father, still insisted on the British envoys kneeling thrice and kowtowing nine times. Amherst in turn insisted that he would only take off his hat and bow, so communication broke down before an accord could be reached.

In order to remedy its trade deficit with China, and after the failure of multiple attempts at diplomacy, Britain resorted to a more underhanded method: selling opium to China. Although the Qing government had already banned the importing of opium in 1799 (the fourth year of the reign of Emperor Jiaqing), the existence of corrupt officials and illegal traders meant that opium imports rose from about 400 crates in the first year of Emperor Qianlong's reign to approximately 4,000 by the first year of Emperor Jiaqing's reign, and thence to more than 30,000 crates per year by the 15th year of Emperor Daoguang's reign (1835). According to official British sources, in the year from July 1837 to June 1838, the total value of China's imports from Britain (including India) was 5.6 million pounds, of which opium accounted for 60% (3.4 million pounds). During the same period, China's exports to the UK were worth 3.1 million pounds, suggesting that China's trade deficit was 2.5 million pounds. That is to

1. He, Xinhua. *Showing Authority to the World: Diplomatic Etiquette and Its Reform in the Qing Dynasty*. Shanghai Academy of Social Sciences Press, 2011, p. 238.

say, in the normal course of trade, without opium, it would have been Britain that was in deficit to China, to the tune of over 900,000 pounds.[1]

Britain made huge profits from the opium trade, and turned its trade deficit with China into a surplus. The import of opium into China not only milked Chinese laborers of their hard-earned money and led to the outflow of cash, but also turned China into 'the sick man of Asia.'

In 1839, Lin Zexu launched his grand campaign against opium, seizing and destroying more than 2.3 million *jin* (approximately 1.15 million kilograms) of opium and destroying it at Humen. He mixed the opium with salt and lime in pits, and then flushed the residue into the sea over the course of 20 days, demonstrating the determination and resolution of the Chinese people in prohibiting the scourge.

From the Chinese point of view, the anti-opium campaign was a righteous one, but the British government and British opium traders saw it (wrongfully) as a serious threat to their interests. Thus, war was inevitable, and it changed China's destiny completely.

In June 1840, in order to protect the illegal opium trade and to forcibly open the Chinese market, Britain – the leading capitalist power in the West – started the Opium War in an act of aggression against China. They launched the 'Eastern Expeditionary Force' under the guise of protecting 'free and equal' trade.

Although the Qing army had the twin advantages of superiority in numbers and of fighting on its own territory, it was roundly defeated by the British army's 28 gunboats and a force of 15,000 men. The Qing troops lacked strength and fighting spirit. Lin Zexu, who had raised the banners of patriotism in in the war against opium, was criticized for having not handled the situation properly, and for having harmed the nation and its people. He was thus dismissed from his post and exiled to Xinjiang. In contrast, Qi Shan – a minister of the court who surrendered and sought a compromise – was considered by Emperor Daoguang to have defeated a hundred thousand men through mere words and pieces of paper.

Considering the decay and stupefaction of the Qing court at the time, was their defeat not thus inevitable?

---

1. Hu, Sheng. *From the Opium War to the May Fourth Movement.* People's Publishing House, 2010, p. 28.

On 29 August 1842, the Qing government signed a humiliating treaty alliance with Britain – the Treaty of Nanjing. In July and October 1843, they signed the Treaty of Humen and the General Regulations of Trade at the Five Ports as supplementary legislation. This was the first of the humiliating unequal treaties that China was subject to in modern history, and it set a precedent for legitimizing the plunder and enslavement of China by foreign forces through a 'legal' treaty:

- Hong Kong was ceded entirely to the British, giving them a colony that they had complete control over. This served as a stronghold, from which the British could push further into China, both economically and militarily.
- 21 million silver yuan were paid to the British as compensation, on the grounds that six million yuan were compensation for the opium that Lin Zexu had confiscated and destroyed in Guangzhou (note that in 1841, the British had already extorted six million yuan for the opium from Yishan, a minister of the time. Three million yuan were designated as repayment for money previously 'owed' to the British merchants in Guangzhou, and 12 million yuan were compensation for the military expenditure of the British army.
- The opening of Guangzhou, Fuzhou, Xiamen, Ningbo, and Shanghai as treaty ports enabled Britain to push its trade frontier from Guangzhou on the south coast to the lower reaches of the Yangtze River, and Shanghai changed from a small, little-known county to a new base for European and American trade with China.
- Tariffs were agreed upon and settled, causing China to lose her autonomy in setting tariff rates.
- British people who committed crimes in treaty ports were not to be dealt with by China, such that foreigners who committed crimes in China were nonetheless not subject to Chinese legal jurisdiction. This began a system of so-called 'consular jurisdiction,' which undermined China's judicial sovereignty.
- One 'official' British ship was permitted to berth at each treaty port, marking the first time in modern Chinese history that foreign military ships could freely enter China's territorial waters as well as inland rivers.

- The British and their families could rent land and build houses to live in within in the five treaty ports, thus giving rise to the so-called 'Concession' system.
- The Qing government would allow any benefits they extended to any particular country to be shared by the British, thus creating the one-sided so-called 'most-favored nation status.' Other powers soon followed suit and used this method to blackmail China into extending benefits to them as well.

Ironically, the door that Britain had failed to open with trade and diplomacy was instead opened with gunboats and warfare. The Qing government had arrogantly refused to open up on the grounds of not kowtowing to the external world, but it was eventually forced to do so anyway, through the humiliation of ceding land and paying reparations.

Thus, history proves several cold truths: Only through opening up can China integrate into the world. Only through integration can it sustain development. Only through development can it be invincible.

2

INVASION BY WESTERN POWERS

THE YEAR 1840 WAS AN important turning point in Chinese history. Its defeat in the First Opium War broke the myth that the Qing Empire was an 'Eastern power' to be reckoned with, and exposed the weakness of the Qing government. This created a kind of 'broken window' effect, in which other Western nations surged forward to launch conflict after conflict against China, pushing it gradually into the abyss of semi-colonization. The old China was seen as a fattened lamb, ripe for the slaughter.

As soon as the Treaty of Nanjing was signed, the American President of the time, John Tyler, sent special envoy Caleb Cushing to China. Caleb was the brother of John Cushing, a man who had smuggled opium into China for many years. In February 1844, Caleb Cushing arrived in Macau with three gunboats, using them as a threat to convince China to sign a "treaty of perpetual friendship and peace." The weakened and ineffectual Qing government lacked the motivation to push back against this, and had no choice but to send an imperial minister to Guangzhou to negotiate with Cushing. This minister was Qi Ying, who had signed the Treaty of Nanjing.

In July 1844, Qi Ying and Cushing signed the Treaty of Wangxia on the outskirts of Macau. Except for not ceding land or paying reparations, the treaty otherwise recognized the USA as enjoying all the same privileges as the British. In fact, some of its provisions were more specific than the British Treaty of Nanjing. They were thus more damaging to China's sovereignty. For instance:

- The tariff clauses in the Treaty of Nanjing used the term "impartial agreement." The Treaty of Wangxia, however, expressly stated that "the Consul of the USA must be consulted, and their consent sought." This established the system of "tariff agreements" in semi-colonial China.

- On the issue of consular jurisdiction, the Treaty of Nanjing only stated that British people who committed crimes at treaty ports were "not subject to Chinese legal jurisdiction." The Treaty of Wangxia made it clear that all criminal and civil cases involving Americans in China (not limited to treaty ports), regardless of whether the plaintiffs were Chinese or foreigners, were "not within the purview of Chinese officials," and could only be handled by American consular officers.
- On the issue of the sailing range of foreign military ships, the Treaty of Nanjing provided freedom of navigation in treaty ports. The Treaty of Wangxia, on the other hand, stipulated that "warship patrols will accompany trade to Chinese ports."[1]

As such, the Treaty of Wangxia between China and the USA became an exemplar for Western powers, who used it as a template when blackmailing China and making unequal treaties. "The USA and other nations must thank Britain for opening China to the world by concluding the Treaty of Nanjing," Cushing, who composed the treaty, triumphantly reported to the US State Department. "But now Britain and the rest of the world have America to thank for opening the door wider."[2]

This was what the daylight robbers called "honorable" logic and "experience" of sharing.

The ink had barely had time to dry on the Treaty of Wangxia when, just a month later, France came in like a greedy animal smelling blood. In August 1844, it followed suit and sent seven military ships to Macau, led by special envoys. In October of the same year, the Treaty of Whampoa was signed between China and France. As for the contents of the treaty, the court official Qi Ying reported to Emperor Daoguang that while "there are similarities and differences regarding the specific words and sentences, the gist is the same" as the Sino-British Treaty of Nanjing and the Sino-American Treaty of Wangxia.[3]

1. Hu, Sheng. *From the Opium War to the May Fourth Movement.* People's Publishing House, 2010, pp. 58–59.
2. Johnson, W. F. *A History of American Diplomacy.*
3. *The Daoguang Emperor's Foreign Affairs*, *Vol.* 5, p. 2879.

Furthermore, the weak, incompetent, and shameless Qing government still tried in vain to pass off such aggressive actions as "equal treatment for all," and tried to keep itself alive by offending no one. However, in doing so, it was merely inviting the wolves into the fold.

Thus, the history of China in the second half of the 19th century was a story of humiliation, bloodshed and tears.

In October 1856, in order to force open the Chinese market as well as to resolve their own domestic economic crisis, the British launched a sudden attack on Guangzhou under the pretext of the 'Yarrow' incident. Since this conflict was a continuation and expansion of the Opium War, it was called the Second Opium War. Furthermore, France and Britain formed an allied force to attack China a mere three months later, using the death of French missionary Auguste Chapdelaine (whose Chinese name was Ma Lai) as an excuse for war. After occupying Guangzhou, the British and French allied forces pushed northward along the coast. In May 1858, they captured the Dagu Estuary, occupied Tianjin, and threatened to attack Beijing. Under the guise of helping the Qing government "mediate" the conflict, but with the true purpose of supporting Western aggression and sharing the spoils, Russia and the USA sent warships to cheat and blackmail the Qing Dynasty. Helpless, the Qing government sent an imperial envoy to Tianjin to negotiate for peace.

The Second Opium War coincided with the upsurge of the Taiping Heavenly Kingdom – a peasants' rebellion that sought to tear down the decadent and corrupt rule of the Qing Dynasty. On the basis of the principle that foreign aggression can only be resisted if one's own house is first set in order, the feudal rulers of the Qing Dynasty always regarded the people of their own country as their biggest enemy. They hence adopted a policy of compromise with regard to the foreign invaders, and tried to avoid any expansion of the war that would be caused by the rupture of relations.

In short, the feudal rulers of the Qing Dynasty considered the demands made by foreign invaders – such as ceding land and making reparations – acceptable, since they did not attempt to overthrow the Qing Dynasty like the peasant uprising. Such foreign demands were not seen as fatal threats. Therefore, when a general proposed to reassign some of the troops that had been sent to the south to suppress the Taiping Kingdom, to resist the allied forces of Britain and France, the imperial court replied, "At this time, the Yue bandits [the Taiping rebels] have not yet been pacified and must still be suppressed by force. The troops must not be hastily withdrawn."[1]

On 26 and 27 June 1858, the Qing government was forced to sign the Treaty of Tianjin with Britain and France. This treaty stipulated that envoys from Britain and France would be resident in Beijing, and that 10 more cities – including Nanjing, Jiujiang, and Hankou – would be opened as treaty ports. The opium trade would be legalized. Britain would receive four million taels in reparations, and France would receive two million.

Enemies who are known should be feared, but an enemy who pretends to be a friend is more insidious.

Russia and the USA, who had claimed to be 'friends' and neutral mediators of the conflict, pre-empted the British and French by enticing the Qing government to sign the Sino-Russian and Sino-American Tianjin Treaties on 13 and 18 June. They thereby obtained everything that Britain and France got from the treaty except reparations.

However, not long after that, the Emperor Xianfeng – who had thus far been hesitant and wavering in the face of conflict – saw the specific provisions of the Treaty of Tianjin, which he himself had already ratified, and found several of the terms difficult to accept. A particular sticking point was the permanent stationing of foreign envoys in Beijing, which he saw as "a most significant source of danger and could never be permitted."[2]

Why?

This particular clause struck at a pain point for the hollow, vain arrogance of the Qing rulers: the Treaty of Nanjing had focused on reparations, and although Hong Kong had been ceded, it could be dismissed as merely a remote piece of territory far from the capital. Although it was humiliating, the Qing government could still wait for the withdrawal of troops and then shamelessly make excuses to the population, claiming that with mere words and paper, they had triumphed over 10,000 military generals, or other such nonsense. As a way of shifting the blame, the Emperor could also claim that he, who was far away in Beijing, had been deceived, and dismiss the ministers and officials who were involved in the negotiations. All this created the illusion that the "foreign

1. *The Xianfeng Emperor's Foreign Affairs, Vol. 12*, p. 24.
2. *The Xianfeng Emperor's Foreign Affairs, Vol. 35*, p. 40.

barbarians" were under the control of the Qing Emperor, rather than the other way around, and thus served to protect his dignity and the authority of his rule.

To have foreign envoys permanently stationed in the capital, however, was tantamount to a public declaration that the Imperial court was being monitored and manipulated by outsiders. Furthermore, according to the Treaty of Tianjin, after a year, the foreign envoys would meet the Emperor to formally exchange the treaty ratification, which would clearly show that it was the Emperor who had sold out the interests of the Qing Empire to the Western powers. This dilemma tormented Emperor Xianfeng, who constantly urged his ministers to communicate with Britain and France and to try and amend the relevant contents of the Treaty of Tianjin.

What all this shows is that making concessions did not bring peace. Rather, it merely emboldened the enemy and fanned the flames of his ambition.

An excessive focus on saving face, accompanied by a refusal to face cruel reality, created a situation where people were only brave after the fact, and thus were forced to accept humiliation heaped on top of shame.

In June 1859, faced with the weak and despicable Qing government's seemingly reneging on the Treaty of Tianjin, the British and French Allied Forces attacked the Dagu Estuary in Tianjin again, but suffered a severe defeat.

As such, in February 1860, Britain and France mobilized 25,000 troops to expand their war of aggression against China. In April, Western forces captured Zhoushan. In August, the Dagu Forts were overrun, and Tianjin and Tongzhou were occupied. Beijing itself was under threat, and Emperor Xianfeng fled to his summer villa in Chengde with most of the members of the royal family.

In October, the British and French allied forces entered Beijing and looted the treasures of the Yuanmingyuan (the Old Summer Palace), stealing the historical relics and treasures of previous dynasties. In order to cover up these crimes, they set fire to the Yuanmingyuan itself. The Yuanmingyuan was known as 'The Garden of Ten Thousand Gardens.' It was filled with the sweat and blood of the Chinese people, and renowned for bringing together the essence of Chinese and Western architectural art. Thus, its destruction was a tragedy, the memory of which still hurts the Chinese psyche to this day.

On 24 and 25 October 1860, the Sino-British Treaty of Beijing and the Sino-French Treaty of Beijing were signed respectively. These treaties stipulated that Tianjin would also become a commercial port, and that foreign countries would be allowed to recruit Chinese coolies to work overseas. Kowloon would be ceded to the British, and reparations to Britain and France totaled 8,000,000 taels each. Thus, the Second Opium War came to an end.

The walls were coming down.

Tsarist Russia took advantage of the difficulties faced by the Qing government during the Second Opium War, fighting the British and French on the external front and the Taiping Rebellion on the internal front. Through the threat of force, it made the Qing government sign the Sino-Russian Treaty of Aigun in 1858, in which Russia claimed over 600,000 square kilometers of Chinese territory north of the Heilongjiang River and south of the Outer Khingan Mountains. Later, in 1860, Russia pretended to "mediate," but instead forced the Qing government to sign the Sino-Russian Treaty of Beijing, which ceded 400,000 square kilometers of Chinese territory east of the Ussuri River. In 1864, Russia forced the Qing government to sign the Treaty of Tarbagatai, which "defined" the northwestern border between the two countries, ceding more than 440,000 square kilometers of land in western China.

By the second half of the 19th century, China had ceded approximately 2.5 million square miles of territory to the great powers – 50 times the size of New York State. Among the forces who invaded China, the Russian Empire had annexed territory that was 11 times the size of New York State, occupying the most territory of ant external power within China.[1]

After its defeat in the Second Opium War, China's national crisis became even more severe. In the two decades from 1840 to 1860, foreign aggression pushed from the original southeastern coastal areas to the coastal provinces, and thence into the interior. China lost more and more sovereignty and territory, and slowly became a semi-colonized country.

As the 1870s went on, Western countries entered an increasingly intense period of colonialization, and the world was carved up between them. Rising powers Japan and Germany also began to invade China, following in the footsteps of Britain, France, Russia, and the USA. Smaller nations bordering China were also prey for the colonizers. In 1876, Russia annexed the Khanate of Kokand, which bordered China's Xinjiang Province. From the same year, Korea

1. Hsiung, James C. *China Into Its Second Rise*. Translated by Li Fang. Hubei Education Press, 2016, p. 77.

was also forced to sign unequal treaties with nations such as Japan, America, Russia, and Germany. In 1879, Japan swallowed up the Ryukyu Kingdom, changing it to Okinawa. In 1874, Vietnam (also called Annam) became a French 'protectorate.' In 1887, Burma was colonized by Britain, and in 1887, Cambodia was incorporated into French Indochina.

As smaller neighboring countries were swallowed up by the great powers, China's decline and crisis also manifested as a series of crises along the border, and it was encircled and sealed off in terms of international traffic. It was from that international macro perspective that China's crisis could most clearly be seen. In *The First Book of the Shangqing Emperor*, Kang Youwei insightfully pointed out that "since the destruction of the Ryukyu Kingdom, the loss of Annam and the fall of Burma, our wings have been broken, and danger will soon pierce the heart and belly."[1]

Just as China was dealing with the border crisis, the French launched a conflict along the Sino-Vietnamese border and the southeast coast, provoking a war. In August 1884, the French navy attacked the garrison of Mawei Port, and the Fujian naval force was wiped out. The Qing government was forced to declare war on France. In March 1885, veteran general Feng Zicai defeated the French army at Zhennan Pass (now the Youyi Pass) in Guangxi. This turned the tides of war, and directly led to the collapse of then-Prime Minister Jules Ferry's Cabinet in France. However, despite the favorable circumstances, the muddle-headed Qing government nonetheless advocated that "victory should be followed by restraint," and bent its knee to plead for peace from the aggressors. In April, a treaty was signed laying out the conditions for a Sino-French armistice, and in June, they signed the Ten Articles of the Treaty of Vietnam. This recognized France's colonial jurisdiction over Vietnam, allowed trade ports to be opened along the China-Vietnam border, and laid down an agreement to build railroads in China, thus enabling France to win without a battle and obtain privileges that it had not won on the battlefield. At this point, China's Guangxi, Yunnan, and other areas became part of France's sphere of influence.

---

1. *The Collected Works of Kang Youwei, Part 1*. Renmin University of China Press, 2007, p. 180.

After the Sino-French War, the Qing Dynasty put several coastal defense measures in place in order to safeguard its interests, including establishing a province in Taiwan in October 1885. Similarly, in the same month, the Naval Office (Yamen) was established to command and manage the navy. In 1888, the Beiyang Maritime Division was completed. Of course, these measures were not completely useless, but they nevertheless remained unable to reverse the decline of the Qing Dynasty.

Besides the aforementioned First and Second Opium Wars and the Sino-French War, there was also the British invasion of Tibet in 1888, the Sino-Japanese War of 1894, the Eight-Power Allied Forces invasion of China in 1900, the Tsar's annexation of three northeastern provinces in 1900, the British invasion of Tibet for the second time in 1903, and the Russo-Japanese War for territorial expansion in the northeast, which took place on Chinese territory in 1904.

These nine conflicts occurred over 13 years and three months. Of the 66 years from 1840 to 1905, the Chinese people spent one-fifth of that time being beaten down by others. According to statistics, during that period, the number of treaties, articles of association, contracts, and special articles that the foreign aggressors forced China to sign totaled 300, and they occupied 1.739 million square kilometers of Chinese territory, which is three times the size of France or seven times the size of Great Britain.

Over those decades, the reparations, city rights, military expenditure, war damages, and the sheer plunder of the exploiters cost China about 100 billion taels of silver, while the income of the Qing government only reached 80 million taels. A simple calculation shows that China would have had to be enslaved for almost a thousand years to repay the reparations and the debt.

If you fall behind, you will be beaten. This was a painful and poignant realization for the Chinese people in that era.

More than a century later, when General Secretary Xi Jinping reviewed that period in history, he lamented, "What a humiliation. What shame. China at that time was simply a fattened lamb ready for the slaughter."

3

THE TAIPING UPRISING

THROUGHOUT HISTORY, THE CHINESE NATION has endured hardship, but its people have remained indomitable. Even when modern China was faced with a serious national and social crisis, the Chinese people refused to be invaded or enslaved.

Who, then, were the first to break the silence and fight back?

If we consider the annals of history, we often find the following phenomenon:

In the face of social or national crisis, it is most often a country's intellectuals who first detect the danger. They raise the alarm, concerned for the nation and its people, but they are often also dismissed as merely blowing hot air, misleading the country, and making bizarre statements. In contrast, it is often the peasants who are first to act directly to bring about social change. The result is that although they typically fail, they are also the ones to strike a blow directly against the old order of things. Of course, there is also a combination of the two: the peasant resistance is often led by a frustrated low-level scholar or intellectual who has repeatedly tried and failed to break into the upper ranks. This thoroughly demonstrates that revolution needs not only theoretical guidance, but the gumption to act when necessary.

Why is that so?

Mao Zedong – who knew the Chinese peasantry best – once incisively put it thus: where there is oppression, there will be resistance. Since the peasantry was at the lowest rung of the social ladder, they were the ones who bore the brunt of the changes and pressures that were wrought by the social and national crises.

Under the oppression of the feudal system and the exploitation and oppression of the landed bureaucracy, Chinese peasants were already in a dire situation. Since the Opium War, the military and war reparations expenditure of the Qing government had increased year on year, and these heavy burdens were transferred to the working people. The fate of the peasants became increasingly miserable: they could not sustain their livelihoods, and some people even saw their families torn apart and broken. As such, their desire to resist such oppression began to grow, and their determination to fight became stronger than ever.

In the middle of the 19th century, the social contradictions and clashes became increasingly acute, leading to pockets of resistance that sprang up one after another. According to statistics, in the decade from 1841 to 1850, there were more than 110 peasant uprisings in various places. In 1851, the Taiping Heavenly Kingdom peasant movement broke out, led by Hong Xiuquan.

Like many earlier peasant uprisings, the Taiping Uprising used religious superstition to drive public opinion. The movement claimed that its leaders had been inspired by the Heavens, and so those who joined would have to be determined to follow said leaders to the death. They thereby won over the hearts of the people and swelled their ranks.

But the difference between the Taiping Heavenly Kingdom movement (which had broken out after the Opium War) and its predecessor peasant movements was that it was influenced by the work of Western missionaries in China, and so the religion that it leaned on was a very "Western" Christianity. In that sense, it was a unique product of the times.

The founder of the Taiping Heavenly Kingdom movement, Hong Xiuquan, was a native of Hua County in Guangdong Province. At the age of seven, he went to a private village school and learned the *Four Books* and *Five Classics*. After he turned 18, he also worked as a village teacher. The villagers thought highly of him and believed that he would surely succeed in the imperial examinations, thereby gaining fame and honoring his family and ancestors. Unfortunately, that was not to be. He repeated his studies three times and went to Guangzhou to take the imperial examinations four times, but failed all of them. He failed to even make it to the most basic rank of *xiucai*, and in 1837, after his third failure, he fell seriously ill. Legend has it that he hallucinated and saw an old man telling him, "I have been sent from God to order you to slay demons and cleanse the earth of evil," handing him a sword with which to do so.

Six years later, Hong found a Christian pamphlet called 'Good Words to Admonish the Age,' which he had received when he had previously gone to Guangzhou to take the examinations. On reading it, he connected the contents of the book with his earlier hallucinations. He believed that the old man in the dream was the God mentioned in the book, that he himself was the second son of God and the brother of Jesus, and that he was on a sacred mission.

At that point in his life, after his academic failures, Hong Xiuquan was particularly frustrated and resentful.

At that point in history, China had suffered defeat in the first Opium War, and as a result, Guangzhou was facing the very forefront of Western military and economic aggression. Hong Xiuquan, as a commoner at the bottom rung of society, keenly felt the rottenness and decadence of the Qing government, the darkness that haunted society, and the cruelty of Western colonial exploitation.

These factors essentially prompted him to abandon his attempts to pass the imperial examinations. He set aside the tablets of Confucius and set up an altar to God instead, making up his mind to evangelize for God.

Interestingly, research shows that 'Good Words to Admonish the Age' was written by Liang A-Fa, a Chinese worker who used to print the Bible for foreign missionaries. Liang himself had become a Christian, and 'Good Words' had been handed out to passersby on the streets of Guangzhou for free.

In 1847, Hong Xiuquan went to Guangzhou to learn more from the American Christian missionary, Reverend Issachar Jacox Roberts (known as Luo Xiaoquan in Chinese), but Roberts was unwilling to consider Hong a true Christian, and thus refused to baptize him. Nonetheless, this did not stop a Chinese peasant from using his own understanding of "God" and his teachings in order to mobilize the people at the bottom rungs of society, and to fight against the weight of feudalism and colonialism.

Hong Xiuquan claimed to be the second son of God and the younger brother of Jesus, and he would proselytize to everyone he met about Christianity as he understood it. After years of hard work, he and Feng Yunshan finally amassed a sizeable congregation of believers in the area around Guiping County in Guangxi province, and thus formed the 'Society of God-Worshipers.'

On 11 January 1851, against the backdrop of uprisings led by the Tiandihui (the Heaven and Earth Society) in Guangxi, Hong Xiuquan launched an insurrection against the Qing government. He was 37 at the time, and led about 20,000 people from Jintian Village in Guiping, calling themselves the Taiping Army. The Army consisted mainly of "charcoal burners" and miners, peasants who had lost their land and been bankrupted, and dockworkers. These people became the backbone of the Taiping Uprising.

The Taiping Heavenly Kingdom was eager to overthrow the Qing Dynasty. To that end, it refused to recognize any of the unequal treaties signed by the Qing Dynasty, and strictly prohibited the opium trade. The Taiping Army fought bravely. During the march from the mountainous areas of Guangxi to Wuhan and Nanjing, they killed corrupt officials and burned land deeds and bonds, being scrupulous about not harming any of the common people. In doing so, they won the support of the masses. The ranks of the Taiping Army were swelled by displaced people, poor miners, barge haulers, boatmen, blacksmiths, carpenters, sedan bearers, as well as some members of the Tiandihui who had turned to banditry. The Qing Army encircled them on multiple occasions, but they persistently broke through, defeating large numbers of troops that the Qing government had recruited from the provinces.

In June 1852, the Taiping Army marched out of Guangxi and entered Hunan. In January 1853, three towns in the Wuhan area were conquered in one stroke, and more people joined the Taiping Army, raising its numbers to 500,000. They went east along the Yangtze River, and captured Nanjing on 19 March. They renamed it 'Tianjing,' and established the regime of Taiping Heavenly Kingdom there. Having established their capital, the Taiping Army carried out northern and western expeditions, pushing into various territories. Along the way, they allied with other uprisings, including the northern Nian Army, the uprisings of various minority groups in the southwest and northwest, the Shanghai Dagger Society, and the Hunan Tiandihui.

For a period of time, peasant uprisings swept through the country, rattling both internal and external powers.

In the winter of 1853, the Taiping Heavenly Kingdom formally promulgated the Land System of the Heavenly Kingdom, in order to solve the central problem of land for farmers. Their revolutionary program repudiated the millennia-old system of feudal land ownership and proposed comprehensive social reforms. They hoped to build an ideal society in which "people will work the fields together, eat together, share wealth and be equal, and no one will need for anything." This program reflected the longstanding desire among peasants to have their own land, and played a critical role in mobilizing and encouraging the peasantry to participate in the anti-feudal struggle. However, with its desire for absolute equality, such a scheme smacked of unrealistic utopianism, and was difficult to carry out in practice.

In the first half of 1856, the Taiping Army broke through the Jiangnan and Jiangbei Battalions, which had encircled their capital, Tianjing. This was the height of its military prowess. The peasant revolution had faced down an attack by its most powerful enemy, but it then had to face down the test of victory. Unfortunately, it failed. Like most peasant uprisings, after having secured their capital at Tianjing, the leaders of the Taiping Heavenly Kingdom became arrogant and complacent. They indulged in hedonistic pleasures and fostered an increasingly bureaucratic style of command, building luxurious palaces in Tianjing, and living in the lap of luxury.

Hong Xiuquan had initially launched his uprising to oppose the emperor, but after settling in Tianjing, he himself quickly 'feudalized,' living an imperial lifestyle and eventually becoming what he had once hated most.

When the King of Heaven arrived at court, his bannermen and officials were required to kowtow in accordance with the old rites and shout, "Long live the Emperor!" No longer was there a sense of brotherhood and equality before God. When a procession left the palace, officials all sat in sedan chairs. The King of Heaven was carried by 64 bearers, the Prince of the East (Yang Xiuqing) had 48, and even the low-level military attachés (called *liang sima*) were carried by four bearers each. Many of them had once been sedan-bearers themselves. Hong Xiuquan's harem of concubines and female attendants numbered more than 2,300. From the moment he entered the palace at the age of 41 to his suicide at age 52, he lived for 11 years in the palace surrounded by beautiful women, and never once took a step out of the gates of Tianjing. Clearly, the leadership of the Heavenly Taiping Kingdom had seriously lost touch with their frontline fighters and the lower masses of society.

Precisely because of this, the peasant leaders who had let victory go to their heads began to struggle for power among themselves despite not having defeated the Qing Dynasty or won sufficient strategic advantage against the Qing Army.

During the internal conflict, Yang Xiuqing (styled 'Prince of the East') and Wei Changhui (styled 'Prince of the North') were both killed, and Shi Dakai ('Prince Yi') left in a fury with 200,000 soldiers under his command. These were all deadly blows to the Taiping Heavenly Kingdom. The Qing Army took this opportunity to mount a vigorous counterattack, and rebuilt the Jiangnan and Jiangbei Battalions to besiege Tianjing once more.

In April 1859, Hong Rengan was granted the title of 'Prince Gan' and became Prime Minister. He proposed a new plan for internal reform and nation building – 'A New Treatise on Aids to Administration.' This was a particularly important document in the late stages of the Taiping Heavenly Kingdom, and it was the earliest program to advocate capitalism in modern China. However, due to the limitations of the peasant class and the fact that the circumstances would not permit such ambitious reforms, the new program did not have a significant effect on the development of the Taiping Heavenly Kingdom's revolution.

In 1861, the Qing general Zeng Guofan led the Xiang and Huai Armies to besiege the Taiping Army on three fronts, and joined forces with British, French, Russian, and American troops to launch a further attack. Tianjing fell in July 1864. Faced with suppression from the Chinese and foreign forces, the once vigorous Taiping Heavenly Kingdom movement finally failed.

Nonetheless, the movement lasted 14 years, sweeping through 18 provinces, conquering more than 600 cities, establishing a government regime that opposed the Qing Dynasty, and promulgating the first complete land reform program in the history of the Chinese peasant movement – the Land System of the Heavenly Kingdom. It was a movement of great scale and rapid development, which also had a complete organizational system and great military strength. In all these respects, it represented the peak of China's olden peasant warfare, dealing a heavy blow to the feudal rule of the Qing Dynasty, and significantly disrupting the old feudal order in general. Simultaneously, it showed foreign powers that the laboring masses of China possessed great revolutionary force, and thus played an important role in preventing the full-scale colonization of China.

However, the eventual downfall of the Taiping Heavenly Kingdom movement suggests the limitations of peasant revolution. In semi-colonial, semi-feudal China, even though the peasantry were a powerful force for anti-imperialism and anti-feudalism, they nonetheless did not represent new productive forces and relations of production, since they were merely small-scale producers. Neither could they provide a scientific, rational, and far-sighted plan for the revolutionary struggle. Without the leadership of the progressive classes, it would be impossible to triumph over powerful enemies or fundamentally root out the old feudal order. New relations of production more suited to the historical development could not be established, the old systems of feudalism and imperialism could not be defeated, and China was still unable to find the right road to independence and prosperity.

Today, the Taiping Heavenly Kingdom appears to be a product of history that is full of contradictions:

It was a peasant movement in China, but it advocated belief in God and opposed Confucianism. It called for the elimination of all Chinese folk beliefs, demolishing temples and smashing statues of the Bodhisattva, as well as those dedicated to Confucius. It triggered great concern about how Chinese civilization was in the midst of crisis, and as a result, it aroused the opposition of Han scholars, officials, and intellectuals.

It raised the banners for a very Westernized kind of worship of God, and put forward a program with strong capitalist leanings in 'A New Treatise on Aids to Administration,' seeking to permit foreign trade and welcoming foreigners who wanted to teach their crafts and technology to the Chinese people. However, it failed to gain recognition and support from Western powers, and was finally suppressed by the joint efforts of Chinese and foreign reactionary forces.

However, the strangest thing about history is this:

In the process of suppressing the Taiping Heavenly Kingdom under the directive of the Qing government, Zeng Guofan built a new type of army, in which individual recruits were armed – the Xiang Army. Later, Zeng Guofan and Li Hongzhang also formed the Huai Army, and introduced the mass usage of Western guns. Later, they became the standing forces of the Qing Army. This broke the old military system of the Manchu Eight Banners and the Green Standard, promoting the modernization of the Chinese forces. It was this new army that launched the revolution in 1911, which was the 'Xinhai' year – a full 60-year lunar cycle after the founding of the Taiping Heavenly Kingdom in 1851. The Xinhai Revolution overthrew the Qing Dynasty in one blow. The Taiping Heavenly Kingdom had failed to realize its goal of expelling the

Manchus and restoring China, but that goal was eventually fulfilled by the enemy who had destroyed the Taiping Heavenly Kingdom itself.

Initially, the Western powers watched and waited, and then they jointly suppressed the Taiping Heavenly Kingdom alongside the Qing government. Over the course of these actions, Western powers arrived at a basic consensus: maintaining the rotten, decadent Qing government was beneficial to themselves, because such a government was more easily pushed around. Demands could be made and concessions obtained. Thus, semi-colonial and semi-feudal China lasted longer. The Taiping Heavenly Kingdom's war to overthrow the Qing Dynasty had led to the alliance of Chinese and foreign reactionary forces, and thus "accidentally" delayed the demise of the Qing government.

This "counterproductive" outcome ultimately contributed to pushing forward the waves of change in society, creating an upward spiral. Such are the dialectics of history, perhaps.

4

THE FAILURE OF SELF-STRENGTHENING REFORM

THE TERM 'MODERN CHINA' IS only useful for dividing sections in world history; it does not refer to a 'modernized' China. In the mid-19th century, China's commodity economy was not yet mature, modern education had not yet started, and industrialization and democratization were not yet possible. Therefore, the most practical and urgent issues facing modern China were:

- How to strengthen itself against imperialist aggression and oppression, and become an independent country.
- How to realize modernization and become one of the major world powers.

Only by solving these two problems could the Chinese nation emerge from the vicious cycle of being beaten because of its backwardness, and falling further and further behind due to the continuous beatings.

What was the solution for China?

In the face of the invasion of Western capitalism, which was "a change unprecedented in thousands of years" for China, Lin Zexu, Wei Yuan, and other people of insight had recognized China's backwardness even before the First Opium War. They advocated viewing the world with open eyes, and put forward the idea of "learning from the barbarians in order to control them." In this regard, Marx once profoundly pointed out, "It seems strange that opium did not have a hypnotic effect, but rather a waking effect."[1]

1. *The Complete Works of Marx and Engels, Vol. 1*, People's Publishing House, 1963, p. 545.

The defeat of the two Opium Wars forced the closed doors of China to open to the outside world; the impact of the peasant movement of the Taiping Heavenly Kingdom caused a serious shock to the feudal order of the Qing Dynasty. These events stirred up a great storm in the stagnant Chinese feudal society. In the face of the new world situation, the serious national crisis, and fierce social contradictions, the Qing government had no way to retreat, forcing self-revolution. It was in this situation that the foreign affairs faction of the Qing ruling class began to seek truth from the West in an attempt to save the country from the crisis of the times, and to push China onto the path of capitalism and prosperity.

In 1861, an enlightened faction within the ruling clique of the Qing Dynasty initiated the Westernization Movement to overcome the crisis. Officials who supported Westernization put forward the slogans 'self-improvement' and 'striving for wealth,' advocating "Chinese traditional values aided with Western modern technology and management." While upholding China's decadent feudal system and ethical principles, they wanted to develop modern industry by picking up advanced technology from the West, so that they could produce new types of weapons and establish a new army. Their aim was to enrich the country, strengthen the army, and continue to maintain the feudal autocratic rule.

In 1864, Li Hongzhang made a proposition to the court that the imperial examinations be changed: "If China wants to strengthen itself, it must understand foreign weapons. To understand foreign tools, we must find the tools that make those tools, and learn their methods without using their people. If we want to find the tools and the people who make the tools, we should create a craftsmanship position for scholars, offering them wealth and fame so that they can focus on their profession, have more time to refine their skill, and develop their talent."[1]

Officials advocating Westernization set up foreign affairs business for the direct purpose of purchasing and manufacturing foreign guns and cannons to suppress the peasant uprisings and to strengthen the naval and border defense. They gave priority to the development of military industry through the state

1. *The Process of Preparing for the Westernization Movement.* Zhonghua Book Company, 1964 (25), pp. 9–10.

power they held, and successively founded the Jiangnan General Administration of Machine Building, the Jinling Machine Bureau, the Fuzhou Bureau of Shipping, the Tianjin Machine Bureau, and the Hubei Gun Factory. In the process, in order to solve the difficulties of military industry such as insufficient supply of raw materials and fuel and backward transportation, they also founded mining, smelting, textiles, and other industrial and mining industries, as well as businesses like shipping, railroads, and telecommunications, such as the Ship Merchants Bureau, the Kaiping Mining Bureau, the Tianjin Telegraph Bureau, and the Shanghai Machine Weaving Bureau.

Except for a few government-run or government-business joint ventures, most of these enterprises were run by government supervisors and merchants. They were basically modern enterprises of a capitalist nature, and laid the foundation of modern Chinese industry.

At the same time, in order to cultivate personnel who understood the advanced technology of the West, the Westernization faction also founded more than 30 new-style academies to cultivate specialists in translation, telegraphy, railroads, mining, and Western medicine. It sent more than 200 young children to the USA and foreign students to Europe at the government's expense, cultivating a cohort of scientific and technological talent.

With the development of the Westernization Movement from the 1870s to the 1890s, the Qing government developed a new military force, building world-class navies in Fujian, Guangdong, Nanyang, and Beiyang. The Beiyang Marine Division was the strongest and largest of the four modern navies of the Qing government, with more than 20 warships of various sizes and nearly 100 auxiliary warships and transport vessels. From an objective point of view, the Westernization Movement played a role in promoting the development of modern Chinese industry and national capitalism.

However, the ultimate failure of the movement was inevitable, because its fundamental purpose was to keep the decadent feudal rule alive, not to push China in the direction of independent capitalism. It also failed because of its dependence on the Western powers and its corrupt and backward management of internal foreign affairs enterprises.

In 1894, the Sino-Japanese War broke out. Faced with the invasion of Japan, whose economy was less than a tenth of China's, the Qing army was defeated first in Korea and then in Liaodong. In February 1895, the Japanese army occupied Liugong Island, and the Beiyang fleet – which was once the first in Asia and the ninth in the world – was wiped out. Faced with repeated military defeats, Emperor Guangxu sent Li Hongzhang as a plenipotentiary to Shimonoseki in Japan, to negotiate for peace at the Japanese border.

On 17 April 1895, Li Hongzhang and Japanese Prime Minister Ito Hirobumi signed the Treaty of Shimonoseki, which stipulated that China: cede the entire island of Taiwan and all its subsidiary islands, the Penghu Islands, and the Liaodong Peninsula to Japan; compensate Japan with 230 million taels of silver, or 365 million yen, which not only exceeded Japan's total economic output of 215 million yen, but also exceeded its total tax revenue for the following three years, which was equivalent to rebuilding a new Japan; open Shashi, Chongqing, Suzhou, and Hangzhou as trading ports, where Japanese ships could sail along the inland rivers to take passengers and load cargo, and the Japanese government could set up consulates at the ports of commerce. The Japanese government could set up consulates in the trading ports; Japanese subjects were free to set up factories in the trading ports in China and import all kinds of equipment; all goods made by Japan in China were exempted from tax, and all Japanese goods could be stored in warehouses; in exchange for prisoners of war, China immediately released Japanese military spies or Japanese subjects suspected of being arrested, and could not arrest traitors in the service of the Japanese army.

The Treaty of Shimonoseki was an unequal treaty of unprecedented severity, imposed on China by foreign invaders after the Treaty of Nanjing. The conditions proposed by Japan were very harsh, and did not allow room for negotiation. In addition to the alarmingly large amount of land cessions and huge reparations, it also included for the first time the freedom to set up factories in China, marking the fact that the economic aggression of foreign capitalism against China had shifted from commodity export to capital export, taking advantage of China's cheap raw materials and labor to deprive it economically. This led to the further loss of Chinese sovereignty and the disintegration of the feudal system, greatly deepening the national crisis and semi-colonization, and basically forming a semi-colonial and semi-feudal ruling order in China. In this way, an ancient civilization of a thousand years was sinking.

The defeat of the Sino-Japanese War caused China – the leading nation in East Asia for 2,000 years – to be replaced by Japan – a comparatively small country. China's international status was in ruins. The cession of Taiwan and the Penghu Islands to Japan was a particularly bitter pill to swallow.

Tan Sitong wrote, "What can show this spring sadness, my sadness? Oh Heaven, Heaven! Only tears can drown it. Ah, eight hundred million eyes are wet! Where is China now, on the map?"[1] These verses expressed the grief and anger of the educated people of China at that time.

Liang Qichao was saddened by the people's numbness and ignorance regarding the national crisis. "Before the Sino-Japanese War of 1894–1895, we did not know that the country was in danger. We still thought that China was noble and prestigious, so no one talked about prevention and national protection."[2] In 'The Coup of 1898' he wrote, "the awakening of China's dream of more than 4,000 years began after the defeat in the First Sino-Japanese War and the cession of Taiwan to pay off 200 trillion."[3]

Wu Yuzhang, who experienced this period of history firsthand, later recalled, "This was really an unprecedented treaty of death. It shook all of China. Our country had only been defeated by the Western powers before. Now we were defeated by a small Eastern country. The defeat was so terrible, and the treaty was so harsh. What a disgrace it was!"[4]

During the Sino-Japanese War of 1894–1895, the new-style army and navy managed by the Westernization faction were completely defeated, marking the complete failure of the 35-year-old Westernization Movement. This cruel fact shows that the effort to modernize China by picking up Western technology and revitalizing industry and military without shaking up the original political and social order was only a benevolent wish that could not succeed. It did not – and could not – serve to save the Chinese nation from peril.

The disgraceful failure of the Westernization Movement, which dealt only with the reform of the apparatus, was a warning to the Chinese people: there is no way out if we follow the old ways; small repairs will not help; the danger of national subjugation is at hand.

1. Tan, Sitong. 'Lines Composed in Reflection', from *The Complete Works of Tan Sitong*, China Book Bureau, 1981, p. 540.
2. Lao, Shike. 'With Respect to the Emperor', *Qing Yi Bao, Vol. 9*, March 22, 1899.
3. *The Complete Works of Liang Qichao, Vol. 1*, Beijing Publishing House, 1999, p. 181.
4. *The Collected Works of Wu Yuzhang, Vol. 2*, Chongqing Publishing House, 1987, p. 955.

As a result, Liang Qichao later criticized the Westernization Movement led by Li Hongzhang and others, saying, "officials advocating Westernization only care about the development of the military and not civil policy. They improve international exchange but not national government; they work for the imperial court and not for people; they focus on Westernization instead of national affairs. They believed that China's political and religious customs were superior to those of other countries, but our guns, cannon, ships, and machines are not as good. If we can improve our backwardness, the goal of Westernization has been achieved."[1]

The failure of the Sino-Japanese War of 1894–1895 further exposed the corruption and incompetence of the Qing government and China's poverty and weakness. It intensified the imperialist scramble for China, and quickly pushed the nation to the brink of partition.

In the 1890s, with the development of Chinese capitalism, a national bourgeoisie gradually developed. Although still weak, this nascent social force represented a new productive force and relations of production. Faced with a national crisis, many Chinese people at that time – especially young students – went to Japan, Europe, and America to learn the mysteries of their rivals' powerful systems and to find solutions to save their country and people. From this, China produced bourgeois reformists such as Kang Youwei, Liang Qichao, Tan Sitong, and Yan Fu. They seized a historical opportunity after the defeat of the Sino-Japanese War, and took a step forward in the self-help movement of the feudal landowners by calling for "salvation and survival," proposing a shift from instrumental to political reform and assisting the Guangxu Emperor in implementing the Reformation.

In 1898 (the year of the 'hundred days' in the lunar calendar), the reformists launched a powerful movement to change the law and reform in China, known as the 'Hundred Days of Reform' or 'Wuxu Reform'. They advocated the establishment of a constitutional monarchy in China through top-down reforms, following the models of capitalist countries such as Britain and Japan, and the participation of the bourgeoisie in power and the implementation of bourgeois improvements to promote the development of capitalist economy and culture in China.

---

1. Jiang, Tingfu. *Modern History of China*, Yunnan People's Publishing House, 2016, p. 131.

However, owing to the fact that the reformists themselves were not powerful enough, the Emperor Guangxu, upon whom they relied, had no authority. The Hundred Days of Reform only lasted for 103 days, ending when the Empress Dowager Cixi launched a coup and Emperor Guangxu was imprisoned. Tan Sitong and the other 'Six Gentlemen of 1898' were beheaded on Caishikou Street in Beijing. In fact, Tan Sitong had a chance to escape abroad, but he chose not to take it, remaining resolute: "Countries evolve with men's blood. China is still backward, as no one has died here in the history of reform. Let me be the first!"[1] In prison, he retained his composure, and wrote the heroic verse, "I leave the two mountains of my loyalty and justice behind!" At the execution site, he looked calm and exclaimed, "I have the heart to kill a thief, but I have no power to return to Heaven. Let me die in the right place – quickly and happily!" Tan is remembered for sacrificing his life to serve his country, and awakening the public in the process.

The bloody facts show that in semi-colonial and semi-feudal China, relying on the feudal rulers to make top-down improvements of a bourgeois nature was simply impossible.

After the failure of the Hundred Days of Reform of 1898, there were rumors that Western powers deliberately asked Empress Dowager Cixi to return authority to Emperor Guangxu. This triggered the Empress Dowager's concern, and harmed her fundamental interests. She therefore utilized the Boxer Rebellion against foreign invaders to declare war on all global leading powers.

The Eight-Nation Alliance launched a war of aggression against China in May 1900. The Qing army and the Boxer regiment, which were dozens of times more powerful than the enemy, were unable to resist the allied forces, which actually numbered fewer than 20,000. The capital city of Beijing fell, and the emperor fled in disarray. The city was ransacked, and left riddled with corpses.

On 7 September 1901, the Qing government signed an unprecedented unequal treaty with 11 countries, namely Germany, Russia, Japan, the USA, France, Britain, Italy, Austria, Belgium, Spain, and the Netherlands. Titled 'Final Protocol for the Settlement of the Disturbances of 1900', it stipulated that a foreign embassy area be allocated near Beijing's Dongjiaomin Alley. This

1. *The Complete Works of Tan Sitong*, China Book Bureau, 1981, p. 546.

area was effectively a state within a state, with countries having the right to "protect" their embassies with their own troops.

It also stipulated that the Dagu Fort be demolished, along with all the forts along the line from Dagu to Beijing. The Chinese army were not allowed to station troops within 20 miles of Tianjin, while the powers had the right to keep troops in the embassy area of Beijing and 12 places along the line from Beijing to Dagu and Shanhaiguan, including Tianjin and Tangshan. The imperial powers thus gained the privilege of stationing troops on Chinese territory.

The Qing government made reparations of 450 million taels of silver to 11 countries, to be repaid over 39 years at an annual interest rate of 4%, with a total of 982 million taels of principal and interest, secured by customs duties, normal tariffs, and salt taxes. These 450 million taels of silver were equivalent to the total revenue of the Qing government for six or seven years.[1] The reason for this figure was that the powers said that China had 450 million people, so it was one tael per capita – a huge insult.

The Qing government's attitude to this unprecedented unequal treaty was disappointing. When the leading powers proposed the outline of the peace negotiation in February 1901, the Qing government – then exiled in Xi'an – immediately signed it and issued an edict, which publicly declared that the leading powers only wanted to "survey China's material resources and enhance national coherence." The Qing government even shamelessly stated, "The present treaty does not encroach on our sovereignty and does not cede our land. In retrospect, we are ashamed and indignant."[2]

Why did the government say that the treaty did not encroach on China's sovereignty, when it had clearly lost its power and humiliated the country?

In *A Sharp Turn Back*, Chen Tianhua wrote, "Listen, do you think the current court is still from Manchuria? It has belonged to foreigners for a long time! If you don't believe me, look at what the court has been doing recently. What has not been at the behest of foreigners?"[3] It turned out that the "our" in "our sovereignty" was not China, but a small group of Qing Dynasty rulers

1. Li, Shaowei et al. *70 Years of Home and Country: The Sharpening and Rebirth of a Civilization* (edited by Southwind Media Think Tank) Journal Press, 2019, p. 52.
2. Sha, Jiansun (editor-in-chief). *General History of the Communist Party of China, Vol. 1*, Hunan Education Press, 1995, p. 10.
3. *The Collected Works of Chen Tianhua*, p. 36.

led by Empress Dowager Cixi. The Eight-Nation Alliance invaded Beijing and demanded the execution of 11 court officials who had expressed support for the Boxer Rebellion, but still admitted that the court headed by Empress Dowager Cixi ruled China. How could she not be "grateful"?

By that point, the Qing government had become a completely 'foreign' court, and China was reduced to a semi-colonial and semi-feudal society.

While the world was celebrating the dawn of the 20th century, China entered it in humiliation.

5

A NATION IN CRISIS

After the Opium War in 1840, the backward Old China fell into passivity. How did the once great civilized country of the East fall into such a miserable situation in modern times? This is the 'question of the century' that haunts Chinese people to this day. In this regard, Mao Zedong pointed out in 1963:

> "From the 1840s to the mid-1940s, a total of 105 years, almost all the world's large and small imperialist countries invaded China and beat us, except for the last time, that is, the war against Japan. Due to various reasons at home and abroad, it ended with the surrender of Japanese imperialism. However, all of the other wars ended with our defeat – the signing of treaties of humiliation and disgrace. The reasons for this were first, the corruption of the social system and, second, our economic and technological backwardness."[1]

Materialist dialectics hold that the development of things is the result of a combination of internal and external factors, of which internal factors are the root cause. By analyzing modern China in this way, we can squeeze out the 'smallness' hidden under the leather robe of the Qing Empire.

Political corruption, official corruption, and bribery prevailed. For example, during the Daoguang era, the Minister of Military Affairs Mu Zhang'a used his power to sell off the government, and acted for personal gain. Incompetent people could be promoted if they gave him a generous gift. Qi Shan, the

1. *The Collected Works of Mao Zedong, Vol. 8*, People's Publishing House, 1999, p. 340.

governor of Zhili, had his house raided in 1841, and the family assets seized were more than 10,000 taels of gold, 18 million taels of silver, and 11 boxes of jewelry. The central officials were even worse, and the local civil and military officials were frequently raided. The widely circulated phrase "local officials can earn 100,000 silvers in three years during the Qing Dynasty" vividly portrays the corruption of officials at that time.

The division between the rich and the poor intensified. Manchu nobles, bureaucrats, and landlords used various means to annex land, which intensified the trend of land concentration, and meant that peasants were less motivated to produce. Meanwhile, outdated farming techniques and the stagnant development of agriculture and handicrafts made the livelihood of ordinary people even tougher, especially for those who lost their farmland.

There was a long period of world peace after Qianlong era. However, the over 800,000 Eight Banner soldiers and Green Battalion troops that the Chinese government had in the mid-Qing Dynasty faced problems such as a lack of armaments, backward equipment, degraded military discipline, and low morale. These former "eagles of the grassland" lacked training, and their power gradually declined. As they spent their days idle, even gambling, drinking, and using prostitutes, their fighting ability deteriorated. Eventually, they became useless, and could no longer bear the important task of protecting the country.

Another important reason was the mentality of blind arrogance. The most typical example was the visit of the British Macartney mission to China in 1793. The mission brought a variety of gifts carefully selected with the fundamental purpose of showing off their advanced technology and strong military power. The aim was to deter the Qing Emperor and the civil and military ministers, and give Britain an advantage in the interaction between the two countries. However, the Qing court's attitude to the British gifts was confusing to the members of the mission:

> "An astronomer gave various skillful demonstrations. He picked a few from a large number of scientific gadgets which he thought he would cause a sensation. He fiddled with these things in front of several high-ranking officials, but he couldn't attract their interest. This disappointed him. 'Some Chinese thoughts are an insult to a European scientist.' The astronomers showed how the Parker lens could melt Chinese coins. He

> Shen used it to light his pipe, as if this instrument was just a 'cumbersome lighter' . . .
>
> There were no more opportunities for military technology to be demonstrated. A British official suggested sending a cannon to the Old Summer Palace for a test shot immediately, but the Chinese thought they were skilled and didn't use our gunners. Were they convinced that they could use the cannon alone? Would they rather have failed than admit that they are at a disadvantage in this sensitive field? The cannon sent by British artillery was given back immediately. In 1860, when the Old Summer Palace was burned, those cannons and shells were founded there intact. They were never used. They were transported back to London."[1]

As for Emperor Qianlong, it is said that when he saw a model of the huge *King* battleship equipped with 110 artillery among the gifts brought by the British mission, he was very interested. When he learned of its power, he was critical, saying "The principles of lethality and kindness cannot be reconciled,"[2] believing that only barbarians would pursue such ominous power.

The search for peace and the prosperity of the country are not contradictory, but complementary. Only when peace-loving nations become strong can they fight the aggressive ambitions and conspiracies of countries bent on theft, and effectively safeguard national security and world peace.

There is no contradiction between benevolence in internal governance and strength in external communication. Only with both can a strong comprehensive national power be formed, thus winning real respect and status in the international arena.

Why did the wise Emperor Qianlong not understand these simple and easy truths? One important reason is that his perception of the outside world and his self-evaluation went awry. To verify this historical fact, we must understand this truth: One cannot win the game without respecting one's opponents and understanding their strategy; being proud and arrogant will lead to defeat.

---

1. Peyrefitte, Alain. *L'empire immobile ou le choc des mondes*. Translated by Wang Guoqing et al. Sanlian Publishing Company, 2013, pp. 237–238.
2. Qin, Guojing. *Emperor Qianlong and Macartney*. Forbidden City Press, 1998, p. 115.

Some people may say that China was one of the world's richest countries at that time, so it would not have been bullied by any other nation if it had invested more in military spending.

Indeed, according to economist Angus Maddison in *The World Economy: A Millennial Perspective*, China's economic output accounted for one-third of the world's GDP in 1830 – more than the 25 percent of the world's economy that the USA now accounts for, making it unparalleled in terms of wealth. But being rich does not necessarily make a country strong.

Under feudal rule the Qing Dynasty was rich, but the wealth was mainly in the ruling group and the landlord class, not in the general public. China was rich in terms of private property, not state property. On the contrary, after the heyday of the Qianlong reign, the Jiaqing Emperor was able to fill the serious financial deficit by seizing the entire family fortune of the corrupt He Shen. It is said that He Shen's personal assets before his death amounted to 800 million taels of silver, more than half of the state's tax revenue during Jiaqing's 20-year reign.[1] This explains the saying "When He Shen fell, Jiaqing ate his fill."

Sadly, although Jiaqing killed He Shen and punished some of the corrupt high-ranking officials, he lacked the courage to carry out a comprehensive reform, failing to completely purge the entire bureaucracy of corruption. Hong Liangji – the head of the Hanlin Academy – was very concerned about this, so wrote a letter criticizing the emperor's lack of courage to purge corruption in the year of He Shen's execution, which was widely circulated in the capital. In the letter, it was stated that:

> "If the officials are not reformed, the people will not be happy; if the people are not happy, the government shall not be counted as successful, as the people will not be at peace. For more than ten years, many governors, vassals, feudal vassals, and lieutenants have been corrupting and deceiving the government."[2]

However, the final result of Hong Liangji's faithfulness was that he was exiled to the northwest.

1. Rowe, William T. *China's Last Empire (History of Imperial China)*. Translated by Li Renyuan and Zhang Yuan. Citic Press, 2016, p. 137.
2. Ibid., p. 138.

After the Jiaqing era, the Qing Dynasty declined, and the social crisis worsened. The luxury of the royal family and the corruption of officials prevailed. The emperor had money to overhaul the palace and gardens, and greedy officials and wealthy businessmen were wealthy enough to buy opium, but the Qing government did not have the funds to develop new weapons or even raise army salaries. Rich, but weak and corrupt, the Qing Dynasty was over-nourished and addicted to excess, with no fighting spirit.

Some may say that, even though China's government was rife with corruption, it was a huge country with a large population. As long as it united against rivals, it could at least draw, if not win. However, as the great modern philosopher Yan Fu wrote, "Since the Qin Dynasty, China has not cared about the world, nor other countries – only itself. One emperor with trillions of officials – his success means prosperity for the whole family, whereas his failure means the failure of the whole family."

In China's feudal system, a change of dynasty was nothing more than the change of the family occupying the emperor's throne. The Han Dynasty belonged to the Liu family, the Tang Dynasty to the Li family, the Song Dynasty to the Zhao family, the Ming Dynasty to the Zhu family, and the Qing Dynasty to the Aisin-Gioro family.

Ordinary people in feudal China got on with their lives without considering the change of dynasties. They didn't care who the emperor was, or what dynasty it was, as long as they could get by. When foreigners came to China to steal royal territory, it was the emperor who had to compensate them; it was nothing to do with the man on the street. That's why Sun Yat-sen later said that the 400 million Chinese people were like scattered sand.

This was an important reason for the humiliation, poverty, and backwardness of modern China.

In addition to political corruption, the division between rich and poor, military backwardness, ideological conservatism, and disorganization of the people, according to Maddison's statistics, from the economic and technical point of view, China's economy had grown continuously for a thousand years, reaching one-third of the world's total economy around 1820. However, despite this, the growth of the Chinese economy had been sustained by a constant increase of labor input, while after 1500, the growth of the West had been achieved mainly by the innovation of technology and production methods. If the growth after 1500 was reflected in the increase in labor productivity, the growth in China during the same period was accompanied by a decrease in labor productivity, which explains why the West, with its small population, created more and more wealth and eventually overtook China.[1]

After clarifying the above internal causes of modern China's backwardness and defeat, one cannot help but wonder why it failed to learn its lessons in time to revive its majesty when it was repeatedly defeated and invaded by so many countries in turn.

The defeat of the Opium War in 1840 shattered the dreams of the Qing Empire, but failed to alert the rulers to the backwardness of China, to recognize the global situation, and to strive to make progress, to reform and to catch up with the trend of human history.

It is one thing to lose a battle, but it is another not to understand why you lost.

On the eve of the First Opium War, many Chinese people still had a very limited and even risible understanding of the West and Westerners. For example, some people thought that Westerners had straight legs and no knees, so as long as they fought in close quarters and managed to knock them to the ground, they would not be able to get up. Also, because Western countries often imported large quantities of Chinese tea, people spread the word that due to the Western diet of beef and milk, they needed Chinese tea or rhubarb to pass stools, otherwise they would die of flatulence. Therefore, as long as China did not sell tea and rhubarb to Westerners, it would defeat them even without a fight.

If you know your enemies and know yourself, you will weather a hundred battles. China was narcissistic and arrogant, with a limited understanding of the outside world and the enemy, so did not foresee defeat. Regrettably, this situation not only existed among the lower-level ordinary people, but also among officials, generals, and even the ruling class.

Between 1842 when the First Opium War was lost, and 1856 when the Second Opium War broke out, there were roughly 12 years, which the ancients called an 'era' (a 'round' today). Defeat without knowing how to change results

1. Han, Yuhai. *Who Writes History in the Past Five Hundred Years: China and the World since 1500*. Jiuzhou Publishing House, 2011, p. 4.

is akin to falling in exactly the same place.

Between 1860 when the Second Opium War was lost, and 1883 when the Sino-French War broke out, there were 23 years.

Between 1885 when the Sino-French War ended to the outbreak of the Sino-Japanese War in 1894, there were nine years.

There were five years between the disastrous defeat of the Sino-Japanese War in 1895 and the invasion of China by the Eight-Nation Alliance in 1900. History did give the Qing Dynasty an opportunity from 1840 to 1900 for a total of 60 years, but the Eastern empire was too old, too rigid in thinking, and too slow in action. It therefore missed opportunities for self-revolution time after time, resulting in the invasion of the Western powers one after another. The intervals between wars grew shorter, and the damage to China's interests became increasingly serious.

In stark contrast, in the mid-19th century, Japan – which had long followed China's example and pursued a 'closed-door' policy – faced almost the same situation as the Qing Dynasty. It was defeated by China in the Sino-Japanese War more than 20 years later, after suffering Western aggression in 1853 and starting the 'Meiji Restoration' reform movement in 1868. In this regard, historian Jiang Tingfu states:

> "From the perspective of national history, the military defeat of the Opium War was not a fatal wound for the nation. After the defeat, the failure to understand the reasons for it, and the failure to pursue reform – that was the fatal wound. If the reforms of the Tongzhi and Guangxu years were transplanted to the Daoguang and Xianfeng years, our modernization would have been 20 years ahead of Japan's. The modern history of the Near East would have been completely different. Unfortunately, the people in the Daoguang and Xianfeng years did not learn the lessons of military defeat. After the war, they were exactly the same as before: insensitive and arrogant."[1]

The Tongzhi Emperor assumed the throne in 1861, just as the Second Opium War was ending and the Westernization Movement was beginning.

1. Jiang, Tingfu. *Modern History of China*, Yunnan People's Publishing House, 2016, p. 28.

This was 21 years after the outbreak of the First Opium War, but seven years before the Meiji Restoration in Japan. If history can be repeated, why were the previous 20 years wasted, making the subsequent reform difficult to complete? Unfortunately, there are no what-ifs in history.

What's even sadder is that some of the most insightful people in modern China, who were the first to open their eyes to the world, were ignored in their efforts to avoid peril and replace the old with the new, and were even criticized by the stubborn rulers.

In early 1839, Lin Zexu, who went to Guangzhou to ban the import and transaction of opium, began to see the gap between China's military and industrial technology and that of modern Western countries from his contact with Western powers, so he actively promoted the purchase of foreign ships and guns. Meanwhile, he sent people to collect books and newspapers from Western countries, and translated and compiled the *Gazetteer of the Four Continents* to explain the situations of various countries in the world. This is the reason why Lin Zexu is remembered as the first Chinese person to awaken from the state of national self-seclusion and see the world with a new attitude.

On the basis of the information collected by Lin Zexu, Wei Yuan later wrote the *Illustrated Annals of Overseas Countries* to impart knowledge of global geography and Western systems and cultures, encouraging Chinese to learn from the West, and introducing the idea of "beating someone at their own game." However, how could the Chinese people – especially the ruling class, who had been superior for thousands of years – accept the views that China was not the center of the world, that Western powers were better than the Qing Empire, and that the Chinese needed to learn from the West? If the general public was made to believe that the Qing Empire, which called itself the 'Heavenly Kingdom,' was lagging behind the global trend, would it not shake the foundation of faith and cause serious political instability? Therefore, when the *Illustrated Annals of Overseas Countries* was published, it was criticized, condemned, and rejected by the ruling and upper classes, and was banned by the Qing government. It failed to attract much attention at the time and, despite its many highlights, had a limited print run in China at that time, and was barely read.

In 1853, when the doors of Japan were forced open by American warships, the Japanese realized that their own backwardness and their national nature of 'learning from whoever is strong' had made them turn to the West. During this process, Japanese literati translated the *Illustrated Annals of Overseas Countries* into Japanese. Once it was published in Japan, it received a lot of attention and had a significant influence, becoming an ideological resource to promote the Meiji Restoration.

The contrast between the different fates of a book in China and Japan is so stark that it is almost heartbreaking. Regarding this, Shioya Shihong from Japan once lamented, "Sadly, patriotic scholars worry that the emperor won't pay attention to their books, but give suggestion to other countries. I do not just feel sorrow for scholars (Wei Yuan's word) but also for the emperor of the Qing Dynasty."[1]

So why did the Chinese not learn from the West?

Li Hongzhang reflects, "Chinese scholars were immersed in the accumulated habits of chapter and verse, and the warriors and soldiers were too stupid to pay attention to them, so they used what they did not learn and learned what they did not use. If there was nothing to do, they would be denouncing foreign weapons as a strange technique, thinking that they did not need to know how to use them. If there was something to do, they would be surprised by the foreign weapons, seeing them as a strange and magical, and thinking that they could not learn how to use them."[2]

For a large country that had failed due to psychological root causes, China refused to face the fact that it lagged behind others, and would not give up its millennium-old high-class identity. When facing the reality of being repeatedly humiliated and beaten by others, the Chinese lost their national and cultural confidence.

This contradictory mentality of looking down on others' blind arrogance and looking down on one's own blind inferiority had fluctuated during the 100 years from the 1840s to the 1940s. Therefore, there were always disputes between favoring the warring factions and the peace-seekers in the Opium War, the Sino-French War, and the Sino-Japanese War of 1894–1895. In the Anti-Japanese War, there was a dispute between the theory of quick victory and the theory of subjugation. It was difficult to completely replace the old system with the new one, as the Westernization Movement aimed to adopt Western

1. Ding, Xianjun. *The History of the Westernization Movement.* Social Sciences Academic Press, 2011.
2. Jiang, Tingfu. *Journal of Modern Chinese History.* Yunnan People's Press, 2016, p. 78.

ideology while keeping Chinese values, and went no further than enacting a constitutional monarchy. The Westernization Movement only sought to make limited reforms, meaning that it difficult to achieve a fundamental revolution.

However, even the most reluctant spirit will bow down when faced with reality.

After losing one war after another, the once-despised "barbarians" slowly became the superior "foreigners."

In 1832, British businessmen such as Hugh Hamilton Lindsay sought to trade in Shanghai. In his reply, the Shanghai Daotai referred to them as the "barbarians" of the "barbarian country." Lindsay and others were very uncomfortable with this.[1]

In 1858, Article 51 of the Treaty of Tianjin signed by China and Britain specifically emphasized that all kinds of official documents, whether in Beijing or other provinces, were not allowed to use the word "barbarian" to describe British officials. From then on, "barbarian" was replaced by "foreigner" in the official diplomatic documents of the Qing government. The "barbarians" who were originally despised by the Chinese had become high-class "foreigners," who were more powerful than most locals.

This shows how important and necessary it is to establish national and cultural self-confidence.

Some may also say that the Qing government let China down because of its closed-door policy. Wouldn't it have been better to get foreign investment, integrate into the global market, and gain development opportunities? However, this idea was only an illusion. The fact is that the imperialists were not willing and would not help China to open up to the outside world on an equal footing and to become democratic and strong on the basis of independence. The money they invested in China was extorted and exploited from China. They only wanted to use China as a market for their surplus products, and as a base for seizing cheap raw materials and labor. It was in their long-term interest to keep China in a backward political and economic system and a state of poverty. If, in the course of this process, some degree of change toward capitalism occurred in China, it was due to the imperialists' need to facilitate their colonial rule.

---

1. Li, Shaowei et al. *70 Years of Home and Country: The Sharpening and Rebirth of a Civilization* (edited by Southwind Media Think Tank) Journal Press, 2019, p. 52.

After the Opium War in 1840, imperialism broke into China like a jackal through a fence. The nation was no longer at peace, and experienced bullying from Western powers. Under the foreign military invasion, the Western powers gained more and more privileges. China, reduced to a semi-colony, was left wide open and at the mercy of others. In those days:

- Foreigners controlled China's customs, and kept the keys to China's gates in their own pockets.
- Foreigners were free to open factories, enterprises, banks, and merchant houses in China, and eventually gained a stranglehold on China's economic lifeblood.
- Foreigners could set up churches and schools in China according to their own rules, forcibly importing Western culture and religion into China and trying to brainwash the Chinese with their so-called "advanced civilization."
- Foreign warships and merchant ships could sail freely along China's coasts and inland rivers. The armies of the powers were stationed on Chinese territory, and the Chinese people were under constant surveillance and threat, with no security for national defense.

Hundreds of unequal treaties, statutes, and special articles bound China like a huge invisible and omnipresent net in all aspects, including politics, economy, military, and culture. Like a parasite, they sucked the blood of Chinese people, making the nation weaker and weaker under the endless demands of the powers. The powers controlled China's ports of commerce, customs, foreign trade, transportation, and other important lifelines, and dumped large quantities of goods, turning China into a market for their products and a base for extracting raw materials.

The military invasion and brutal exploitation by the Western powers led to the bleeding of the modern Chinese economy and the outflow of silver. In *The Great Divergence: Europe, China, and the Making of the Modern World Economy*, American historian Kenneth Pomeranz points out, "the additional funds that exceeded the power of Britain several times between 1689 and 1815 were raised from the London capital market, while after 1840, the deficit was filled by Chinese reparations."[1] This shows that the Opium War caused great losses in the economy of the Qing Dynasty. A large amount of silver flowed to the Western powers and became part of the "dirty blood" of the original capitalist accumulation.

There is no doubt that modern China has always been in the tragic situation of being invaded, looted, and oppressed. The poverty and backwardness of modern China were caused by imperialist colonial rule and cruel exploitation.

1. Pomeranz, Kenneth. *The Great Divergence: Europe, China, and the Making of the Modern World Economy*. Translated by Shi Jianyun. Jiangsu People's Publishing House, 2003, p. 174.

PART 2

China Awakens:

From Institutional Transplants to Cultural Enlightenment and Revolutionary Thinking

China is a famously peace-loving nation, but will never submit to foreign aggression and bullying.

The outbreak of the Opium War in 1840 ended modern China's global isolation, and brought it into closer contact with the rest of the world. The Chinese people thus had their eyes opened to the changes that had taken place and were taking place in the outside world. However, modern China was connected to the world as a semi-colony, and the awakening of the Chinese nation was a tortuous process of resistance to invasion and oppression.

In world history, the relationship between intellectual and political revolutions has always been inextricably linked, both in China and abroad. In Europe, the Renaissance – which lasted nearly 300 years from the mid-14th century to the end of the 16th century – broke the bonds of ecclesiastical theology, and put an end to the particularly 'dark' era of the Western European Middle Ages, thus giving rise to the bourgeois revolution. In China, revolutionaries used the pen as a gun, advocating revolutionary and republican ideas, and fighting to break the feudal ideological and cultural 'black room,' triggering the Xinhai Revolution, which ended the feudal imperial system that had lasted for more than 2,000 years. The New Culture Movement used literature as a banner to promote democracy and science, break spiritual shackles, and spread new ideas. It give birth in turn to the May Fourth Movement, which kicked off the New Democratic Revolution.

1

THE 1911 XINHAI REVOLUTION

While many people thought that the Qing Dynasty had restored the Tongzhi regime to become the first-class power in Asia, and was getting closer to the Western powers because of the seemingly remarkable achievements of the Westernization Movement, Sun Yat-sen had long recognized the decadent nature of the Qing Dynasty's feudal rule and its declining fate. While the Sino-Japanese War was still in progress, Sun had already begun to make further preparations for its overthrow.

On 24 November, 1894, Sun united with like-minded anti-Qing aspirants and founded the Xingzhong Society – the earliest bourgeois revolutionary group in China – in Honolulu, USA. They coined the slogan "Revive China," and began to plan the armed overthrow of the Qing Dynasty.

In February 1895, Sun Yat-sen established the headquarters of the Society in Hong Kong; in October, the Society launched an uprising in Guangzhou and later in Huizhou. Although both armed uprisings failed, they had a significant impact both in China and abroad.

The failure of the bourgeois Hundred Days of Reform in 1898 reinforced the conviction of Sun Yat-sen and other revolutionaries that it was undesirable to hope for self-reform within the Qing government system, and that revolution was the only fundamental way out for national revitalization.

However, most of the members of the Xingzhong Society were overseas Chinese, and had little influence in China. Under these circumstances, the question of how to awaken the general public to rise against the Manchu government and the feudal imperial system and form a revolutionary torrent became a problem for revolutionary aspirants struggled to explore at that time. In order to awaken the people, the revolutionaries formed groups, published revolutionary books and newspapers, and actively spread democratic revolutionary ideas.

In 1903, Chen Tianhua's *The Warning Bell* and *A Sharp Turn Back* were published – two popular books with a strong patriotic spirit and revolutionary courage, which profoundly exposed the corruption of the Qing government and the unprecedented crisis of the Chinese nation. In the books, Chen regretfully depicted China's tragic situation at the beginning of the 20th century under imperialist aggression and serious military threat: "Russia in the north has surrounded me on three sides; the British, under the pretext of commerce, have poisonous plans for China and Tibet; France, occupying Guangzhou, has its eye on Yunnan and Guizhou; Germany, with its Jiaozhou territory, is looking to the East; New Japan is taking Taiwan and then Fujian; the USA, too, wants to cut off its territory." Faced with the critical situation of "the country's demise and extinction," Chen wrote, "If we want to resist the foreigners, we should only talk about revolutionary independence, not about the king."[1]

Soon after, Zou Rong's famous book *Revolutionary Pioneers* was published, in which he wrote with fire-like enthusiasm and poetic language, "Aha! I, China, must not be revolutionary today! If China wants to be free from the bondage of the Manchurians today, it must be revolutionary. If China wants to be independent, it must be revolutionary. If China wants to be equal to the world powers, it must be revolutionary. If China wants to survive in the new world of the 20th century, it must be revolutionary. If China wants to be a famous country and the master of the earth, it must be revolutionary," for "Revolution is the common law of the evolution of the heavens; revolution is the axiom of the world."[2] Zou Rong's popular, emotionally-charged writing and strong revolutionary calls shook the Chinese intellectual world, and inspired the ideals and passion of advanced elements to recreate China by revolutionary means.

Around 1904, revolutionary groups such as the Huaxing Society, the Guangfu Society, and the Yuewang Society emerged, spreading throughout Jiangsu, Zhejiang, Hunan, Hubei, Anhui, Fujian, Jiangxi, Sichuan, and

1. Liu, Qingbo and Peng, Guoxing. *The Chen Tianhua Collection,* Hunan People's Publishing House, 1982, p. 37.
2. Zou, Rong. *Revolutionary Pioneers*, China Bookstore, 1958, pp. 1–2

Shaanxi. This indicated that a new type of social and political force – a bourgeois revolutionary faction – had taken shape.

In 1905, two major events occurred in China, with far-reaching effects. The first was the establishment of the Chinese League. On 20 August 1905, Sun Yat-sen contacted the Xingzhong, Huaxing, and Guangfu Societies and other revolutionaries with a view to establishing the Chinese League in Tokyo. At the founding meeting, Sun was elected as the premier, and it was stipulated that under the premiership there would be three ministries – executive, deliberative, and judicial – in accordance with the principle of the separation of powers. In November, in the League's organ, the *People's Daily*, Sun outlined the 16-word (in Chinese) motto of the organization as 'The Three Principles of the People – nationalism, civil rights, and the people's livelihood.' These principles constituted a complete bourgeois-democratic revolutionary program, reflecting the Chinese people's urgent desire for national independence, democratic rights, and livelihood. They also played a significant role in promoting and facilitating the revolutionary struggle.

After the establishment of the League there were fierce debates between royalists and reformists. After two or three years of discussions on such important issues as whether to overthrow the Qing Dynasty by violence, whether to establish a bourgeois democratic republic, and whether to change the feudal land system, the reformists were finally defeated, and the enthusiasm for democratic revolution became even higher. Meanwhile, they actively expanded their organizations, developed revolutionary forces, and launched a series of armed uprisings in China. From 1906 to 1910, the League organized and launched the Ping Liuli Uprising on the border between Hunan and Jiangxi, the Huanggang Uprising in Chaozhou, Guangdong, the Qinuhu Uprising in Huizhou, the Fangcheng Uprising in Qinzhou and Lianzhou, the Nanguan Uprising in Guangxi Zhen, the Hekou Uprising in Yunnan, and a series of armed struggles such as the famous Guangzhou Uprising. All of these uprisings quickly failed because they were essentially purely military actions detached from the masses, and the feudal ruling forces were still strong. However, they expanded the revolutionary influence among the people. The bloodshed stirred up a fighting spirit against the Qing Dynasty, and contributed to the climax of the revolution.

The second thing was the abolition of the imperial examinations and the establishment of new-style schools. On 2 September 1905, the Qing government was forced by the development of the New Deal to stop all imperial examinations from the following year. Soon after, provincial administrators were appointed to take charge of the affairs of the academies, and new-style academies were gradually set up throughout the country.

The abolition of the imperial examinations was a major event in the millennia-old feudal society, and had far-reaching effects. As a result, hundreds of thousands of students, millions of children, and many more intellectuals who sought to change their fate by reading classical texts and history and writing 'eight-legged' essays, lost out on a chance to take the imperial examinations. They had to abandon their studies and give up their dreams of earning a living. Many resentful intellectuals turned from loyalty to their country to opposing feudal rule.

The imperial examinations emphasized national studies, classical texts, and history, while the new-style academies focused on Western science. A large number of students were sent abroad to study, especially to Japan. By 1906, the number of students studying in Japan topped 8,000. By 1909, there were more than 800 students studying in the USA. After returning to China, many of these foreign students taught in new-style schools in various provinces, which in turn promoted domestic education. By 1909, there were 460 middle schools with 40,468 students and 51,678 elementary schools with 1,522,746 students.[1]

Most of these exchange students and the pupils at the new-style schools in China came from the lower and middle classes. They were less blindly arrogant and pedantic than the old-style scholars and intellectuals, who saw China as the world and the Qing Dynasty as the great heavenly power. They felt the national and social crisis more directly, and experienced it more deeply; they were young, and more easily accepting of new ideas, new concepts, and new propositions. Full of confidence in their personal and national future, they had strong patriotic feelings and a fierce desire for innovation.

Li Da, a delegate at the First Party Congress, recalled attending a new-style school in 1905:

---

1. Sha, Jiansun (editor-in-chief). *General History of the Communist Party of China, Vol. 1*, Hunan Education Press, 1995, pp. 21–22.

> "At the age of 15, I was admitted to a publicly funded high school. I began to gain some new knowledge and gradually learned about some national events. For example, from looking at the map, I knew that the 'foreign devil' countries often talked about in the past were Britain, the USA, Germany, France, Italy, Japan, Russia, and Austria, and they had all invaded China. China's poverty and backwardness were due to political darkness, and the Qing court's pandering to foreigners... I began to develop some patriotic consciousness, and became patriotic."[1]

As increasing numbers of foreign students and new intellectuals took the revolutionary path out of frustration with the Qing government, the emerging social forces were immature but growing. With the continuous organization and mobilization of the League, the climax of the democratic revolution soon arrived.

In April 1911, the Huanghuagang Uprising broke out in Guangzhou, with revolutionaries such as Huang Xing leading a fierce attack on the governor's palace. They were eventually defeated by the arrival of large numbers of Qing troops, and 72 martyrs died for their country. Around this time, the people's struggle against the Qing Dynasty developed rapidly in various places. The movement to protect the roads also rose widely, meaning that the subjective and objective conditions were ripe for overthrowing the Qing Dynasty. After the failure of the Huanghuagang Uprising, the League decided to shift the center of the revolution to the Yangtze River valley. In September, the Hubei Revolutionary Society and the Communist Progressive Society united and held a joint meeting. They decided to launch an armed uprising, and set up a leading body. On 9 October, leaders including Liu Fuji, Peng Chufan, and Yang Hongsheng were arrested, and gave up their lives for the cause. However, the revolutionaries were not deterred, and continued to intensify their preparations for the uprising.

On 10 October, Xiong Bingkun of the Eighth Battalion of the New Army Engineers led the revolutionaries of the battalion to fire the first shot of the Wuchang Uprising. With the cooperation of soldiers from all battalions, they killed the reactionary officers who blocked the uprising, occupied the armory

1. Li, Da. 'Advance Along the Road to Revolution,' *China Youth*, No. 13 and 14, 1961.

and Chu Wangtai in one fell swoop, and captured high points such as Snake Hill and Phoenix Hill. Then, the insurgents divided into three groups and attacked the governor's palace. The new troops in Hanyang and Hankou also revolted, and occupied the two places. On 12 October, the Hubei military government was established.

The news of the Wuchang Uprising spread around the country, and all provinces responded, setting off a revolutionary storm throughout China. Between 11 October and 9 November, the city of Shanghai and 13 of the 24 provinces declared independence and joined the revolutionary camp. On 29 December, representatives of the provinces elected Sun Yat-sen – by then a recognized revolutionary leader – as the provisional president in Nanjing.

On 1 January 1912, Sun was formally sworn in as the first provisional president of the Republic of China in Nanjing, and renamed the country the Republic of China. On 3 January, provincial representatives co-opted Li Yuanhong as vice president. On 28 January, the provisional Senate was established as the legislative body of the provisional government. The establishment of the Provisional Government of the Republic of China in Nanjing marked the birth of the first bourgeois republic in the nation's history.

The new government enacted the Provisional Treaty of the Republic of China, which was a bourgeois republican constitution, and promulgated a series of new measures to abolish feudal customs. These included changing to the solar calendar and using 1 January 1912 as the beginning of the Republic of China calendar year, as well as cutting men's braids, unbinding women's feet, and stopping the prostration of subordinates to superior officials. This reflected the revolutionary spirit of removing the old and bringing in the new, and aspiring to republicanism.

The Xinhai Revolution overthrew the Qing Dynasty, and put an end to the monarchical dictatorship that had lasted for more than 2,000 years in China. It established a republican system of government, opened the floodgates of progress in China, and spread the concept of democracy and republicanism. It also greatly promoted the liberation of the Chinese nation's thinking, and sparked major social changes.

2

THE DIFFICULTIES OF CREATING A DEMOCRATIC REPUBLIC

After the Taiping Uprising, Western powers became even more hostile to China's revolutionary movement. As soon as the news of the Wuchang Uprising spread, they tried to stifle the revolution by every means possible. For one thing, they isolated the revolutionary camp politically, militarily, economically, and diplomatically; for another, they chose Yuan Shikai as a new agent to defend imperialist interests in China when the Qing court's power had already waned. Under the pressure of imperialism, the Qing government appointed Yuan as premier of the cabinet.

After Yuan Shikai had seized true power, he played two sides against the southern revolutionary camp. He hastily mobilized the Beiyang Army to suppress the revolutionary forces in the south, and gave a high profile to the 'North-South Peace Talks,' but his fundamental purpose was to prevent the revolutionary forces in the south from developing in the north, and to divide and discourage the revolutionaries.

Sun Yat-sen was initially opposed to peace talks between the north and the south. On returning to Shanghai from abroad, he publicly stated that there would be no peace talks until the revolutionary aims were achieved. After the establishment of the Provisional Government, Sun himself became the commander-in-chief of the Northern Expeditionary Army and announced a northern expedition. The Northern Expeditionary Army defeated the Qing army in Suzhou and Xuzhou, and achieved some victories in other areas as well.

However, due to the intervention of the Western powers and the fact that the revolutionary forces were still at a disadvantage compared to the Beiyang

Army, the North-South Peace Talks were endorsed by many people within the revolutionary faction, and the Northern Expedition was aborted halfway through. Sun Yat-sen was forced to declare that he would give provisional presidency to Yuan Shikai as long as he truly favored the republic and forced the Qing Emperor to abdicate.

The ambitious Yuan Shikai called the Provisional Government of Nanjing to express his 'support' for the republic, claiming that it was the best state system in the world. He also forced the Qing emperor to abdicate. On 12 February 1912, the Qing Emperor announced his abdication under the conditions that he would not abrogate his imperial title, would remain living in the palace temporarily, and would receive four million taels of money per year. After Sun Yat-sen learned of this abdication and Yuan Shikai's approval of the republic, he immediately submitted his resignation to the Senate, and recommended that Yuan succeed him as the provisional president. On 15 February, the Senate elected Yuan as provisional president. On 10 March, he was sworn in as the provisional president of the Republic of China in Beijing. The fruits of the Xinhai Revolution were finally usurped, and China entered the period of the Beiyang Warlord rule.

The ultimate failure of the Xinhai Revolution showed that the Chinese national bourgeoisie was weak and compromising. It could not lead the semi-colonial and semi-feudal nation to a complete victory of the democratic revolution against imperialism and feudalism, meaning that the program of the bourgeois republic could not be realized in China.

After Yuan Shikai became president of the Republic of China, he soon reneged on his previous promises. He became a dictator, making a series of moves to undermine the democratic republic, and suppressing Sun Yat-sen's 'Second Revolution.' He signed the 'Twenty-one Demands' with Japan to destroy China, and finally staged the scandalous act of naming himself emperor on 12 December 1915.

In 1916, after the death of Yuan Shikai – who had been emperor for 83 days – the essence of warlord rule did not change. Although the Republic of China nominally had only one president, it was already divided among warlords, and the feudal economy, politics, and ideology were still dominant. In July 1917, the scandalous drama of Zhang Xun's restoration of the empire was staged, but lasted only 12 days from the beginning to the end.

After the death of Yuan Shikai, the Northern Warlords divided into the Zhi, Wan, and Feng branches.

The Wan branch was headed by Duan Qirui, with the support of Japanese imperialism, controlling the central government in Beijing and ruling provinces such as Shandong, Henan, Anhui, Fujian, and Zhejiang.

The Zhi branch was headed by Feng Guozhang and his successors Cao Kun and Wu Peifu, with the support of British and American imperialism, ruling Zhili, Jiangsu, Jiangxi, Hubei and other provinces, and competing with the Wan for controlling the Beijing central government.

The Feng branch was headed by Zhang Zuolin, and ruled northeastern China. With the support of Japanese imperialism, it gradually expanded its power into the capital, and competed with the Zhi and Wan branches for control of the central government in Beijing.

In order to consolidate and expand their territories and fight for control of the Beiyang government, with the support of imperialism, the warlords engaged in frequent contests and even wars, which not only plunged the country into long-term division and turmoil, but also sank China ever deeper into the abyss of a semi-colonialism and semi-feudalism by constantly selling out national interests and borrowing money from the powers to support the war. The actions of the warlords were described as follows:

> "These people do nothing, and only know how to ride in a car and owe foreign debts. The first thing they do is sell their country, little by little, to foreign thieves; the second thing they do is sell themselves to foreign thieves every day, every hour, every minute."[1]

Mao Zedong pointed out that the Revolution of 1911 "had its triumphs and its failures. You see, the Xinhai Revolution drove out the emperor, so was it not a victory? To say that it failed is to say that it only drove away an emperor. But China was still under the oppression of imperialism and feudalism, and the revolutionary task of anti-imperialism and anti-feudalism was not completed."[2]

As Cai Jimin wrote in his poem 'The Book of Indignation':

1. *The First Appearance of the Communist Party of China on the International Political Stage.* Memorial Hall of the First Congress, p. 267.
2. *Selected Works of Mao Zedong, Vol. 2*, People's Publishing House, 1991, p. 564.

"The situation changes, with the vicissitudes of life,
When you repel the tiger, the wolf comes instead;
Boundless money and bloodshed have only bought a fake republic."

A series of historical facts after the Xinhai Revolution proved that the bourgeois republic program could not be realized in China under the rule of imperialism and local warlords. The Northern Warlords made the 'Republic' a mere formality – a mere signboard. Faced with the huge contrast between the democratic and republican ideals and the oppressive reality, people grew tired of the situation. A Qing Dynasty legacy compiler wrote a couplet to satirize the status quo of the 'Republic' at the time:

"The people are the same, the country is the same –
what is the difference between north and south?
In a word, in a nutshell, they are neither east nor west."[1]

This situation deeply affected advanced elements and people who had expectations of the bourgeois revolution in China, and immersed them in extreme bitterness and uncertainty. In the fall of 1916, Zhou Enlai – who was studying at the Nankai School – was filled with worry for his country, and wrote:

"The continent is in the grip of a storm, and the country is in a daze.
The saddest thing is that fall has come again, and the sound of insects is unheard."[2]

Faced with this situation, Sun Yat-sen launched the 'Second Revolution' and the Constitutional Protection Movement, but without a reliable revolutionary army, a strong revolutionary organization, or the ability to rouse the people, both ended in failure. In May 1918, Sun – who had been expelled from the military government of Guangdong by the Southwestern Warlords – wrote bitterly in his telegram of resignation from the post of Marshal: "China's greatest

1. Pu, Yi. *From Emperor to Citizen*, People's Publishing House, 1964, Chapter 2.
2. *Selected Poems and Writings of Comrade Zhou Enlai Before and After May Fourth,* Tianjin People's Publishing House, 1979, pp. 32–33.

problem is the struggle of the martial artists. The South and the North are like raccoons. Although they are called the provinces of law protection, they are not willing to bow down under the law and public opinion."[1] Thereafter, he went to Japan to conduct activities, but was treated with indifference. Upon his return to Shanghai, without a single soldier in his possession, without a revolutionary organization around him, and without the right direction for his advance, Sun became upset, and developed a negative attitude towards political activities, intending to put his energy into writing books and developing industry instead.

Faced with a deepening national and social crisis between the Xinhai Revolution in 1911 and the May Fourth Movement in 1919, patriots from all echelons of society continued to struggle. The task of salvation and survival faced by the national democratic revolution in modern China became even more urgent. What was the way out for China? This was still the most urgent question of the times.

1. *Chronology of Sun Yat-sen*, p. 227

3

A CULTURAL ENLIGHTENMENT OF DEMOCRACY AND SCIENCE

ALTHOUGH THE REVOLUTION OF 1911 deposed the Manchu Emperor, the revolution was in no way thorough. Feudal thought and imperial consciousness were still entrenched in the minds of some Chinese people. As a result, Yuan Shikai was able to rise up as 'Great Leader,' installing himself as an autocratic emperor with hereditary power. Yuan began to reinstitute elements of state Confucianism. He was quickly ousted by the people, but the harsh reality indicated that while it might be easy to overthrow a regime using violent tactics, it is far more difficult to change the mindset of a generation.

The autocratic dictatorship and dark rule of the Beiyang warlords led a group of advanced intellectuals to reflect on the fundamental reason for the failure of the Revolution of 1911, namely that it did not awaken the ideological awareness of the majority of citizens, because it did not eradicate the feudal mindset. Since it did not arouse the general public's ideological awareness and participation in action, the transplantation of Western political systems alone was not enough to save China. Neither did it make sense to shout about the Constitution and the separation of powers. Therefore, it was necessary to launch a new cultural movement to awaken people's consciousness, so as to liberate the masses from the state of ignorance bound by feudal thought.

As Lu Xun pointed out in the preface to *Call to Arms*, "The people of a weak and backward country, however strong and healthy they may be, can only serve to be made examples of, or to witness such futile spectacles; and it doesn't really matter how many of them die of illness. The most important thing, therefore, is to change their spirit."

Lu Xun's views were shared by Chen Duxiu. In June 1915, 36-year-old Chen returned to Shanghai from Japan, furious about the traitorous 'Twenty-one Demands' treaty that had just been signed between the Beiyang government and Japan. However, unlike other young radical patriots, he did not just stop at protest and opposition. He pointed out that unless anti-republican thought was washed completely from people's minds, the old system of monarchy would prevail, and the democratic republic would not be stable. Therefore, in order to carry out a political revolution in China, it would have to "start with a spiritual revolution" and "change the Chinese people's minds and spirits" first.[1]

This was because Chen Duxiu had experienced the pain of Republican disillusionment, which had led him to realize that the success of political revolution depended on the awakening and participation of the majority, rather than the movement of a few political party elites. He wrote, "Nowadays, the so-called 'republic' and the so-called 'constitution' are the ideas of a few political parties; most citizens do not have a sense of what is at stake, nor a sense of choice. The majority of people are aware that the minority can be the forerunner, but not the substitute. The major cause of the constitutional republic can be advocated by the minority, but not realized by it."[2]

So, how could they awaken and involve the majority? According to Chen Duxiu, "If you want to make the republic worthy of its name, you must change people's minds. To change minds, you must start with words."[3]

On 15 September 1915, Volume 1 of *The Youth Magazine* was officially published in Shanghai, founded by Chen Duxiu. This magazine was originally a comprehensive academic journal for young people, with about 100 pages in each issue. One volume contained six issues.

Before the publication of *The Youth Magazine*, Shanghai Young Men's Christian Association had founded a weekly newspaper called *Shanghai Youth*. Soon after the launch of *The Youth Magazine*, the association wrote to its sponsor

---

1. Selected from the Modern History Research Room at the Chinese Academy of Social Sciences, and the Party History Research Room at the Museum of the Chinese Revolution: *Before and After the First National Congress of the Communist Party of China, Vol. 2*, People's Publishing House, 1980, p. 214.
2. *Selected Essays of Chen Duxiu, Vol. 1 of 3*, Sanlian Publishing Company, 1984, p. 107.
3. Ren, Zhuoxuan. 'Chen Duxiu's Life and My Comments,' *Biographic Lit*, Vol. 30, No. 5.

– the Chun Yui Book Company – claiming that *The Youth Magazine* was "so similar to *Shanghai Youth* that they should change the name quickly to avoid misunderstandings."[1] So, from Volume 2, published on 1 September 1916, *The Youth Magazine* officially changed its name to *New Youth*. The word 'New' expressed its main purpose of spreading new ideas, promoting new culture, enlightening new consciousness, and inspiring new youth. This was the origin of the New Culture Movement.

In January 1917, the renowned educator Cai Yuanpei was appointed President of Peking University. He put forward the concept of "following the principle of freedom of thought,"[2] encouraging academic research, publishing, and carrying out community activities. He also recruited a wide range of newcomers with genuine talent and knowledge to teach at Peking University.

In the same month, Chen Duxiu was hired as Dean of the School of Letters at Peking University, and was inaugurated in Beijing, taking the editorial department of *New Youth* with him. Famous scholars such as Li Dazhao, Lu Xun, Hu Shi, Qian Xuantong, and Liu Bannong soon joined the editorial department, and became the main contributors.

The team of writers for *New Youth* grew rapidly. In January 1918, an editorial committee was formed. From the first issue of the fourth volume, the style was changed to written vernacular Chinese. New punctuation was used, and new-style poems were published, encouraging other publications to follow suit. The influence of *New Youth* expanded rapidly. According to Zhang Guotao, who was a student at the School of Letters at Peking University at that time, the publication was "not well known" among his classmates until it switched to written vernacular Chinese. Thereafter, it "attracted wide attention from students, and each issue sold out quickly."[3] As a result, Peking University and the editorial department of *New Youth* became the main sites of the New Culture Movement.

1. Wang, Yuanfang. *Memories of the Yadong Library*, Academia Press, 1983, pp. 31–32.
2. Cai, Yuanpei. 'Letter to *Public Voice* and Reply to Lin Qinnan,' *Journal of Peking University*, March 21, 1919.
3. Ren, Jianshu. *Biography of Chen Duxiu*, Shanghai People's Publishing House, 2012, p. 102.

The basic slogan of the early New Culture Movement was to support 'Mr. De' and 'Mr. Sai'[1] i.e. democracy and science. This was because ignorance and autocracy depended on each other, and democracy and science complemented each other. Democracy is the bane of autocracy, while science is the adversary of ignorance. Therefore, these two slogans had strong practical relevance at that time. The purpose of promoting democracy was to oppose the dictatorship of the Beiyang warlords, as well as the autocratic ideology, hierarchy, and ethical principles of feudalism, which were still dominant in China. The purpose of promoting science was to oppose the tide of feudalism and retrogression, as well as the tendency towards superstition and blind obedience instead of progress.

Chen Duxiu put forward six points of hope for young people in his article 'Call to Youth,' published in the first issue of *New Youth*: "To be independent instead of servile, progressive instead of conservative, aggressive instead of retiring, cosmopolitan instead of isolationist, utilitarian instead of formalistic, and scientific instead of imaginative." He wrote, "The Chinese people want to escape from the age of ignorance, and they are ashamed to be shallow, so they rush to catch up. They should pay equal attention to science and human rights. What is science? It is our concept of things combined with objective phenomena, without contradictions in terms of subjective rationality."[2] Chen Duxiu thus established the banner of democracy and science, pointing directly at the key point of decadent feudal culture, and showing an unprecedented revolutionary spirit that was in complete opposition to feudalism.

Chen believed that democracy and science were the two wheels that would push Chinese society forward. On 15 January 1919, he wrote an article titled 'An Answer to the Crimes of *New Youth*' in the first issue of the sixth volume of *New Youth*: "My colleagues were originally innocent of these crimes. They committed them only because they supported democracy and science. To support democracy, they have to oppose Confucianism, etiquette, chastity, old ethics, and old politics. To support science, they have to oppose old art and old religion. To support both, they have to oppose the quintessence of Chinese culture and old literature." Finally, he made a clear-cut stand: "We

1. Mr. De means 'democracy,' transliterated as *demokelaxi*, which refers to democratic thought and politics. Mr. Sai means 'science,' transliterated as *saiyinsi*, which refers to modern natural science.
2. *Selected Essays of Chen Duxiu, Vol. 1 of 3*, Sanlian Publishing Company, 1984, pp. 77–78.

now believe that only science and democracy can cure the darkness in China's politics, morality, academics, and ideology. If we support these two 'gentlemen,' we cannot resign ourselves to the oppression of the government, attacks from society, or the shedding of blood."[1]

In order to establish a democratic concept, it was necessary to conduct a thorough struggle against feudal autocracy. Therefore, the thinkers of the New Culture Movement pointed their finger directly at the feudal ethics that had ruled China for more than 2,000 years.

On 15 January 1916, in response to the historical cross-current of Yuan Shikai's proclaiming himself emperor, Chen Duxiu published an article titled '1916' in the fifth issue of the first volume of *The Youth Magazine*, violently criticizing Confucian feudal ethics such as 'The Three Rules' and 'loyalty, filial piety, chastity, and righteousness.' He wrote: "If a ruler guides a subject, the subject is only the accessory of the ruler, and is not independent. If a father guides a son, the son is only the accessory of the father, and is not independent. If a husband guides a wife, the wife is only the accessary of the husband, and is not independent. If all men and women in the world serve as subjects, sons, and wives, nobody will be independent. 'The Three Rules' and 'loyalty, filial piety, and chastity' are not ethics; they are slave morality.[2]" Therefore, he demanded that these moralities be abolished in order to strive for independence.

On 15 February, Chen Duxiu published 'The Last Enlightenment' in the sixth issue of the first volume of *The Youth Magazine*. He emphasized that "if China wants to survive in the world, we must abandon the bureaucratic politics that have been handed down for thousands of years, and adopt free and autonomous national politics instead." He asserted that "there is no way for our politics, laws, and social morality to move from dark to bright if we do not break down feudal ethics."[3] He pointed out that 'The Three Rules' were incompatible with the Republican system, and all the old feudal thoughts against the Republic had to be washed from citizens' minds. Only in this way would the ideology of restoring the monarchy be eradicated in order for the Republic to be consolidated.

---

1. Chen, Duxiu. 'The Answer to the Crimes of *New Youth*,' *Selected Essays of Chen Duxiu, Vol. 1 of 3*, Sanlian Publishing Company, 1984, pp. 317–318.
2. *Selected Essays of Chen Duxiu, Vol. 1 of 3*, Sanlian Publishing Company, 1984, p. 103.
3. *Selected Essays of Chen Duxiu, Vol. 1 of 3*, Sanlian Publishing Company, 1984, p. 169.

Li Dazhao also launched strong attacks on feudal ethics. In May 1916, he wrote in his article 'Human Relations and Politics,' "The people and their monarch cannot coexist; freedom and despotism cannot coexist; therefore, if the monarch lives, the nation dies; if despotism lives, freedom dies."[1] Later, in his article 'The Ethics of Nature and Confucius,' he used the point of view of modern materialism to illustrate that old morality was not suitable for modern society. He pointed out that the universe is a natural entity with no beginning and no end. All natural and social phenomena are developing and changing, as is morality. Therefore, in order to establish new morality, we must use human power to accelerate the collapse of the outdated morality. "I will not hesitate to risk destroying the name of the holy and unlawful."[2]

The fundamental purpose of these fierce words and profound insights was to put forward a comprehensive challenge to feudal ethics, and shake the dominant position of feudal orthodoxy. These statements were also designed to break down the old masters and idols that bound Chinese people's thoughts, and to encourage people to become new citizens in control of their own destiny under the guidance of new ideas and new culture.

Science was another slogan of the New Culture Movement. To promote science, it was necessary to fight against feudal superstition – a major focus of the thinkers of the New Culture Movement.

After the failure of the Revolution of 1911, the resulting rise of retrogressive thinking meant that feudal superstition spread through society. In January 1918, Ding Baofu's article 'The Ghost in My Ideal' was published in the first issue of *Psychic Philosophy Magazine*, founded by the Shanghai Spiritual Society. He wrote that after people died, they became ghosts with shapes and substance. They were not visible to the human eye, but animals could see them. Obviously, this was an absurd view, couched in feudal superstition. On 15 May 1918, the fifth issue of the fourth volume of *New Youth* was published, in which Chen Duxiu and others wrote in opposition to Ding's theories.

Chen wrote an article titled 'Questioning the Belief in Ghosts.' At over 700 words in length, it raised six questions that were difficult to answer for those who claimed ghosts existed. He wrote, "Things that we can feel can probably be

1. *The Complete Works of Li Dazhao, Vol. 1*, People's Publishing House, 2006, p. 163.
2. *The Complete Works of Li Dazhao, Vol. 1*, People's Publishing House, 2006, p. 247.

explained by science. However, people who hold superstitious beliefs argue that ghosts are 'beyond feeling and beyond scientific explanation.' So how can you see their shapes and hear their voices? Besides, 'If a person can become a ghost, anything can become ghost.' Why do we 'just see the ghosts of people and not of animals?"[1] Using materialistic monism to oppose the dualism of matter and spirit, Chen's questions received no reply from the ghost theorists.

Lu Xun was another advocate of science. In October 1918, he summed up the struggle between science and superstition in 'Random Records' in the fourth issue of the fourth volume of *New Youth*. He wrote, "There are some people who hate science and pursue superstition. Because science can help people to understand and think clearly, it becomes their enemy." He added, "As far as I can see, in order to save this China, which has fallen into ruin, the method of 'Zhang Tianshi and the Confucian sage preaching from Shandong' is all wrong. Only science – real science – can save China, which has been destroyed by national subjugation."[2] Thanks to the resolute efforts of the leaders of the New Culture Movement, spirituality and feudal superstition were hit hard, and gradually lost their power.

Old morality and old literature were often dependent on each other. In the eyes of the feudal literati, only the use of literary language (used in ancient texts, poems, and lyrics) constituted authentic literature, which belonged to the upper class society. Operas and novels written in vernacular slang were side stories, and belonged to the lower class. For this reason, as the struggle to criticize feudal ethics was becoming increasingly popular. The likes of Chen Duxiu and Hu Shi initiated a literary revolution, using written vernacular Chinese as a tool to spread democracy and science, leading the ideological liberation movement across a wider range.

In terms of form, the literary revolution advocated easy-to-understand written vernacular Chinese, and opposed the classical form of the language. In terms of content, it used democratic 'new literature' written in vernacular Chinese to oppose feudal 'old literature.' As one of the advocates of the New Culture Movement, Hu Shi made great efforts to promote the literary

---

1. *Selected Essays of Chen Duxiu, Vol. 1 of 3*, Sanlian Publishing Company, 1984, pp. 264–265.
2. 'Random Records,' No. 33, *New Youth*, Vol. 4, Issue 4, October 15, 1918.

revolution. In January 1917, when the editorial department of *New Youth* moved to Beijing, he published an article titled 'Ruminations on Literary Reform' in the fifth issue of the second volume of *New Youth*, focusing on the reform of literary style. He proposed eight things: "Firstly, we should have something to say; secondly, we should not imitate the ancients; thirdly, we should emphasize grammar; fourthly, we should not complain unless we are ill; fifthly, we should not use clichés; sixthly, we should not use allusion; seventhly, we should not write antithetical sentences; eighthly, we should not avoid common words and sayings. All of this advocates the unity of language and literature, so written vernacular Chinese is the most authentic literature."[1]

In February, Chen Duxiu published 'Theories of Literary Revolution' in the sixth issue of the second volume of *New Youth*, officially beginning the 'Literary Revolution' in China. He revealed the reasons and original intention of initiating such a revolution, claiming that "Entrenching deep-rooted ethics, morality, literature, and art in our spiritual world is always a shady and dirty business. Today, if we want political innovation, we have to create literature that is entrenched in the world of politicians."

With regard to how to carry out the 'Literary Revolution,' he proposed three great doctrines. The first was "Abolish the polished aristocratic style, and build an easy and lyrical national literature instead"; the second was "Abolish the stale and extravagant classical style, and build a fresh and honest realistic literature instead"; the third was "Abolish the tedious work of recluses, and build a clear and common social literature."[2] He stated, "To improve Chinese literature, written vernacular Chinese is regarded as the most. Its rights and wrongs are very clear, which does not allow its opponents to have further discussion. Moreover, it must support what our people advocate, and stand for it unswervingly."[3]

Chen Duxiu's 'Theories of Literary Revolution' had clear-cut aims, strong momentum, sharp language, and a firm attitude, providing a theoretical weapon with which to criticize old literature, and pointing the way towards a new style

1. *The Collected Works of Hu Shi, Vol. 1*, Huangshan Publishing House, 1996, pp. 4–12.
2. *Selected Essays of Chen Duxiu, Vol. 1 of 3*, Sanlian Publishing Company, 1984, p. 172, p. 174.
3. *Selected Essays of Chen Duxiu, Vol. 1 of 3*, Sanlian Publishing Company, 1984, p. 208.

of literature. It was a manifesto that cast Chen as the leader of China's 'Literary Revolution.' The publication of this article was an attack on the old feudal literature, and attracted a lot of attention from literary circles. The likes of Qian Xuantong and Liu Bannong immediately responded, throwing themselves into the fray in support.

As a result, from the first issue of the fourth volume in January 1918, *New Youth* switched to publishing most of its articles in written vernacular Chinese, and began to include vernacular poems by Hu Shi, Shen Yinmo, and Liu Bannong from the second issue. In this way, they took practical actions to promote breakthroughs in the literary field and create a new style.

However, it was Lu Xun (who was later praised by Mao Zedong for being "the master of China's cultural revolution" and "a man of unyielding integrity") who produced the most epoch-making work in Chinese literature. In May 1918, 37-year-old Zhou Shuren published the first novel ever written in vernacular Chinese – *Diary of a Madman* – under the pen name 'Lu Xun.' His first vernacular novel was also his first shot at feudal ethics.

In this work, Lu Xun angrily exposed the true face of the feudal ethics that had prevailed for thousands of years, through the words of the 'madman': "I tried to look this up, but my history has no chronology, and scrawled all over each page are the words 'Virtue' and 'Morality.' Since I could not sleep anyway, I read intently half the night, until I began to see words between the lines, the whole book being filled with the two words – 'Eat people.'"[1]

Diary of a Madman was inspired by the New Culture Movement's spirit of advocating democracy and science, and was a vicious takedown of feudal ethics. Lu Xun went on to publish other exceptional works in vernacular Chinese such as *Kong Yiji*, *The Real Story of Ah-Q*, and *Medicine* in *New Youth*, criticizing the old feudal morality, reflecting the weakness of the national character, and arousing people's consciousness. His articles set a good example for the literary revolution, and laid a solid foundation for the development of new Chinese literature.

In this regard, in the article 'Crossing the River and Leading the Way,' Lu Xun pointed out that the goal of the literary revolution was not only to advocate for written vernacular Chinese, but also to improve thought. "If the

1. *The Complete Works of Lu Xun, Vol. 1*, People's Literature Publishing House, 1981, p. 425.

thought is still the same, no improvement will be made. Improving thought is the priority."[1] This idea of combining innovations in form and content pushed the literary revolution of the New Culture Movement to a deeper level. Under the influence of Lu Xun and others, a large number of writers of 'new literature' emerged in China.

The New Culture Movement of the early 20th century was a time of great ideological liberation in modern Chinese history, and was known as the 'Chinese Renaissance and Enlightenment.' It was unprecedented in the intensity of its attack old ideas, old concepts, old institutions, and old traditions, breaking the feudal confinement that had lasted for more than 2,000 years. It enlivened Chinese society and shook the rule of feudal orthodoxy, liberating people's thinking and invigorating the nation. Mao Zedong spoke highly of it in *On New Democracy*: "There had never been such a great and thoroughgoing cultural revolution since the dawn of Chinese history."[2]

Of course, while people today recognize the significance of the New Culture Movement, they also often point out that its attacks on traditional Chinese culture were somewhat excessive and biased. There was a subjectivist and one-sided bias in its approach and attitude of absolute affirmation or absolute negation, pitting tradition and modernity, and China and the West against each other. Furthermore, it was not good at dialectically analyzing and scientifically criticizing the essence and dross of Chinese traditional culture, nor the advancements and disadvantages of Western capitalist culture, such as improper handling of the relationship between the criticism and inheritance of Chinese traditional culture, represented by the likes of Confucius.

However, it is worth noting that major initiators of the New Culture Movement such as Chen Duxiu, Li Dazhao, Hu Shi, Lu Xun, and Liu Bannong were themselves renowned scholars of traditional Chinese culture. The reason why they lashed out so violently at traditional Chinese culture was to awaken the Chinese people as quickly as possible. As Lu Xun wrote in *Silent China*,

> "By temperament, the Chinese love compromise and a happy mien. For instance, if you say that a room is too dark and a window should be

1. *The Complete Works of Lu Xun, Vol. 7*, People's Literature Publishing House, 1981, pp. 34–35.
2. *Selected Works of Mao Zedong*, People's Publishing House, 1991, p. 700.

opened, everyone is sure to disagree. But if you propose taking off the roof, they will compromise and be glad to open a window."

From this point of view, the New Culture Movement opened a window through full-scale fire and fierce attack, awakening a people who were sleeping in the 'iron house' of decadent feudal culture.

Historically, whenever there is a major social change, there is always an ideological revolution that goes along with it. The New Culture Movement was a revolutionary ideology that was used for ideological enlightenment and cultural promotion for political mobilization. It not only paved the way for the May Fourth Movement, but also created important conditions for the spread of Marxism thereafter.

4

THE PARIS PEACE CONFERENCE AND THE MAY FOURTH MOVEMENT

In November 1918, Germany signed a contract to surrender, bringing the First World War to an end.

The Beiyang warlord government had declared war on Germany on 14 August 1917, and Duan Qirui personally served as the war supervisor. He borrowed money from Japan many times, received arms and instructors from it, and trained three participating troops. These troops were nominally built to participate in the First World War, but they did not actually enter combat. Duan Qirui's true goal was to develop a direct army of his own, which could consolidate the rule of the Anhui warlords and be used against Sun Yat-sen's southern military government.

Although the Chinese army did not participate in the actual war, as many as 140,000 Chinese workers made significant sacrifices in the service of the Allied forces in the European theater, and China rightfully became one of the eventual victors in the conflict.

This news was a great source of excitement for many Chinese people, coming as it did in a period of oppression. The government in Beijing declared a three-day holiday. Tens of thousands took to the streets to celebrate with lanterns, and people in Shanghai and many other cities held various kinds of celebrations. Not since 1840 had the Chinese people felt such a sense of victory.

They were even more heartened by President Woodrow Wilson's speech on the day the war ended. In his speech, Wilson made 14 recommendations for world peace, including no secret diplomacy, respect for the opinions of colonial and colonized nations, equal rights for all nations, large and small, and justice instead of might. The equality and friendliness shown by the USA gave the Chinese people hope for the future. The Chinese press and publishers wrote articles claiming that China had thus turned a corner and would abolish unequal treaties, end 100 years of international defeat, and be on par with Britain, France, and the USA. Some students in Beijing rushed to the US Embassy in high spirits, shouting, "Long live President Wilson!"

In January 1919, the victorious powers of Britain, France, the USA, Italy, Japan, and China met at the Palace of Versailles in Paris for a peace conference.

The Paris Peace Conference, which was advertised as a meeting that would ensure international peace and security, was in fact designed to divide the spoils of the world among the imperialist countries. The conference was attended by more than 1,000 delegates from 27 countries. China, as a victorious nation, sent five delegates, including Foreign Minister Lu Zhengxiang and Ambassador to the USA Wellington Koo (Gu Weijun).

The Peace Conference initially established a 'Council of Ten' consisting of the heads of state and foreign ministers of the USA, Britain, France, and Italy, and two special representatives of Japan. Later, a 'Council of Five' was established, consisting of the foreign ministers of the USA, Britain, France, and Italy, and the representative of Japan, which became the decision-making body of the Council, and decided on all major issues.[1] This mechanism allowed the USA, Britain, and France to manipulate the meeting.

China was placed at a disadvantage even before the conference. According to promises made by Britain and France, China would be treated as great power after the war. The participating countries were divided into three classes, with five, three, and two delegates respectively. The Chinese government took it for granted that, as a large and victorious country, it should send five delegates to attend the conference. Therefore, it sent Foreign Minister Lu Zhengxiang, Ambassador to the USA Wellington Koo, Ambassador to Britain Shi Zhaoji, Ambassador to Belgium Wei Chenzu, and Southern military government representative Wang Zhengting, with Lu Zhengxiang as the chief representative. However, after arriving in Paris, they were informed that China could only have two delegates. The Chinese delegation was unable to achieve anything,

1. Sha, Jiansun. *History of the Communist Party of China (1921–1949), Vol. 1*, Central Literature Publishing House, 2006, p. 130.

despite its efforts, to the frustration and embarrassment of Foreign Minister Lu Zhengxiang. It was finally decided that the five delegates would take turns to attend the conference.

At the beginning of the Paris Peace Conference, under the influence and pressure of national public opinion, the Chinese delegates put forward three proposals. Firstly, they raised seven propositions against the privileges of the imperialist countries in China, namely (1) abandoning the sphere of influence, (2) withdrawing foreign troops and patrols, (3) abolishing foreign postal and telegraph organs, (4) revoking consular jurisdiction, (5) returning leased lands, (6) returning leased territories, and (7) tariff autonomy. Secondly, they demanded the cancellation of the 'Twenty-one Demands,' which had been signed between Japan and Yuan Shikai in 1915, calling for the destruction of China. Thirdly, they demanded the return of the former German-leased lands, railroads, mines, and other rights and interests in Shandong, which had been seized by Japan during the First World War.

However, no sooner than the Chinese delegation's first two proposals had been submitted, they were rejected. In a letter to the Chinese delegates, French Prime Minister Georges Clemenceau – president of the Peace Conference's Supreme Council – wrote, "Recognizing the importance of the issue, it cannot be considered within the competence of the Peace Conference."[1] In this way, all that the Chinese delegates could fight for was the question of Shandong.

Although the question of Shandong was discussed, the Japanese representatives firmly refused to return the former German interests there to China, citing the secret agreement of understanding signed between Japan and Britain, France, Russia, and Italy in 1917, as well as the exchange of letters to which Zhang Zongxiang had "readily agreed" when the railroad loan agreement was signed between China and Japan. After the meeting, Japan exerted pressure on the Chinese government through diplomatic channels.

The discussion of the Shandong issue was reported in China, and immediately aroused strong righteous indignation across all echelons of society. In February and March, rallies were held in Beijing, Shandong, and other parts of the country. Telegrams were sent out, strongly requesting the Beiyang

---

1. Sha, Jiansun. *History of the Communist Party of China (1921–1949), Vol. 1,* Central Literature Publishing House, 2006, pp. 130–131.

government and the Chinese delegates at the Peace Conference to negotiate seriously, argue on the basis of reason, and recover the sovereignty of Shandong.

The Paris Peace Conference had a long debate on the Shandong issue, but it remained inconclusive. When the American, British, French, and Italian heads of state met to discuss it, Japanese delegates were invited to attend the meeting. However, Chinese delegates were excluded, as members of a sovereign state, and were not even entitled to see the minutes of the meeting. The US representative proposed that the former German rights and interests in Shandong should be temporarily administered by the Peace Conference or handed over to the 'Five Powers' of the USA, Britain, France, Italy, and Japan, but Japan still resolutely opposed it, and threatened to withdraw from the Peace Conference if its demands were not met. The USA, Britain, France, and other countries reneged on their promises, and made compromises to Japan in order to ease the conflicts among the imperialists.

On 30 April, regardless of the repeated requests from Chinese delegates, the manipulator of the Paris Peace Conference finally decided to transfer all of the former German privileges in Shandong to Japan, and explicitly included it in the Treaty of Versailles.

At this point, China's diplomatic efforts at the Paris Peace Conference failed completely. It had participated in the conference as a victorious nation, but was treated as a loser, and suffered an unprecedented humiliation. However, when Lu Zhengxiang reported the situation to the Beiyang government, the latter informed the Chinese delegates that they should sign the peace treaty. Such a result was hugely unexpected.

The stark contrast between the past glory of the Chinese nation and the reality of being trampled upon by others, the people's legitimate demands as a victorious country, and the weak and incompetent warlord government made the humiliation and misfortune unbearable for a Chinese population bent on reprisal.

More importantly, this humiliation, along with the decline of the country since the late Qing Dynasty, made the Chinese people realize for the first time that faced with the 'law of the jungle' of the Western powers, the promise that justice would prevail over might was only an illusion; thanks to the weak and incompetent warlord government, both the victorious and defeated countries were trampled over. The hope of the Chinese nation lay nowhere else but in rising up to save itself.

On 1 May 1919, the English-language Beijing newspaper *China Times* published a report from the Chinese delegation, stating the reasons for the failure of diplomacy at the Paris Peace Conference. On the same day, the Shanghai-based English-language newspaper *The China Press* also published the news that "the government received a call from the Chinese delegation in Paris, saying that the diplomatic war against Japan over the return of the Jiaozhou lease had failed."

It was also on this day that Li Dazhao – who had been concerned about the fate of China and the progress of the Paris Peace Conference – suggested in his article 'Thoughts on May Day' in *The Morning Post:* "May Day is the day when the only weapon of the workers of the world – direct action – was created."[1] The meaning of direct action is to organize and act spontaneously without the approval of the authorities in order to achieve revolutionary goals. On the eve of May Fourth, Li Dazhao's article mentioned it openly and distinctly for the first time, sending out a battle cry for the coming revolutionary storm of the May Fourth Movement.

The deep ideological foundation laid by the New Culture Movement, the grief and anger inspired by China's humiliation, and the shock and inspiration of the October Revolution in Russia finally ignited anti-imperialist and patriotic fury in the Chinese people.

The second of May in Beijing was a seemingly calm day with a beautiful breeze and high clouds. However, beneath this calm surface, a storm was brewing.

Early in the morning, Cai Yuanpei – President of Peking University – arrived at his office in a hurry, dressed in a long shirt and carrying a briefcase. He instructed the janitor to bring in some of the student class presidents and student club leaders, and showed them an article entitled 'Diplomatic Alert to the Nation' that had just been published in the *Beijing Morning Post.* The article said, "Yesterday I received a call from Mr. Liang Rengong in Paris, saying that the issue of Qingdao, and the Japanese ambassador's efforts to fight for it, had

1. *The Complete Works of Li Dazhao, Vol. 2*, People's Publishing House, 2006, p. 335.

moved the British and French. I heard that it would be handed over directly to Japan. If this is the case now, Jiaozhou is dead, Shandong is dead, and China is no longer a country."

The author of this article was Lin Changmin, who was an advisor to Xu Shichang – the great president of the Beijing government – and a member and chief of the Foreign Affairs Committee. The article conveyed Liang Qichao's alarming news from Paris that China's efforts at the Peace Conference had finally failed, and that none of the German interests in Shandong would be returned to China, but would be "ceded" to Japan. This confirmed the news of China's diplomatic failure, which had been published the day before in the Shanghai-based English-language newspaper *The China Press*. Seeing this news, the students present immediately expressed righteous indignation: "We must immediately petition to prevent the government from signing the agreement!"

In the afternoon of that day, more than 100 members of the 'National Magazine Society' from various schools in Beijing held an emergency meeting in the Xizhai Dining Hall at Peking University, not far from the university headquarters. Cai Yuanpei told the attendees about the collusion of the imperialists at the Paris Peace Conference at the expense of China's sovereignty, and called on the students to rise up to save the country. The students were so angry that they decided to spread the news to all of the colleges and universities in Beijing, and then take collective action. The next morning, wall posters were put up on the campuses of Beijing's secondary and higher education establishments, stating that an emergency assembly of students from secondary and higher institutions would be held that night at 7pm in the auditorium of the Law School at Peking University on the north riverside.

Thus began a political frenzy that was destined to influence the direction of Chinese history.

On the evening of 3 May, more than 1,000 students and representatives of 13 Beijing universities gathered for the meeting. A series of patriotic speakers took to the stage, criticizing the hypocrisy and aggressive nature of the powers, and denouncing the weakness and traitorousness of the Beiyang government. Xie Shaomin, a law student from Peking University, bit his middle finger, tore off his lapel, and wrote the words "Give back Qingdao" in blood and held it high. The students chanted passionately: "Never let Shandong fall into the hands of the invaders! Give back Qingdao! Give back Shandong!"

In the afternoon of 4 May, a huge anti-imperialist and patriotic march began. More than 3,000 students from a dozen schools in Beijing gathered in Tiananmen Square, carrying banners and slogans, chanting "Fight for sovereignty from the outside and eliminate traitors from the inside!" and distributing leaflets. Among them, the 'Declaration of the Whole Beijing Academic Community' read:

"The survival of China is at stake!
I make two creeds with my compatriots today.
China's land can be conquered but not surrendered!
The people of China can be killed but not bowed down!
Our country is dying. Rise up, fellow countrymen!"

When the student procession reached the west entrance of the Legation Quarter, it was blocked by an iron fence. The staff of the British, French, American, and Italian embassies said that the ministers were out of town and could not receive submissions in support of the Chinese people's right to reclaim Shandong. The student representatives then negotiated with the inspector, and demanded that the procession be allowed to pass through the embassy area. The inspector said that the President had to give his consent, and that he had to contact the Presidential Office by telephone, but he did not return for two hours.

The students stood waiting in the sun for two hours, and grew increasingly impatient. They felt that their country had not died, but their territory was no longer passable, and their own government was standing in the way. At that moment, someone shouted, "Let's all go to the Foreign Ministry! Let's go to Cao Rulin's house to settle accounts with the traitors!" This proposal was immediately accepted, and the marching crowd headed for Zhaojialou Hutong.

During the Yuan Shikai era, Cao Rulin had served as the Undersecretary and Director General of Foreign Affairs, and was the chief negotiator of the traitorous 'Twenty-one Demands.' That day, President Xu Shichang was giving a lunch for Zhang Zongxiang, the Ambassador to Japan, who had just returned. Cao Rulin, who was the Head of Transport at that time, was attending as well, so was not at home. During the lunch, people advised him not to go back for the time being, and to take refuge instead. However, Cao Rulin did not think that a group of unarmed students could do anything to him, and invited Zhang Zongxiang to go home with him.

At 4pm, the marching students arrived at Zhaojialou Hutong. They banged on the door and shouted, "Cao Rulin, the traitor! Come out!" The military police came forward to stop them. At that moment, someone in the crowd shouted, "We're in! We're in!"

The first to enter Cao Rulin's house was Kuang Husheng – a 22-year-old from Shaoyang in Hunan Province, who had practiced martial arts since childhood. The military police in the courtyard did not expect the students to act in this way, and they panicked and rushed forward to stop them. Kuang Husheng cried excitedly, "Brothers, China is going to die! We are here to seek justice from the traitor Cao Rulin. I hope you will not interfere on the basis of national justice!"

Moved by the students' courage and patriotic enthusiasm, and shocked by the crowd and slogans outside, the military police stood by and watched. The students who had come in over the wall opened the gate and let in the tidal wave of people.

Cao Rulin and the others who were in the living room panicked when they heard the students barge in. Cao rushed to hide in a box room next to his bedroom, and Zhang Zongxiang was dragged by a servant into the Cao family's underground boiler room.

The students poured into the house, shouting, "Where is the traitor?" and looking everywhere. They saw that Cao's house was full of Japanese things. There was even a statue of the Japanese emperor hanging on the wall. Some of the students shouted, "Burn down this den of thieves! Let's see where the traitors are hiding!" A few of them rolled up a carpet and set it on fire. Someone got gasoline from the garage and poured it on the carpet, and the fire grew.

In the boiler room Zhang Zongxiang saw the smoke and ran out, trying to escape through the back door. Seeing that he was wearing a suit, the students mistook him for Cao Rulin and shouted, "Here is Cao, the traitor!" As they shouted, they rushed up and hit him with their flags and fists. Shortly after, a large number of military police arrived, and most of the students withdrew. Only 32 were arrested.

This came to be known as the 'Burning of Zhaojialou' incident.

In order to rescue their comrades who had been arrested, the Beijing students held a general strike on 5 May, and sent telegrams to the rest of the country. Students everywhere responded by missing classes. Two days later, the Beiyang government was forced to release the students they had arrested, but ignored their political demands.

On 1 June, the Beiyang government issued two orders. One was to 'honor' the pro-Japanese officials Cao Rulin, Zhang Zongxiang, and Lu Zongjiu, who were denounced by the public as traitors to the country. The other was to outlaw all patriotic actions carried out by students.

In this way, traitors were given merit, but patriots were guilty.

The students were so angry at the perverse actions of the Beiyang government that they decided to resume street speeches, which had not taken place since 3 June. The authorities were determined to redouble their efforts until all the students were arrested by the reactionary military police, and would not give up their struggle.

On 3 June, more than 2,000 students poured into the streets to give mass public speeches. More than 170 people were arrested by the reactionary military police, and the Law Department of Peking University was used as a temporary prison. The next day, more than 4,000 students took to the streets to give speeches, and more than 700 people were arrested.

On 4 June, the news reached Shanghai, which was then the largest industrial city in the country. The city's working class, with its glorious revolutionary tradition, expressed deep sympathy and support for the patriotic actions of the Beijing students, as well as extreme indignation at the atrocities of the Beiyang government. They came forward at the critical moment and joined the anti-imperialist patriotic struggle, launching the far-reaching 'June 5th' political strike.

This general strike started in the Japanese factories, and was directed at the Japanese imperialists. In the course of the strike, the workers united to break the barriers that existed between the original gangs and factory associations, and jointly discussed the steps and strategies of the struggle. Even though they were not paid during the strike, they donated their hard-earned money to support the patriotic movement. In this way, the workers' strike began to shift from an economic struggle to a political battle.

Then, all Shanghai universities, high schools, and elementary school went on strike. The students took to the streets and went door to door to mobilize merchants to go on strike as well. If a store owner did not want to close his store, they knelt in front of the door and cried, begging him to join the patriotic action for the sake of the nation.

By 12am on 5 June, all stores in Shanghai had gone on strike. Some barbershops put up slogans that read: 'The country is in such a state, I don't want to have a face-lift, so please don't give me your custom.' Students from various schools were worried that the merchants would not be able to hold out, so they took to the streets every day to maintain order and urge them to stick to the strike.

On 6 June, the scope of the strike expanded rapidly, and workers in various industries took action. On 10 June, workers on the Shanghai-Nanjing and Shanghai-Hangzhou railroads went on strike, along with all seafarers, and Shanghai's external land and water transport was completely cut off. At this point, there was a tri-fold situation of citywide strikes, academic strikes, and market strikes. The struggle reached its climax, creating unprecedented momentum.

Meanwhile, strikes were burning like wildfire across the country. Workers from the Shanghai-Nanjing, Shanghai-Hangzhou, Peking-Hankou, and Peking-Mukden railroads went on strike, as did workers in hundreds of cities including Tianjin, Hangzhou, and Jiujiang. Chinese workers began to take the political stage independently and with large-scale actions, which was unprecedented in Chinese history.

On 10 June, under pressure from the public, the Beiyang government publicly announced the removal of Cao, Zhang, Lu, and other traitors from their posts. By this point, the May Fourth Patriotic Movement had achieved a stage victory.

However, the Shandong issue was still unresolved. The reactionary army and police were still swaggering around in Beijing. At a time when people did not know where to go, Chen Duxiu – who was later hailed by Mao Zedong as the "Commander-in-Chief of the May Fourth Movement"[1] and was then a

1. *The Collected Works of Mao Zedong, Vol. 3*, People's Publishing House, 1996, p. 294.

professor at Peking University – came forward and drafted the 'Beijing Citizens' Manifesto.'

On 11 June, Chen Duxiu was arrested by secret agents when he went to the New World amusement venue to distribute leaflets. Student groups and social figures from all over the world sent out telegrams to protest against this atrocity of the Beijing government.

On 17 June, the Beiyang warlord government ordered the Chinese envoys attending the Paris Peace Conference to sign the Paris Peace Treaty. This event was disclosed by the newspapers, and immediately sent shockwaves throughout the country. A patriotic movement once again rose up across all echelons of society, with the goal of refusing to sign the treaty. Telegrams from all over the country arrived in Beijing and Paris. According to the *Weekly Review*, the Paris delegation received more than 7,000.

The date of the signing of the Paris Peace Treaty was 28 June. Before dawn that day, the apartments of the Chinese delegates in Paris were surrounded by Chinese workers and students. They forbade the delegates to go out, and said that if any of them did, they would be killed immediately, whether they were going to a meeting or not. No Chinese delegate would be allowed to appear at the signing of the Paris Peace Treaty that day. In order to prevent anyone from backing out, they met in advance to sign a list. If any delegate did come out and was killed, they would take their lives in the order of the list of signatures. Each delegate's life was paid for with the lives of three men.[1] This momentum and determination eventually kept the Chinese envoys away from the signing of the treaty.

At 2pm on 28 June, the delegates found the seats of the two Chinese delegates empty at the signing ceremony in the Palace of Mirrors in Versailles. By 3pm, when the treaty was signed, those two seats were still empty. Just as the peace treaty with Germany was being signed, a statement explaining the reasons for the Chinese envoys' refusal to sign was sent to the other delegates. At the same time as the delegates received this statement, a copy of the document was sent to the major newspapers in Paris. The refusal of the Chinese delegates to sign immediately caused a worldwide sensation.

1. *New Journal of Current Affairs*, July 6, 1919.

Since the beginning of the modern era, China had signed one unequal treaty after another under imperialist coercion. The Chinese delegates had only accepted (and were never allowed to lower, let alone refuse) the conditions proposed by the powers that had humiliated it. This time, at the signing ceremony of the Paris Peace Conference, the Chinese delegates' refusal to attend was a feat of resistance against imperialist domination.

If the New Culture Movement was confined to the intellectual class and had limited influence, the May Fourth Movement gradually shifted its main force from students to workers, thus breaking out of the narrow scope of intellectuals and becoming a mass movement on a national scale with the participation of the working class, petty bourgeoisie, and bourgeoisie, and converging to form an impressive revolutionary force.

The May Fourth Movement swept away the dreary atmosphere that beset Chinese society after the Xinhai Revolution. It carried out a thorough and uncompromising struggle against imperialism and feudalism, with a gesture that had not been seen in the Xinhai Revolution. It awakened the consciousness of the masses and promoted the unity of revolutionary forces, thus becoming an epoch-making event in the history of Chinese revolution.

China's situation after 1919 was deeply marked by the May Fourth Movement. During this period, various political trends were introduced into China or emerged in Chinese society. It was in the process of widespread dissemination, debate and identification, and social experimentation of various new trends that Marxism finally emerged as the theoretical weapon that would guide the Chinese revolution.

Many advanced elements entered the political arena during the May Fourth Movement. They exercised and grew in the practice of struggle, and began to accept Marxist beliefs, becoming the pioneering force of China's new democratic revolution.

The labor movement, youth movement, and women's movement, all of which started during the May Fourth period, fully demonstrated the great power hidden in the general public, and became the main form of revolutionary activity before and after the founding of the Communist Party of China. It is for this reason that General Secretary Xi Jinping stated in his speech at the conference commemorating the centenary of the May Fourth Movement that:

"With its revolutionary nature of complete anti-imperialism and anti-feudalism, its progressive nature of pursuing the truth to save and strengthen the country, and the widespread participation by the masses of all nationalities and circles, the May Fourth Movement promoted social progress in China, and facilitated the spread of Marxism. It also promoted the combination of Marxism and the Chinese labor movement, prepared the ideology and cadres for the founding of the Communist Party of China, and created the conditions for new revolutionary forces, revolutionary culture, and revolutionary struggles to enter a new phase. This was the turning point of China's old democratic revolution towards a new democratic revolution. It was also a milestone in the historical process of the Chinese nation's pursuit of national independence, development, and progress in modern times."[1]

1. Xi, Jinping. 'A Ceremony to Mark the Centenary of the May Fourth Movement,' April 30, 2019, *People's Daily*, May 1, 2019 (Second Edition).

PART 3

Justice Restored:

From Mr. De and Mr. Sai to Mr. Ma

The New Culture Movement made the Chinese people realize that feudal dictatorship and its ideology and culture were destined for decay and extinction, and that they would have to learn about democracy and science from the West in order to keep pace with the development of the times.

The First World War and the Paris Peace Conference were like a blow to the head. They made the Chinese people understand that there was no diplomacy for a weak country, and that an independent and strong China was impossible to obtain from the Western powers. Although democracy and science were positive things, the aura of Western democracy and institutional civilization was no longer there, and could not save the Chinese people from the double oppression of colonial exploitation and feudal dictatorship.

The May Fourth Movement made China understand that the people are the masters of history. As for the traitors Cao Rulin, Lu Zongjiu, Zhang Zongxiang, and other high-ranking officials of the Beiyang government, "when we rise up and cry out, the traitors will stand up and tremble, and will run for their lives."[1] Under pressure from the people, the Chinese delegates had refused to attend the signing ceremony of the Paris Peace Treaty, which was drafted by the largest imperialist countries in the world, including the USA, Britain and France. This was unprecedented in the history of China since 1840.

---

1. Mao, Zedong. 'The Great Union of the People,' *Xiangjiang Review*, No. 2, July 21, 1919.

This series of practical struggles made the Chinese people much more aware of the truth of their own emancipation. As Li Dazhao noted in his article 'The Real Liberation' in the *Weekly Review:*

> "True liberation does not mean begging others to be generous and set us free; it means relying on our own strength to resist so that they have to let us free ourselves. It does not mean relying on the grace of authority to unlock the chains around our heads; it means relying on our own efforts to break out of the prison of darkness and let in the light."[1]

After the May Fourth Movement, salvation and survival became the greatest concerns of the Chinese people, and finding a new way forward became the most urgent task.

At the time when Chinese advanced elements were struggling to find a new way forward, the October Revolution propelled Marxism-Leninism into China like a cannon shot. After repeated comparisons and debates, a group of intellectuals finally chose Marxism as their ideology.

From this, we can see that the New Culture Movement, with the May Fourth Movement as its boundary, was manifested in two interrelated but distinct stages of development.

Before the May Fourth Movement, the New Culture Movement was mainly a cultural enlightenment that violently criticized traditional feudal culture, and gave the Chinese people 'Mr. De' (democracy) and 'Mr. Sai' (science), so that they had the theoretical weapons to deal with the ideological bondage of feudalism.

After the May Fourth Movement, the New Culture Movement was mainly an ideological revolution that analyzed and criticized various new trends in the West, actively spread Marxism in China, and gradually occupied a dominant position in the field of thought. It gave the Chinese people 'Mr. Ma' (Marxism), so that they had the correct guiding ideology for salvation and national revival.

Moving from Mr. De and Mr. Sai to Mr. Ma constituted the course of the Chinese ideological revolution, and was a theoretical turn-around of the Chinese nation from suffering to revival.

---

1. *The Complete Works of Li Dazhao, Vol. 2*, People's Publishing House, 2006, p. 363.

1
THE OCTOBER REVOLUTION

Hegel predicted that ancient China needed external ideological stimulation in order to come alive. However, before Russia's October Revolution, this prediction did not seem to have been completely fulfilled. China had learned and adopted almost all influential Western thoughts and doctrines in an effort to save itself, but all of them had failed. At the time when the New Culture Movement was advancing with great vigor, the First World War (1914–1918) further exposed in an extreme way the insurmountable contradictions inherent in the capitalist system, which had entered the age of imperialism. This caused advanced elements in China to doubt and waver in their views of Western thought and civilizational values, and they began to reflect on and criticize the Western capitalist system.

On 23 August 1917, Mao Zedong wrote in his 'Letter to Lai Jinxi' that Eastern thought was certainly not relevant to practical life, and that "Western thought may not be all, but a few more parts should be transformed at the same time as Eastern thought."[1]

In June and July 1918, Li Dazhao stated in his article 'The Fundamental Differences between Eastern and Western Civilizations' that the First World War "cast great doubt on the authority of European civilization. The Europeans themselves had to reflect on the true value of their civilization."[2]

The Chinese people had tried to learn from the West, and had made all kinds of attempts to do so, but had failed repeatedly. This cruel fact showed that capitalism was not a viable way out for China, as a semi-colonial and semi-

1. *Early Manuscripts of Mao Zedong*, Hunan Publishing House, 1990, p. 86.
2. *The Complete Works of Li Dazhao, Vol. 2*, People's Publishing House, 2006, p. 218.

feudal society. These reflections and doubts pushed Chinese advanced elements to abandon the bourgeois republican program and to explore new ways to save the nation from peril.

The seventh of November 1917 was a late fall day in Beijing, and leaves were flying in the chilly wind. It was 25 October in Russia – China's neighbor to the north. This was the day that the Great October Revolution began. The first salvo came from the cruiser *Aurora*, which attacked the Winter Palace – the seat of the Provisional Government. Headed by Vladimir Lenin, the Bolshevik Party led the workers, peasants, and soldiers to overthrow the bourgeois provisional government and establish the dictatorship of the proletariat.

A new global tide arrived like a raging storm. The victory of the October Revolution began a new era in history. It marked the collapse of the old world and the establishment of a new socialist order, and greatly inspired the world proletarian revolution, with national liberation movements in the colonial and semi-colonial countries. Marked by the First World War and the October Revolution, the world entered an era of war and revolution. The tide of the proletarian revolution changed the world and triggered a revolutionary storm that swept the globe:

In 1918, there was a general strike of workers in Berlin, and the Soviet of Workers' Deputies was established.

In April 1919, a Soviet Republic was established in Bavaria.

In 1918, soviets of workers' deputies were formed in Vienna and other Austrian cities, and the revolutionary movement spread throughout the Austro-Hungarian army.

In 1918, a general political strike took place in Prague and many other cities, and on October 28 that year, the Czechoslovak Republic was founded.

In 1918, the French people held demonstrations on May Day.

At the beginning of 1918, the workers of Finland formed a Soviet of People's Deputies.

In November 1918, workers in Brazil staged an armed uprising.

At the end of 1918, workers in Romania went on strike.

In 1918, there were 417 strikes in Japan, and 'rice riots' in April and September.

In 1919, there were mass political strikes and large demonstrations in Poland, Bulgaria, Italy, and Spain.

In 1919, British railroad workers held a general strike.

In 1919, there were 3,577 strikes by workers in the USA.

In March 1919, the famous 'March 1st Movement' against the Japanese colonialists broke out in Korea, with more than two million people participating in the uprising.

In March 1919, mass meetings, demonstrations, and strikes were held all over India. In addition, in many colonies and dependent countries such as Indonesia, Burma, Afghanistan, Egypt, Iraq, Iran, Morocco, Syria, Lebanon, Turkey, and the Philippines, national liberation movements were held to varying degrees under the influence of the October Revolution.[1]

At that time, world capitalism was in a period of relative stability, and the proletarian revolutionary movement in Europe and North America soon entered a low ebb under imperialist repression. At the same time, the national liberation movements in the colonies and semi-colonies in the East flourished, constantly moving from one climax to another. With this tide, the center of the revolution shifted from the West to the East, and Marxism spread throughout the world.

Three days after the October Revolution, the Shanghai newspaper *Republican Daily* reported the news under the title 'The Sudden Russian Coup,' stating that "the Petrograd garrison and labor society have overthrown the Kerensky government."[2] From then on, news about the Russian Revolution appeared frequently in Chincse newspapers and magazines.

Unfortunately, the initial reports were confusing. The angle was not very clear, and the Bolshevik Party was even referred to as the 'party of excesses,' showing a certain degree of hostility to the Russian Revolution in the mainstream media at the time.

This hostility was due to the fact that the Beiyang warlord government was rattled by the attitude of the Western imperialist powers. In November 1917, the Soviet government had tried to establish diplomatic relations with it, but was refused. Moreover, the Russian minister in Beijing at that time continued to maintain relations with the Beiyang government even though he had been removed from his post by the Soviet leadership.

1. Peng, Ming. *History of the May Fourth Movement* (revised), People's Publishing House, 2019, pp. 132–134.
2. *Shanghai Republican Daily*, November 10, 1917.

Later, with the passage of time and the stabilization of the revolutionary situation in Russia, especially at the beginning of 1918, the Soviet government proposed to abolish the unequal treaties imposed on China by the Tsarist government through concrete negotiations, and to sign new agreements in order to establish equal diplomatic relations. This proposal was very unusual and extremely favorable for China, which had long been bullied by foreign powers. However, the Beiyang warlord government did not adopt the proposal. Seemingly in order to win the trust and favor of the imperial powers, it took a hostile stance against Soviet Russia.

In contrast, the victory of the October Revolution pushed Chinese advanced elements to see the light of day after the bitterness and uncertainty of the failed Xinhai Revolution. Those who had looked to the West for a way out began to turn their eyes back to the East for the salvation of the Chinese nation.

In May 1918, the *Republican Daily* – a progressive newspaper under Sun Yat-sen's direction –published an article preaching to the Chinese people about the foreign policy of the Soviet government and its far-reaching effects, and stating clearly that China should learn from the Russians. Sun also called Lenin and the Soviet government to congratulate them on the success of the October Revolution. Lenin was touched by the congratulatory telegram from the Far East at a time when Soviet Russia was isolated by enemies on all sides.[1]

While it was Sun Yat-sen who first expressed respect to Lenin and the Russian Revolution on behalf of the Chinese people, it was Li Dazhao who was the first to raise the banner of the October Revolution on Chinese soil and to analyze and systematize its great significance in depth.

Li had been exposed to Marxist doctrine from 1913 to 1916, while studying in Japan. In the spring of 1917, he studied the February Revolution in Russia, and the role of the Bolshevik Party in it. After the successful October Revolution, he worked hard to explain the situation in Russia to his comrades back home.

In January 1918, Li Dazhao succeeded Zhang Shizhao as Director of the Peking University Library, and in July he published his first essay on the October Revolution – 'A Comparative View of the French and Russian Revolutions.'

1. Peng, Ming. *History of the May Fourth Movement* (revised), People's Publishing House, 2019, p. 137.

This essay focused on the differences between the Russian October Socialist Revolution and the French bourgeois revolution, and pointed out that the former was "different in the spirit of the times and in its revolutionary nature, and therefore not comparable." So, "we can only look forward to the dawn of a new civilization in the world, to the news of a new Russia built on freedom and humanity, and to new global trends."[1] In this way, he made an essential distinction between the two revolutions, thus profoundly clarifying the great political and historical significance of the October Revolution.

At the same time, in his capacity as director of the library, Li purchased and collected Marxist works, and books and journals explaining the Russian Revolution, such as *The Communist Manifesto*, *Capital*, *Marxism*, and the foreign-language periodical *Soviet Russia*, turning the library at Peking University into a study and research center for Marxist theory. Zhang Guotao, who was a student there in those days, later recalled:

> "At that time, the library at Peking University was still poorly equipped. It was not very spacious, and there were not enough books, but it was very attractive. It was often crowded, mostly with left-leaning people searching for new ideas, and the few socialist books and journals were often borrowed. In the lounge, groups of young people talked. Marxism and anarchism were often the main topics of conversation. The library director's suite had two rooms. One was Mr. Li's office, and the other was a reception room. The reception room was a place where socialists and radicals gathered in those days. There were several seminars, which attracted large numbers of people, and the debates were very serious."[2]

In time, Peking University became a center for the dissemination of new ideas in China, especially the propagation of the October Revolution and Marxism.

In November 1918, the First World War came to an end. While the Allied powers and the Beiyang warlord government were celebrating humanity and

---

1. *The Complete Works of Li Dazhao, Vol. 2*, People's Publishing House, 2006, p. 228.
2. Su, Hang and Su, Ruoqun. *Zhang Guotao in the Declassified Archives*, People's Publishing House, 2015, p. 11.

justice, Li Dazhao asked a question that would make people think: Who actually won the war?

Subsequently, Li published two articles in quick succession in *New Youth* – 'The Triumph of the Common People' and 'The Triumph of Bolshevism.' He used an analysis of historical materialism to point out that, by nature, the First World War was a war of contention between imperialist thieves, while the proletarian revolution in Russia stopped the war between imperialist countries. All reactionary forces were bound to perish, while socialism and Bolshevism would surely triumph throughout the world. He pointed out that "the Russian Revolution of 1917 was the precursor of the world revolution in the 20th century… a victory for freedom, a victory for democracy, a victory for socialism, a victory for Bolshevism, a victory for the Red Flag, a victory for the world working class, and a victory for the new trend of the 20th century." Regarding the new global revolutionary situation after the October Revolution, Li wrote with confidence and enthusiasm that:

> "From now on, we will see the victory flag of Bolshevism everywhere. Everywhere we will hear the sound of the triumphal song of Bolshevism. The alarm bell of humanity is ringing! The light of freedom is dawning! The world will be filled with red flags!"[1]

In order to adapt to the drastic changes of this global revolutionary situation, the zeitgeist and the people demanded a publication that was faster, shorter, and more directly related to reality than *New Youth*. Thanks to the efforts of Chen Duxiu, Li Dazhao, and their colleagues at *New Youth*, the *Weekly Review* was launched in Beijing on 22 December 1918. It contained the first weekly commentary on current affairs in China, called 'Commentary,' and its purpose was "to advocate justice and oppose power." From January 1919 until the May Fourth Movement, the *Weekly Review* published many reports on the socialist revolution.

On New Year's Day 1919, Li Dazhao wrote an article entitled 'A New Era' for the third issue of the *Weekly Review*, stating:

---

1. *The Complete Works of Li Dazhao, Vol. 2*, People's Publishing House, 2006, pp. 256, 259, 263.

"The blood of the World War of 1914, the blood of the Russian Revolution of 1917, and the blood of the German-Austrian Revolution of 1918 is like a great flood. A new era has emerged. This is because the working class, with weapons in their hands, will turn around and defend the rights of labor and attack their public enemies. The working class has the means to defend itself, and the handful of thieves who plundered the labor surplus should be silenced. Starting from now, the system of production will undergo a great change, and the working class will unite with their compatriots all over the world to make a reasonable union of producers, to break the national boundaries and defeat the capitalist class all over the world."[1]

Lu Xun, who was known for his skepticism and critical mind, later wrote about the influence that the October Revolution had on him:

"I was aware of the corruption of the old society, and I hoped for the rise of a new society, but I did not know what the 'new' society should be; nor did I know whether the 'new' society would necessarily be good. Only after the October Revolution did I realize that the creator of the 'new' society was the proletariat."[2]

Issue 16 of the *Weekly Review*, published on 6 April the same year, included in its 'Masterpieces' section a translated passage from Chapter 2 of the *Communist Manifesto*, 'The Proletarians and Communists,' which stated, "The first step in the labor revolution is to exalt the proletariat. The first step of the labor revolution, which we hope for above all else, is to raise the proletariat up and put them in a position of dominance, and … to put all the organs of production in the hands of the government." The editor's special 'Note' before this translation stated, "This manifesto is the first and most significant opinion of Marx and Engels … Its thrust is to advocate class warfare, to call for the union of labor everywhere, and to express the instruments of the new generation."[3]

1. *The Complete Works of Li Dazhao, Vol. 2*, People's Publishing House, 2006, pp. 266–268.
2. 'Essay on Qiejieting,' *The Complete Works of Lu Xun, Vol. 6*.
3. Ren, Jianshu. *The Great Biography of Chen Duxiu*, Shanghai People's Publishing House, 2012, p. 151.

This was the first time that the Chinese press published the main points of the *Communist Manifesto*, more than a year before Chen Wangdao's full translation was published in Shanghai.

At first, Chen Duxiu was slightly confused about the October Revolution, but with Li Dazhao's explanation and propagation, it gradually became clearer.

On 20 April 1919, he wrote in issue 18 of the *Weekly Review*, "The political revolution in France in the 18th century and the socialist revolution in Russia in the 20th century were cursed by the people of that time, but later historians have to treat them as the great key to the change and evolution of human society."[1]

Although the above-mentioned articles were not yet a systematic introduction to Marxist doctrine, they introduced some of the important points of Marxism and initially revealed the difference between scientific socialism and other schools. It was sufficient to show that under the influence of the October Revolution in Russia, Chinese advanced elements led by Li Dazhao had made a qualitative leap in their ideological understanding. They had begun to shift from revolutionary democracy to Marxism, gradually attempting to use it as a theoretical tool for observing social realities and exploring the fate of the country.

As Mao Zedong pointed out in 'On the People's Democratic Dictatorship':

> "The salvoes of the October Revolution brought us Marxism-Leninism. The October Revolution helped progressives in China, as throughout the world, to adopt the proletarian world outlook as the instrument for studying a nation's fate and considering their own problems anew. Follow the path of the Russians – that was their conclusion."[2]

Along with active introduction and propagation by advanced elements in China, there was another important channel to convey the truth about the October Revolution and Bolshevist ideas to the general public, namely Chinese workers returning from Russia.

In 1915, when the First World War was in full swing, all countries experienced a shortage of labor in their industrial sectors. Allied Powers such

1. Chen, Duxiu. 'The Russian Revolution in the 20th Century,' *Weekly Review*, No. 18.
2. *Selected Works of Mao Zedong*, People's Publishing House, 1991, p. 1471.

as Britain, France, and Tsarist Russia put pressure on the Beiyang warlord government, thus allowing free recruitment of laborers from China. Tsarist Russia recruited about 100,000 Chinese workers. After the outbreak of the October Revolution, these enslaved and abused laborers joined the struggle with the Russian working masses, and tens of thousands of Chinese laborers volunteered to join the Red Army. In addition, with the help of the Soviet government, about 40,000 Chinese laborers returned to China via Siberia from the October Revolution until the summer of 1919.[1]

The Chinese workers who returned to China after the October Revolution told of the changes that were taking place in Russian society from their own experiences. For example, more than 2,000 workers from the Kailuan coal mine had worked in Russia. After the October Revolution, some of the workers who had returned to China told their colleagues about what had happened. They said, "The capitalists were brutally exploiting and oppressing the workers, and the Russians were well aware that the capitalists were their mortal enemies and that their method of struggle was to strike." Of the newly established Soviet Russia, they said with admiration:

> "In post-revolutionary Russia, the capitalists' factories were under workers' management. The Russian workers had a week's holiday, and quite a lot of benefits. There were no capitalists there, and no contract workers. Workers were not oppressed and exploited anymore. If we struggle, we can also rise up."[2]

These after-work conversations, with their simple but realistic words, resounded and touched the hearts of those at the bottom of the pile.

After the October Revolution, revolutionary scholars in China used their influential writings to introduce grand theories with thousands of articles, driving the people forward. By word of mouth, ordinary workers spread the revolutionary truth that they had seen and heard, which was hugely thought-provoking.

1. *Pravda*, August 26, 1919.
2. Kailuan Coal Mine History Editorial Committee Compilation Group. *History of the Kailuan Coal Mine* (preliminary draft of the labor movement section), mimeograph from March 1959.

In this way, the October Revolution and its revolutionary theory were introduced to China through a variety of channels, pointing out a new way for the Chinese people to save themselves.

2

TRUTH LIGHTS THE WAY

Russia's October Revolution brought Marxism-Leninism to the Chinese people. However, the introduction and discussion of Marxism had already begun in China before it.

As early as the Westernization Movement in the late Qing Dynasty, cultural exchanges between China and Western countries created the conditions for introducing Marxism into China. In 1871, Wang Tao and others compiled the *Chronicle of the Franco-Prussian War*, which was the earliest introduction of the revolutionary Paris Commune to China. In 1891, Li Fengbao recorded the activities of the German Social Democratic Party and socialists in other countries in the *Diary of Being a Diplomat in Germany*.

According to currently accepted sources, the earliest mention of Marx and Engels in the Chinese press was in the *Universal Gazette*. From February to May 1899, this publication serialized *The Great Learning*, which was translated from *Social Evolution* by British missionary Richard Timothy and rewritten by Cai Erkang. The first chapter of *The Great Learning*, published in February, stated, "The one who is famous as the leader of the workers is the Englishman Marx."[1] Since Marx had been engaged in writing and revolutionary struggle in London since 1849, and was buried in London after his death, the author of the article mistook him for British. In the eighth chapter, published in May, it was written, "There are two famous scholars who are engaged in raising the German people up. One is Marx, and the other is Engels."[2] Although the author of this article did not really know Marxism, and his presentation was not very accurate, it

1. *Universal Gazette*, No. 121, February 1899, pp. 11–13.
2. Sha, Jiansun. *History of the Communist Party of China (1921–1949), Vol. 1,* Central Literature Publishing House, 2006, p. 203

was the first time that the Chinese people heard about Marx and his doctrine.

At the beginning of the 20th century, the Chinese press began to publish increasing numbers of articles about Marxism and the socialist movement. In 1902, the reformist leader Liang Qichao mentioned Marx in an article in *Xinmin Congbao*. However, it was not translated as 'Marx,' but instead said "Marcus, a German man – the deity of socialism."[1] In 1904, in his article 'Socialism in China,' Liang wrote, "The ancient Chinese well-field system, which is widely known today, is the same as modern socialism."[2] However, Liang Qichao's fundamental goal in introducing Marxism and socialism was not to push China onto a socialist trajectory. He wrote that China was "currently still far from nationalism, not to mention the ideal of great socialist unity. Since I know it is impossible to reach great unity immediately, I intend to build a solid foundation for it. What is the foundation of great unity? It is to force the imperial court to change from an autocratic regime to a constitutional one."[3]

Sun Yat-sen – the forerunner of China's democratic revolution – and his comrade Zhu Zhixin came to admire socialism through their learning from the West. Because the ideology of the 'ideal society' already existed in traditional Chinese culture, Sun Yat-sen believed that socialism would have a bright future in China. In a speech, he remarked, "Throughout history, our country has always stood for socialism. The well-field system is the origin of egalitarianism and communism. Generations living together is the precursor of communism. It shows that the spirit of socialism has existed in the Chinese mind for a long time. Thus, carrying out socialism in China will take place at a speed of a thousand miles per day."[4]

As a great man of his generation, Sun Yat-sen thought about the long term. He believed that when learning from the West, China had prevented and avoided the existing ills of European and American societies. Meanwhile, he also opposed the view that China was very backward and did not have the conditions for socialism. He stated, "People denounce advocating socialism in

1. Liang, Qichao. 'The Theory of Kidd – A Revolutionary Evolutionism,' *Xinmin Congbao*, No. 18, September 15, 1902.
2. Liang, Qichao. 'Socialism in China,' *Xinmin Congbao*, No. 46, 47, 48, February 14, 1904.
3. Sha, Jiansun. *History of the Communist Party of China (1921–1949), Vol. 1*, Central Literature Publishing House, 2006, pp. 203–204.
4. *The Collected Works of Sun Yat sen, Vol. 2*, Zhonghua Book Company, 1982, pp. 506–507.

our country as 'complaining when you are not ill.' This is because people are unaware of the function of socialism. In today's China, socialism can prevent the appearance of capitalism and its proponents."[1]

Zhu Zhixin was known as the "true researcher of Marxism"[2] in the Chinese Revolutionary Alliance. In 1906, he published the 'Biographies of Germanic Revolutionists' in *Min Bao*. Entitled 'Marx,' the first biography gave a preliminary introduction to Marx's life along with a summary of the *Communist Manifesto* and *Capital*, with an emphasis on the theory of class conflict and surplus value. This was the first time that Marx's name had appeared as a title in an article by a Chinese writer. Mao Zedong spoke about this the Seventh National Congress of the Communist Party of China, saying, "Zhu Zhixin was a member of the Kuomintang, so it seems that the Kuomintang embraced Marxism earlier than we did."[3]

Sun Yat-sen and others' admiration for Marxism and socialism laid the ideological foundation for Sun's later proposal of the 'Three Principles of the People' and the implementation of Kuomintang-Communist cooperation. However, they neither had a real understanding of Marxist historical materialism and the theory of class struggle, nor did they agree with them. Therefore, they were not scientific Marxist socialists. They simply extracted some ideas from Marxism to prevent possible disadvantages when developing capitalism in China.

The early anarchists also played a certain role in the initial discussions of Marxism, because ideological circles at that time did not strictly distinguish Marxism from anarchism. In 1907, anarchists represented by the likes of Zhang Ji and Liu Shipei set up a group called the Socialist Seminar, to study socialism in Tokyo. They published work about Marxism in their publications *New Century* and *Heng Bao*. In March 1908, Liu Shipei published the 'Preface to the *Communist Manifesto*' in *Tianyi Daily*. He stated, "This manifesto describes every detail of the social change in Europe. Accordingly, the most crucial thing is to unite all working people in the world to implement class struggles, but this is not easy. The manifesto refers to a communism of democracy, not of

---

1. *The Collected Works of Sun Yat-sen, Vol. 2*, Zhonghua Book Company, 1982, p. 509.
2. Sha, Jiansun. *History of the Communist Party of China (1921–1949), Vol. 1*, Central Literature Publishing House, 2006, p. 204.
3. *The Collected Works of Mao Zedong, Vol. 3*, People's Publishing House, 1996, p. 290.

anarchy."[1] Based on the understanding that "communism and anarchism share the same spirit," the purpose of anarchists was still to propagate anarchism when introducing Marxism.

Thus, Marxism was introduced successively to the Chinese people through the foreign affairs faction of the Qing ruling class, the reformists who advocated constitutional monarchy, bourgeois revolutionaries, and anarchists. However these introductions were sporadic and fragmentary, and the proponents themselves did not believe in Marxism. Strictly speaking, before Russia's October Revolution, Marxism in China had neither been systematically and correctly explained, nor widely spread, with no practical movement.

Mao Zedong stated, "The October Revolution taught a lesson about communism to the proletariat and other progressives all over the world. Marx and Engels created Marxist theory in 1843 (three years after the Opium War). However from 1843 to 1917, for 74 years, the influence of Marxism was mainly limited to Europe. Most people in the world did not know that there was such a thing. Marxism originated in Europe and developed slowly there. At that time in China, most people did not know about it, except very few students abroad."[2]

Two major events in the early 20th century promoted the spread of Marxism in China: the October Revolution in Russia and the May Fourth Movement in China.

The October Revolution broke out in Russia in 1917, leading to the establishment of the world's first socialist country. This was a great victory for Marxism in guiding revolutionary practice. It also provided a successful example for backward semi-colonial and semi-feudal countries to overthrow imperialism and exploitation. China had similar national conditions to Russia at that time. The success of the October Revolution prompted the Chinese people (who had been learning from the West for a long time) to turn their attention to Soviet Russia.

The Soviet Government had renounced its privileges in China during the era of Imperial Russia. This made a good impression the Chinese people, and won their trust. It also strengthened the concepts of learning from Russia and

1. *Tianyi Daily*, Joint Issue, No.16, 17, 18, 19, March 15, 1908.
2. *The Collected Works of Mao Zedong, Vol. 3*, People's Publishing House, 1996, p. 290.

fostering friendship with it, thus promoting the spread of Marxism in China.

In this regard, Cai Yuanpei wrote in his preface to *The History of Socialism* published in 1920, "Western socialism was imported to China only 20 years ago. Through translating books such as *Modern Socialism*, students who studied in Japan imported socialism indirectly. It was also imported directly by students studying in France... After the establishment of the majority government in Russia, increasing numbers of people began to introduce Marxist theory. Such topics were often seen in daily and monthly magazines."[1]

In the May Fourth movement, the Chinese working class began to step onto the political stage independently. They supported the students, and became the main force in the later period of the movement. For the first time, Chinese people saw the strength of the masses, especially the great power of the new working class. This aroused a great interest in Marxism as a hope for the future.

Lu You, a great poet of the Southern Song Dynasty, wrote, "Knowledge you learn from books is shallow; only practice can help you master it thoroughly." The October Revolution in Russia and the May Fourth Movement in China gave people a true feeling and understanding of Marxism – the most up-to-date and avant-garde revolutionary theory in the world at that time. They saw its great power in terms of truth and practical function. Hence, in China – a country with thousands of years of civilization – Marxism began to spread widely. A group of advanced intellectuals such as Li Dazhao and Chen Duxiu emerged to propagate it, along with a number of progressive journals such as *New Youth* and *Weekly Review*. According to the publishing industry at the time, "Many socialist magazines have been launched in the past year. Although some of them were short-lived, it seemed that they all carried the socialist spirit. A publication that does not discuss socialism cannot be called a publication of the New Culture Movement."[2]

The fifth of May 1919 was the anniversary of the birth of Karl Marx – founder of the world communist movement. This day coincided with the rising tide of the May Fourth Movement in China. Guided by Li Dazhao, the supplement of the *Beijing Morning Post* launched a special column called 'Marx Studies.' This was a bold pioneering move. The column ran from 5 May

1. Lin, Daizhao and Pan, Guohua. *Marxism in China: From the Introduction of Influence to its Spread, Vol. 2*, Tsinghua University Press, 1983, p. 99.
2. 'Implementing socialism and developing industry,' *New Youth*, Vol. 8 and No. 5.

to 11 November, and had a significant social impact. To explore and spread Marxist theory further, Li Dazhao edited issue five of volume six of *New Youth* as 'Marxist Research,' and wrote a 20,000-word article called 'My View of Marxism.' In it, he stated:

> "Since the Russian Revolution, 'Marxism' has swept around the world. Originating from it, there have been social revolutions in countries such as Germany, Austria, and Hungary.... Although our research on 'Marxism' was extremely poor, scholars all over the world revived their interest in studying it after the centenary of Marx's birth in 1918... We have taken these fragmentary materials, sorted them out a little, and used the publication of this journal 'Marxist Research' to introduce him to readers, so that this doctrine, which is the original motive for the transformation of the world, can be interpreted correctly in our discourse."[1]

Li also stated the three components of Marxism, namely historical materialism, political economics, and scientific socialism. He pointed out that they "have inseparable relations, while the theory of class competition connects these three principles fundamentally, like a golden thread."[2] This article introduced Marxism systematically for the first time, and played a pioneering role in its spread.

In March 1920, Li Dazhao and the progressive teachers and students at Peking University initiated the first Marxist Research Association in China. Progressives such as Deng Zhongxia, Gao Junyu, He Mengxiong, Luo Zhanglong, and Zhang Guotao all joined. As a result, in north China, the main epicenter for the spread of Marxism was Beijing, with a strong backbone represented by Li Dazhao – the first proponent of Marxism in China.

Based in Guangdong, Yang Pao'an was the earliest disseminator of Marxism in south China, during the May Fourth Movement. As a middle school teacher in Guangzhou and a reporter for *Guangdong Zhonghua New Daily*, Yang had reported on the October Revolution on the eve of the May Fourth Movement. In 1919, he wrote a series of articles to propagate Marxism in *Guangdong*

1. *The Collected Works of Li Dazhao, Vol. 3*, People's Publishing House, 2006, pp. 15–16.
2. Ibid., p. 19.

Zhonghua New Daily, including more than 40 freely translated articles in the 'World Theories' column. His article 'Marxism' was serialized over 19 days in 1919, from 11 November to 4 December, providing a thorough introduction to the history of the appearance of Marxism and its various components (historical materialism, class struggle, and surplus value). At the end of the article, Yang asserted, "Marx's words have been proven correct! Today, Western countries have realized that it is impossible to eliminate Bolshevism by force."[1] This article had far-reaching influence, and can be regarded as a companion piece for 'My View of Marxism' by Li Dazhao, which was published at a similar time.

In Shanghai, in the 'Consciousness' supplement of the *Republic of China Daily*, Li Da published articles such as 'What is Socialism?' and 'The Purpose of Socialism' in June 1919. He stated, "Socialism is an effective solution to eradicate the civilized shortcomings of the 19th century."[2] From the fall of 1919 to the summer of 1920, he translated three more works, namely the *Interpretation of Historical Materialism*, *Marxist Economic Theory,* and *An Overview of Social Problems*, which systematically expounded Marxist philosophy, political economy, and scientific socialism.

In the early spring of 1920, Chen Wangdao, who was in Hangzhou, was both surprised and excited to receive an invitation from the *Shanghai Weekly Review* magazine to translate the *Communist Manifesto* in its entirety. Soon after, he received the copy to be translated – a Japanese version – from Shanghai. He took it back his hometown of Yiwu in Zhejiang Province. To translate it accurately, Chen used several versions for reference. He asked Chen Duxiu to borrow an English version from Peking University Library through Li Dazhao. It was nearly Spring Festival when Chen Wangdao arrived home. To avoid being interrupted by New Year visitors, he hid in the woodshed next to his old house. There were no tables or chairs, and half of the room was piled with firewood for warmth against the winter chill. Using two benches and a plank of wood as a desk, and bundles of straw as a stool, Chen devoted himself to the translation, usually working until midnight with an oil lamp, forgetting to eat and sleep. Completely isolated from the outside world, he was deeply moved by Marx's profound thoughts and passionate words – "a ghost, a ghost of communism,

1. Peng, Ming. *History of the May Fourth Movement* (revised), People's Publishing House, 2019, pp. 362–363.
2. *The Collected Works of Li Da, Vol.1*, People's Publishing House, 1980, p. 6.

wandering in Europe...."

In April 1920, after finishing the translation of the *Communist Manifesto*, Chen Wangdao received a telegram in his hometown. The *Weekly Review* was inviting him to work as editor of the magazine in Shanghai. Overjoyed, he packed up and set off immediately. However, he did not expect that the *Weekly Review* would be compelled to shut down by the Beiyang government not long after his arrival in Shanghai. The *Communist Manifesto*, which was ready to serialize, could not be published. Chen Wangdao took the translated manuscript to Li Hanjun and Chen Duxiu, and asked them to proofread it. Chen Duxiu appreciated Chen Wangdao's exceptional language skills, and was fully aware of the significance of publishing the full Chinese version of the *Communist Manifesto*. In August, it was officially published with the help from Chen Duxiu, and became very popular. The print run of over 1,000 copies were sold and given away, and soon ran out. It was reprinted many times, in 39 editions. Seventeen of these editions were printed exclusively by the People's Publishing House, and were widely circulated in the community. It became the most widely disseminated, influential, and prestigious Marxist work in China in the early 20th century.

When the full version of the *Communist Manifesto* was published in Chinese, Chen Wangdao sent a copy to Lu Xun. After reading it, Lu Xun remarked, "Nowadays, everyone is talking about 'over-radicalism,' but no one has really introduced this 'doctrine' to China. In fact, this is the most urgent task at present. Wangdao has done a great service to China by putting his head down and working hard to translate this book."

In an interview with American journalist Edgar Snow in 1936, Mao Zedong said:

> "During my second visit to Beijing, I read many articles about what was happening in Russia. I searched eagerly for Chinese versions of the few Communist documents I could find at that time. Three books became deeply engraved upon my heart, setting up my belief in Marxism. I fully accepted it, believing it to be the correct interpretation of history. I have never vacillated. The three books were the *Communist Manifesto* translated by Chen Wangdao, which was the first Marxist book published

> in Chinese, *Class Struggle* by Kautsky, and *History of Socialism* by Kirkup. By the summer of 1920, I had become a Marxist in theory and to some extent in practice, and I have considered myself a Marxist ever since."[1]

Around that time, following Chen Duxiu's relocation from Beijing to Shanghai in February 1920, *New Youth* also moved south. In May, Chen Duxiu initiated and established the Marxist Research Association in Shanghai. In September, the early party organization in Shanghai led by Chen Duxiu decided to turn *New Youth* into a Party publication from the first issue of the eighth volume. From then on, *New Youth* began to spread Marxism-Leninism with a brand-new look, and launched a special column called 'Russian Studies.' This column helped progressives who were inclined towards socialism to strengthen their faith through developing a better understanding of the real situation in Soviet Russia.

In this way, a new pattern was formed for the spread of Marxism in China: the north was centered on Beijing, then the seat of the Beiyang government, while the south was centered on Shanghai –the largest industrial city and economic center of China – and Guangzhou, a port city. The north and the south echoed one another, forming a greater spread of momentum. Linking with Hunan, Hubei, Shandong, Zhejiang, and a large number of overseas progressives who were deeply influenced by the May Fourth Movement, these communication centers radiated to all parts of the country. This effectively promoted the wide spread of Marxism in China. More importantly, a group of progressives established their belief in Marxism while researching and explaining it. They considered the future and destiny of China by taking Marxism as a complete scientific world view and a theoretical weapon to alter the fate of the country.

On the centenary of the October Revolution, General Secretary Xi Jinping stated:

> "In the history of human thought, no ideological theory can reach the height of Marxism, nor has any theory had such a tremendous impact on

---

1. Snow, Edgar. *Mao Zedong's Talk with Snow in 1936*, People's Publishing House, 1979, p. 33.

the world in terms of science, truth, influence, and dissemination. This reflects the great power and vitality of Marxism, and shows that it is still irreplaceable in the human understanding of the world, and our ability to transform it and promote social progress."[1]

1. *Xi Jinping's Talk on Governing the Country, Vol. 2*, Foreign Language Press, 2017, p. 65.

3

IDEOLOGICAL DEBATES

AT THE BEGINNING OF THE 20th century, China was in a period of great social upheaval and ideological liberation. The old democratic revolution led by the bourgeoisie was gradually transformed into a new democratic revolution led by the proletariat. Social thought was unprecedentedly active, with a hundred new ideologies competing and mixing. While Marxism was spreading at a faster pace, trends like pragmatism, anarchism, and idealistic socialism jostled for attention, and competed to express themselves in different ways. Therefore, it was not easy for Marxism to stand out from the various '-isms' that were popular in China at that time, and to be recognized by the revolutionaries of the day.

Meanwhile, the imperialists and feudal warlords regarded the widening spread of Marxism as a major threat, and treated it with great hatred and fear. They falsely referred to socialism as 'radicalism,' and from time to time ordered strict censorship of the 'radical party' and 'radicalist' publications. The *Weekly Review* and *Xiangjiang Review* were banned, as were many publications and books promoting anarchism. By the start of 1920, 83 publications had been banned by order of the Beiyang warlord government.[1]

However, while the press can be censored, the truth cannot be blocked. In the midst of three orders and repeated bans, Marxism grew tenaciously, like grass in the crevices of a stone. In the process of continuous dissemination, what did socialism really look like? Did it fit China's national conditions? Could it save China from the crisis? In those days there was a distinct lack of clarity of

1. Peng, Ming. *History of the May Fourth Movement* (revised), People's Publishing House, 2019, p. 368

thought among the people. Around these questions, there were three ideological encounters between Marxism and other schools of thought.

The first was the debate over 'problems' and '-isms.' Before the May Fourth Movement, intellectuals with different ideological tendencies all participated in the New Culture Movement, and did not have obvious differences in criticizing feudal rituals and advocating science and democracy. However, with the spread of Marxism, this group gradually diverged. Led by Hu Shi, some bourgeois intellectuals were very reluctant to see the New Culture Movement develop into an ideological movement that included Marxism. Hu said, "The 'new' elements in China kept quiet about specific political issues, but talked about anarchism and Marxism. I couldn't stand. As I believe in experimentalism, I was determined to talk about politics."[1]

In June 1919, Chen Duxiu was arrested for distributing the 'Beijing Citizens' Manifesto' during the May Fourth Movement, while Li Dazhao was preparing to leave Beijing to avoid being arrested. At this point, Hu Shi took over from Chen Duxiu as editor of the *Weekly Review*. In July, Hu published an article entitled 'More Research on Problems, Less Talk of "-isms".' Issues 26 and 27 of the *Weekly Review* were also devoted entirely to the lectures of his mentor Dewey. This provoked a debate between 'problems' and '-isms.'

In his article, Hu advocated experimentalism, and opposed the propagation of all kinds of '-isms,' including Marxism. He wrote, "It is extremely easy to talk about '-isms' – something that can be done by a cat or a dog, by a parrot or a phonograph machine." At the same time, he argued that "empty talk about foreign imported '-isms' is of little use."[2]

Playing on Dewey's pragmatic ideas, Hu Shi advocated a bit-by-bit approach to social improvement, and opposed revolution in China. He advised people to "ask more questions and talk less about academic matters. Please think about how to solve issues, and do not talk about how new and subtle this '-ism' is." He argued, "China has so many problems that need to be solved immediately, from the livelihood of rickshaw drivers to the authority of the great president;

1. *The Collected Works of Hu Shi (Series 2, Vol. 3)*, Huangshan Publishing House, 1996, p. 331.
2. *The Collected Works of Hu Shi (Series 1, Vol. 2)*, Huangshan Publishing House, 1996, p. 250.

from prostitution to traitorous officials and the state."[1]

Hu Shi's proposition sounded quite pragmatic, but its essence was to replace Marxism and social revolution with experimentalism and reformism. This was confusing, especially to young students.

Soon after Hu's article was published, it was criticized by advanced elements, most notably Li Dazhao. Li, who was temporarily living in the Wufeng Mountains in Changli, Hebei, published an article entitled 'On Problems and "-isms" Again' in August 1919 to counter Hu Shi's remarks. Li proclaimed in unequivocal terms that "I like to talk about Bolshevism" and that "the popularity of Bolshevism is really a great change in world culture. We should study it, introduce it, and spread its reality to human society. We should not just listen to the rumors that people have created about it in order to discredit it with cruel and violent words."[2] He believed that the propagation of idealism and the study of practical problems were not incompatible, but rather intertwined and parallel. Indeed, the studying and solving of problems had to be guided by '-isms.' However, socialism had the potential to be applied to practice, and was not just empty talk. Notably, in his article Li Dazhao also expressed the idea of combining the basic principles of Marxism with the concrete reality of China. He pointed out that "every '-ism' has both ideal and practical sides," and that "the application of this ideal to practical politics varies somewhat according to the time, place, and nature of the situation."[3]

Based on this, Li Dazhao also pointed out the necessity of first having a common ideal and doctrine, writing, "Only when there is a fundamental solution can we hope to solve all of the specific problems." He also stressed, "According to Marx's materialistic view of history, the spiritual constructions of law, politics, and ethics in society are all superficial. The economic structure is the basis for all of them. Once the economic problem is solved, all political issues, legal problems, problems of the family system, issues of women's emancipation, and problems of workers' emancipation can be solved."[4] To solve economic problems, class struggle must be waged, and revolution must be carried out.

1. *The Collected Works of Hu Shi (Series 1, Vol. 2)*, Huangshan Publishing House, 1996, pp. 251–252.
2. *The Collected Works of Li Dazhao, Vol. 3*, People's Publishing House, 2006, pp. 4–5.
3. Ibid., p. 3.
4. Ibid., p. 6.

In December 1920, Chen Duxiu published an article entitled 'Doctrine and Effort' in *New Youth*. He pointed out that Marxism-Leninism was like the direction of a ship, and that "the transformation of society is the same as rowing a boat: direction and effort are both indispensable." The controversy over problems and '-isms' was not only a war of words between Li Dazhao and Hu Shi. It also spread through the entirety of the New Culture circle. Discussions of a similar nature were held within many societies, thus beginning the division within the New Culture Movement.

The essence of the debate was the question of whether China needed Marxism or pragmatism, and whether China's issues should be solved through social revolution or social improvement. In the course of the debate, Li Dazhao and others defended Marxism. Many progressive youths wrote articles in support of Li's and others' views.

Although the debate between Li Dazhao and Hu Shi on this topic was significant, the personal relationship between the two men at the time was remarkable in that both came from rural backgrounds, and were colleagues and associates at Peking University. They clearly shared a common will to revitalize the Chinese nation, promote social reform, and oppose feudal dictatorship, but they differed in their understanding of the methods of social reform and certain doctrines. After the debate, the pair continued to communicate and discuss the various '-isms.'

The second debate was about socialism.

After the May Fourth Movement, Chinese society began to explore solutions for national salvation, researching and propagating new ideas. In particular, the victory of the October Revolution made 'socialism' a buzzword in China. All kinds of people were talking about it, even warlords and politicians. For example, the Guangdong warlord Chen Jiongming mentioned it in his magazine *Minxing* in southern Fujian, writing that "socialism is the common idea of mankind now and in the future."[1] He also declared that "a worldwide revolution is inevitable."[2]

However, in addition to scientific socialism, the new trends circulating in Chinese society at that time included the anarchism of Proudhon, Bakunin, and

1. 'The Struggle for Power Has Ended and the Class Struggle has Begun,' *Minxing*, Vol. 1, No. 5, December 15, 1919.
2. 'The Red Tide Has Crossed the Atlantic Ocean,' *Minxing*, Vol. 2, No. 8, January 26, 1920.

Kropotkin, the 'new villagism' of Mitsutoshi Koji, the ideal socialism of Owen and others, the pan-laborism of Tolstoy, the parliamentarism of Bernstein and Kautsky, and Penty's guild socialism. For a while, there was a dizzying mix of different ideologies, leading Sun Yat-sen to exclaim, "There are 57 kinds of socialism. I don't know which one is true."[1] Qu Qiubai summarized the situation: "The discussion of socialism at that time often aroused boundless interest, but it was like the thinking of the youth in Russia in the 1840s – driven by vague influences. It was like looking at the dawn fog through the window. The socialist schools and the meaning of socialism were confusing and unclear."[2] For a while, people could not distinguish what was true Marxism, and were not sure what to believe.

Influenced by this diversity of thought, in November 1920, Zhang Dongsun published 'Another Lesson from a Trip to the Mainland.' In December, he published 'The Present and the Future,' which openly opposed the Marxist doctrine of class struggle and strongly distorted class relations in China. He claimed that there was only one way to save China, namely to increase wealth and power, and that empty talk about socialism would be fruitless. In February 1921, Liang Qichao also published articles such as 'Reply to Zhang Dongsun's Letter on the Socialist Movement,' supporting and elaborating on Zhang arguments.

Unlike Hu Shi, Zhang and Liang also talked verbally about socialism. However, they believed that China was economically backward, and that the majority of the people were uneducated, meaning that there was no basis for the establishment of a proletarian party. Therefore, China could not build a working class state, nor establish a communist party. Propagating socialism should be done sparingly, otherwise it would only create a "pseudo-laboring peasant revolution." They did not deny that imperialist plunder and oppression were the root cause of China's poverty and backwardness, but they believed that the only way to save China was to rely on the "gentry and merchant class" to develop capitalism, smooth out labor-management relations, establish public utilities, and then move peacefully toward socialism. These seemingly pertinent

1. Peng, Ming. *History of the May Fourth Movement* (revised), People's Publishing House, 2019, p. 450.
2. *History of the Communist Party of China, Vol. 1*, Central Literature Publishing House, 2006, pp. 209–210.

views created a certain amount of ideological confusion at the time.

Zhang Dongsun and Liang Qichao claimed that there was no working class in China. In response to this, Chen Duxiu pointed out, "If there are no workers in China, where does the rice you eat, the clothes you wear, the house you live in, and the cars and boats you take come from? Who prints the newspapers that Mr. Zhang runs?"[1] Li Da wrote in an article, "The labor force in China is in surplus. We cannot say that there is no working class. They are just not organized. In this aspect, there is a confrontation between international capitalism and the Chinese working class."[2] On this basis, Li Dazhao stated, "If we want to develop industry in China today, the government must be organized by pure producers to eradicate the domestic plundering class, resist global capitalism, and operate industry according to socialist organization."[3]

In response to the statement from Zhang Dongsun and others that China's current task was to develop industry, Li Da emphasized that "As far as the present situation in China is concerned, there are very few new organs of production in the country. The best way to develop industry today is to adopt socialism, i.e. to adopt socialist methods in order to develop Chinese industry, and try to avoid all the evils born of the industrial society of the capitalist system in Europe and America."[4] Meanwhile, although it was important to develop industry, society would still be monopolized by a few people if the focus was on promoting material civilization without sharing its fruit with the masses through proper distribution.

The discussion lasted for more than a year before it was won. In essence, it was a debate on whether China should take the socialist road or the capitalist road, and whether a proletarian party should be established. During the discussion, the early Chinese Marxists were able to use Marxist theory to analyze the contradictions inherent in the capitalist system and point out that the way out for China could only be socialism. To transform Chinese society, a communist party had to be established.

---

1. Chen Duxiu, 'Duxiu's Reply to Zhang Dongsun' (December 1920), *New Youth,* Vol. 8, No. 4.
2. *The Collected Works of Li Da, Vol. 1*, People's Publishing House, 1980, p. 48.
3. *The Collected Works of Li Dazhao, Vol. 3*, People's Publishing House, 2006, pp. 277–278.
4. *The Collected Works of Li Da, Vol. 1*, People's Publishing House, 1980, p. 74.

Lasting from the end of 1920 into 1921, this discussion was the preparatory period for the creation of the Communist Party of China. It allowed a group of activists who originally did not have a clear understanding of Party building to strengthen their Marxist beliefs. In his reply to Cai Hesen and others, Mao Zedong pointed out that capitalists now held power and education, and that "it is impossible to ask [them] to believe in communism" because "in history, all authoritarians, imperialists, or militarists who did not wait until others came to overthrow them, were never willing to close themselves down. They are not willing to give up… In my opinion, the Russian Revolution was the only choice. There was no other way. It is not that we are specifically choosing this terrifying way while ignoring the other possible better methods."[1]

The third debate was to criticize anarchism.

Anarchism, which originated in Europe, was a petty-bourgeois ideology with worldwide influence, and was introduced to China in the early 20th century. The ideas of abolishing authority and opposing exploitation propagated by anarchism were adapted to intellectuals' negative mentality toward the state, politics, and law in the dark reality of Old China at that time. Such ideas had played a positive role in overthrowing the feudal rule of the Qing Dynasty and criticizing the autocratic rule of the feudal warlords. In particular, in China – which had long been suppressed by feudal rituals, and was a sea of petty-bourgeois thought – anarchist thinking resonated more easily, and thus spread widely and deeply. It was particularly popular among the youth, yet even some advanced elements with initial communist consciousness were influenced to a greater or lesser extent. However, while opposing authoritarian rule, anarchism also directed its attacks at the Marxist doctrine of the state and the dictatorship of the proletariat in Russia.

From 1919 to 1921, anarchists led by Huang Lingshuang and Ou Shengbai published articles such as 'Criticism of Marx's Doctrine' and 'We Oppose the Bolsheviks,' openly challenging Marxism. Politically, anarchists opposed all states and authorities, all political struggles and violent revolutions, instead advocating bourgeois pacifism and humanitarianism, individualism, and

1. Liu, Shenghui and Jin, Chongji. *Biography of Mao Zedong, Vol. 1*, Central Literature Publishing House, 2011, p. 71.

absolute freedom. In economic terms, they called for free joint management of production, opposed centralized and planned production, and advocated the immediate implementation of the 'take what you need' method of distribution.

In response to this attack, early Marxists such as Chen Duxiu, Li Dazhao, and Li Da fought back resolutely. In the inaugural issue of the monthly *Communist Party*, they wrote, "Anarchists! You are also opposed to capitalism and private property, so please do not give your precious freedom so indiscriminately to the capitalist class. It is our creed that all the instruments of production belong to the productive worker, and that all power belongs to the worker. It should also be your creed if you do not willingly connive with the evil of the capitalist who refuses to engage in productive work."[1]

On the question of freedom, Li Dazhao wrote, "Imagine a person who, at birth, left the social environment and lived a life of total isolation and silence. What is the meaning of such a person's individuality?"[2] In other words, there can be no freedom from social relations. Meanwhile, Chen Duxiu astutely pointed that society is a combination of many groups. In a group, each person has their own opinion; in a society, each person has different opinions. If the people in a group do not agree with each other, they can withdraw from the group, but how can members of a society withdraw from that society if they do not agree with each other? This shows that absolute freedom is impossible to achieve.

With regard to the principles of production and distribution, Chen Duxiu noted that the realization of socialism was not a break with centralized mass production, but a change in the bourgeois ownership of the means of production. If the organs of production were delegated to individuals according to the anarchist view, they would not be able to cope with the most complicated modern economic problems, much less achieve the socialization of agriculture and industry in China. Li Da also pointed out that it was absolutely impossible to implement demand-based distribution when the level of production was not sufficiently developed, as it would inevitably undermine the social and economic order and the development of the social productive forces.

---

1. *Selected Essays of Chen Duxiu*, Sanlian Publishing Company, 1984, pp. 50–51.
2. *The Collected Works of Li Dazhao, Vol. 3*, People's Publishing House, 2006, p. 253.

The essence of this controversy was the question of whether to have violent revolution, organizational discipline, and the dictatorship of the proletariat. As a result of the debate, more advanced elements came to realize that the nature and ultimate goal of the Communist Party was to seize power, establish the dictatorship of the proletariat, and then build socialism.

The more the truth is debated, the clearer it becomes. Through the many discussions, Marxists repelled the theoretical attacks of non-Marxists. As a result, Marxism spread widely and deeply in China, and became the mainstream among the new, socially-recognized thought trends, thus laying a solid ideological foundation for the creation and development of the CPC. At the same time, during the many controversies, a group of advanced elements improved their theoretical abilities, and became firmer in their political stance. They were eventually able to draw a clear line between Marxism and non-Marxism, thus firmly assembling under the Marxist banner.

By choosing Marxism, the Chinese revolution achieved the right direction and the hope of victory. It also meant that after many setbacks and failures, debates, and choices, the Chinese people had finally found a powerful ideological weapon to achieve national independence and liberation.

4

THE BACKBONE OF THE PARTY'S FOUNDING

Only when Marxism was accepted and grasped by the masses could it show its power and become the theoretical basis for guiding the revolution.

Because of China's specific national conditions and political environment, the spread of Marxism there was relatively difficult and convoluted. Led by Li Dazhao, advanced elements worked hard and made many efforts to propagate it. They founded progressive newspapers, translated the original works of Marx and Lenin, wrote articles introducing Marxist views, and actively participated in polemics against bourgeois ideology. Eventually, they succeeded in spreading Marxism widely in China.

In March 1920, Li Dazhao led the establishment of the Marxist Research Association at Peking University after much discussion. It was only on 17 November 1921 that the group was publicly announced in the *Peking University Journal*. The fundamental purpose of the Association was to study and research Marxism, unite progressive students, and train advanced elements.

When the Marxist Research Association was first established, there was no fixed place for its activities. After several negotiations, with the support of President Cai Yuanpei, the university allocated two spacious rooms in the Xizhai dormitory for the Association, one as an office and the other as a library. The library was known as 'Kangmuyi Zhai.' Outsiders would not have understood the meaning of this name. In fact, 'Kangmuyi' was transliteration of communism, while 'Zhai' referred to the dormitory. Therefore, 'Kangmuyi Zhai' meant 'communist room.' Located close to the President Cai's office, it was relatively concealed. Public access was forbidden, and it was guarded by the university police.

The Association collected and translated a wide range of Marxist books, organized thematic studies, and held events such as lectures, seminars, and debates. Through these organized study sessions and publicity activities, the Association united progressive youths, expanded the influence of Marxism, and raised the ideological awareness of members and non-members. It deepened their understanding of Marxism, and created a group of advanced youths with strong communist ideas. At that time, Deng Zhongxia and other young students went to the three courtyards of Peking University every morning to read Marxist books. They engaged in political and social activities in the afternoon, and gathered in the evening to discuss revolutionary issues or exchange ideas from their studies, never going to bed before midnight.

The Marxist Research Association was the first group of its kind in China. The influence of its colorful research activities expanded from Peking University to the rest of Beijing and then to the whole country. Revolutionary intellectuals in Shanghai, Wuhan, Changsha, Guangzhou, and Jinan followed suit and set up similar organizations. They launched various forms of study, research, and publicity events, bringing the spread of Marxism to a more organized stage.

In Tianjin, Zhou Enlai and his classmates set up a society to promote the new ideas of the May Fourth Movement, called the Awakening Society. In early 1920, members of the Society joined the anti-Japanese movement, and Zhou Enlai was arrested. The reactionary authorities took a delaying approach, neither referring him to the court for public interrogation nor releasing him. The delay lasted for more than two months.

On 2 April, Zhou and his friends launched a hunger strike after a secret meeting. Due to strong demands from the students and representation from school teachers, students, and lawyers, the reactionary authorities were pressured to transfer the arrested students to the local prosecutor's office. Here, the students' conditions of detention were somewhat improved: with the exception of the two female delegates, they could live in the same place, move around freely, and be able to read books and newspapers. They were allowed to exercise every morning and hold plenary sessions in the evening. They elected Zhou Enlai and others to organize a reading group, and decided to hold lectures every Monday, Wednesday, and Friday to introduce various new ideas.

This was the start of learning activities under special conditions. The prison was used as a classroom to study revolutionary theories, starting with a lecture on the history of the global industrial revolution. This was followed by five lectures given by Zhou Enlai from 28 May to 7 June, explaining the life of Marx and the materialistic view of history, the history of class competition, and the doctrine of surplus value. The lectures were very popular. This organized and relatively systematic dissemination of Marxism in prisons was rare both in China and elsewhere. It proved that the advanced elements in China never stopped in their pursuit of truth, even in the face of adversity.

For the purpose of strengthening external publicity and guiding study, from the first issue of the eighth volume published on 1 September 1920, the Shanghai-based magazine *New Youth* became an organ and an open theoretical publication of the early Communist Party organization there. From then on, it spread Marxism-Leninism publicly, with rich contents and a new look, putting forward political ideas for the transformation of China in a clear and affirmative manner.

In the same month, Chen Duxiu wrote a long essay entitled 'On Politics' for the third issue of the eighth volume of *New Youth*, in which he pointed out that "without the class war, without the era when the working class occupies the position of the ruling class, democracy will always be the exclusive property of the bourgeoisie, that is, the bourgeoisie will always hold power over the working class." He declared, "I recognize that the building of the working class (i.e. the productive class) by revolutionary means –the creation of politics and laws that prohibit all plunder, both internal and external – is the first requirement of modern society."[1] Chen Duxiu, who had previously advocated for the establishment of a bourgeois republic in China, following the example of Europe and the USA, abandoned this idea, arguing that "republican politics are held by a minority of the capitalist class" and that "it is simply a delusion to use it for the wellbeing of the majority."[2] These statements and actions show that Chen Duxiu had come to the Marxist standpoint, and had become an early Chinese Marxist. His change of heart was a powerful example and encouragement for the progressive youth.

1. *Selected Essays of Chen Duxiu, Vol. 2*, Sanlian Publishing Company, 1984, pp. 9–10.
2. Ibid., p. 37

On 7 November, coinciding with the anniversary of the October Revolution, the early Communist Party of Shanghai established a semi-public, highly political monthly publication called *Communist Party*, which published fragments or abridged translations of important writings by Marx and Lenin. It explained the Marxist doctrine of Party building, and imparted knowledge about the Communist Party, the October Revolution in Russia, the Comintern, and the Communist Party of Russia, receiving wide praise from advocates of Communism. This new publication openly flew the flag of the Communist Party. It had a circulation of 5,000 copies, and was disseminated throughout the country through various channels, playing a significant role in the establishment of the CPC.

In Changsha, Mao Zedong began to spread Marxism, seeking like-minded 'true comrades.' He set up groups such as the Culture Press and the Russian Research Society on the platform of the New People's Society, and adopted various methods to strengthen the spread of Marxism.

From 18 December 1919 to 11 April 1920, Mao led the 'Expelling Zhang Delegation' from Hunan to Beijing to petition for the second time, staying at Peking University for almost six months and joining the Young China Society. During his time in Beijing, Mao interacted closely with Li Dazhao, Deng Zhongxia, He Mengxiong, and Luo Zhanglong, and often studied and discussed issues concerning the October Revolution and Marxism-Leninism. After the establishment of the Marxist Research Association, Mao took full advantage of its extensive collection of progressive books and journals, reading everything he could find about the October Revolution and Marxism, thus building his faith in the ideology. He later recalled:

> "During my second visit to Beijing, I read many articles about what was happening in Russia. I searched eagerly for Chinese versions of the few Communist documents I could find at that time. Three books became deeply engraved upon my heart, setting up my belief in Marxism. I fully accepted it, believing it to be the correct interpretation of history. I have never vacillated. The three books were the *Communist Manifesto* translated by Chen Wangdao, which was the first Marxist book published in Chinese, *Class Struggle* by Kautsky, and *History of Socialism* by Kirkup. By the summer of 1920, I had become a Marxist in theory and to some

extent in practice, and I have considered myself a Marxist ever since."[1]

Under the influence of Mao Zedong and others, by the fall of 1920, the progressive New People's Society had more than 100 members, and wielded considerable social influence. On New Year's Day 1921, 18 members held a New Year's Conference in Changsha, with three consecutive days of meetings focusing on three questions: 'What should be the common purpose of the New People's Society?' 'What methods should be used to achieve the purpose?' and 'How can we proceed immediately with these methods?'

There was a discussion and a vote. On the first question, 14 people were in favor of transforming China and the world. On the second question, 12 were in favor of Bolshevism, two were in favor of social democracy, one was in favor of communism by moderate methods, and three abstained. In this regard, Mao Zedong stated, "Social policy is a policy of patching up loopholes, not a solution. Social democracy uses parliament as an instrument of transformation, but in fact parliamentary legislation always protects the proletariat. Anarchism, which denies power, will never be able to do so, I am afraid. A moderate approach to communism, such as Russell's advocating extreme freedom and letting the capitalists off the hook, will also never work. The communism of the radical method, that is, so-called labor-agriculturalism, is the most appropriate because it can be expected to be effective by the method of class dictatorship."[2] On the third issue, all agreed to establish a Socialist Youth League as one of the methods of proceeding.

Thanks to Mao's efforts, most of the members of the New People's Society made the right choice, and gathered under the banner of Marxism.

By the early 1920s, a group of intellectuals with initial communist consciousness had emerged in Chinese society, led by Li Dazhao and Chen Duxiu. They included Mao Zedong, Deng Zhongxia, Zhang Guotao, Gao Junyu, He Mengxiong, Miao Boying, Luo Zhanglong, Chen Tanqiu, Dong Biwu, Wang Jinmei, Deng Enming, Yu Xiusong, Zhang Tailei, Bao Huiseng, He Shuheng, Shi Cuntong, Zhang Wentian, and Yun Daying. There were also Li Hanjun, Li Da, and Chen Wangdao, who had studied in Japan; Cai Hesen,

1. Snow, Edgar. *Mao Zedong's Talk with Snow in 1936*, People's Publishing House, 1979, p. 33.
2. *95 Years of Struggle and Progress of the Communist Party of China, Vol. 1 (1921–1949)*, p. 1.

Li Weihan, Zhou Enlai, Xiang Jingyu, Li Lisan, Zhao Shiyan, Chen Gongpei, Nie Rongzhen, Wang Ruofei, Li Fuchun, Liu Qingyang, Chen Yannian, Cai Chang, Chen Yi, and Deng Xiaoping who had studied in Europe; and Qu Qiubai, Ren Bishi, Xiao Jinguang, and Liu Shaoqi who had studied in Russia.

It was this group of advanced elements who first believed in Marxism and became the backbone of the founding of the Communist Party of China. They established Marxist belief, and used it as a tool for observing and understanding the country's destiny, thereby pushing the Chinese revolution forward in a correct and positive direction.

On the eve of the founding of New China, Mao Zedong wrote his famous work 'The Bankruptcy of the Idealist Conception of History,' in which he stated, "The reason why Marxism-Leninism had such a great effect in China is because China's social conditions needed it – because it is connected with the practice of the Chinese people's revolution, and because it is controlled by the Chinese people."[1] Later in this eloquent article, Mao declared with immense pride, "As soon as the Chinese people heard about Marxism-Leninism, they moved from passivity to initiative. From this point on, the era in modern world history when the Chinese people and culture are looked down upon will come to an end."[2]

On 29 September 2017, while presiding over the 43rd collective study of the Politburo of the CPC Central Committee, General Secretary Xi Jinping stated:

> "Although the times we live in have changed dramatically and profoundly from the times of Marx, we are still in the historical era indicated by Marxism from the perspective of the 500 years of world socialism. This is the scientific basis for our firm confidence in Marxism and our belief in the triumph of socialism. Marxism is the root of the continuous development of the cause of our Party and people, and the source of our continuing advancement. If we depart from or abandon Marxism, our party will lose its soul and direction. We must be steadfast on the fundamental issue of adhering to Marxism as a guide. We cannot waver at any time or under any circumstances."[3]

1. *Selected Works of Mao Zedong, Vol. 4*, People's Publishing House, 1991, p. 1516.
2. Ibid.
3. Xi, Jinping. *On Governance, Vol. 2*, Foreign Languages Press, 2017, p. 66.

PART 4

The Sanctity of Labor:

From Spontaneous Strikes to Conscious Struggle

Before and after the Xinhai Revolution, the Chinese people pinned their hopes for national salvation on the implementation of heroic, virtuous, and sage politics. It was not until the First World War and the victory of the October Revolution that people with initial communist consciousness gradually began to realize the great power of the masses and the working class in promoting the progress of society.

On 11 November 1918, the First World War ended with the victory of the Allies, and China was among the victorious nations. On receiving the news, Cai Yuanpei – President of Peking University – made a celebratory speech in Tiananmen Square on 16 November, titled 'The Sanctity of Labor.' In it, he stated, "The labor to which I refer is not only metalworking, carpentry, and the like. Anyone who benefits others with his work, either physically or mentally, is undertaking labor. Thus, farmers do the labor of planting, businessmen do the labor of transferring, and school staff, writers, and inventors do the labor of education. We should recognize the value of labor. It is sacred!" He went on to predict that "from now on, the world is a world of labor!"[1]

---

1. Gao, Pingshu (editor). *Political Works of Cai Yuanpei*, Hebei People's Publishing House, 1985, p. 178.

During the May Fourth Movement, the Chinese working class mostly did away with guilds and gangs. They organized and carried out alliances and strikes, showing a highly conscious form of patriotism, as well as the determination to thoroughly oppose imperialism and feudal warlords. Thereby, the working class began to step onto the political stage independently, and played a decisive role in the movement.

After the May Fourth Movement, the wide spread of Marxism in China and the continuous development of the Chinese labor movement needed to be combined. Recognizing the awareness and strength of the working class in the practice of struggle, the elites and advanced groups that emerged from the May Fourth Movement realized that the Chinese revolution could only succeed by working together rather than relying on the efforts of a handful of intellectuals. Therefore, they put forward the slogan "Go to the People" and began a social movement called 'Join the Workers' to promote the combination of Marxism with the Chinese labor movement.

1

TRIPLE OPPRESSION OF THE CHINESE WORKING CLASS

CHINA'S WORKING CLASS WAS NOT entirely a product of the independent development of capitalism within Chinese society. It gradually emerged and developed during the nation's evolution from a feudal state to a semi-colonial and semi-feudal society under invading Western powers and the plunder of foreign capitalism after the Opium War in 1840.

China's working class was born out of modern industry. The founding of China's modern industry came from three main sources:

The first was foreign-invested industries. With a series of unequal treaties signed after the Opium War, China was forced to open up to the outside world. In order to dump commodities and plunder raw materials, the major capitalist countries set up a number of modern industrial enterprises, such as shipyards, repair plants, shipping companies, silk reeling plants, printing plants, and flour mills in Shanghai, Guangzhou, Xiamen, and Ningbo, taking advantage of China's cheap labor and raw materials for economic exploitation.

The earliest modern industry invested and operated by foreign countries in China was the shipyard industry. In 1845, John Couper – the representative of the Peninsular and Oriental Shipping in Huangpu, Guangzhou, who was overseeing the overhaul of the company's ships – rented several mud docks from the Chinese and transformed them into the new 'Couper Dock,' employing around 1,000 Chinese workers.[1] According to incomplete statistics, in

1. Liu, Mingkui and Tang, Yuliang. *A History of the Chinese Labor Movement, Vol. 1*, Guangdong People's Publishing House, 1998, p. 18.

the half-century from 1840 to 1894, foreign capitalists opened more than 100 industrial enterprises in China, employing about 34,000 Chinese workers. This is where the earliest group of industrial workers in China came from. After the Sino-Japanese War, and with the signing of the Treaty of Shimonoseki, the imperialists were given the privilege of running factories, opening mines, and building railroads in China. Foreign-capital industries developed rapidly, and the number of Chinese industrial workers increased as well.

In this regard, Mao Zedong once pointed out, "The emergence and development of the Chinese proletariat came not only with the Chinese national bourgeoisie, but also with the direct operation of imperialist enterprises in China. Therefore, a large part of the Chinese proletariat is more senior and more qualified than the Chinese bourgeoisie, and thus its social force and social foundation are also more extensive."[1]

Second, the government-run industries operated by Qing government officers advocated for the use of advanced Western technologies to strengthen the army and enrich the country. From the 1860s, some key Qing officials, including Zeng Guofan, Li Hongzhang, and Zuo Zongtang, started to set up the modern military industry. In 1861, Zeng Guofan established the modern Anqing Military Factory, which was the first of its kind. In 1865, Li Hongzhang set up the Jiangnan Manufacturing Bureau in Shanghai, which was the largest government-run military industry, with factories equipped with high-quality machines for guns, artillery, ammunition, steel making, and machine building. It also had one medium-sized dockyard employing more than 2,000 workers. In 1866, Zuo Zongtang set up the Fuzhou Shipyard Bureau – the largest government-run ship-repairing plant, employing about 2,000 workers. From 1862 to 1894, before the Sino-Japanese War, the Qing government opened a total of 19 military factories and 28 civilian industries for mining and transport services, employing nearly 40,000 workers as part of the Westernization Movement.[2] The emergence of China's modern military industry and its associated industrial enterprises produced many industrial workers.

The third source took the form of the national industries set up by Chinese capitalists. In the 1870s, due to the increase of foreign investment and the

1. *Selected Works of Mao Zedong, Vol. 2*, People's Publishing House, 1991, p. 627.
2. Liu, Mingkui and Tang, Yuliang. *A History of the Chinese Labor Movement, Vol. 1*, Guangdong People's Publishing House, 1998, p. 22, 27.

stimulus and influence of China's early government-run enterprises, the natural economy gradually disintegrated. The number of bankrupt farmers and handicraft workers increased, and the commodity market and labor market continued to expand. What resulted was the rise of modern industries invested by Chinese national capital. Some landlords, bureaucrats, merchants, and buyers, who had amassed large monetary wealth, began to invest in new forms of industry, and gradually transformed themselves into China's early national bourgeoisie by running modern industries.

Among the national capital enterprises, machine silk reeling was the first to emerge. In 1872, Guangdong merchant Chen Qiyuan founded the Jichanglong Silk Reeling Plant in Nanhai, employing over 600 female workers. Two years later, there were five silk reeling plants around Guangzhou, and 11 in the following 10 years. In 1878, a group of Shanghai merchants set up the Shanghai Mechanical Textile Bureau, employing 4,000 workers. At the same time, national capital enterprises such as flour, matches, papermaking, and printing also began to appear. In 1880, coalmines were founded in Chizhou (Anhui), Yixian (Shandong), Jingmen (Hubei), Xuzhou (Jiangsu), and Lincheng (Zhili). From the very beginning, the development of modern national capital industry was beset with major problems between foreign capital and the feudal forces of the country, leading to a state of contradiction and dependence. After more than 20 years of hard work, more than 100 enterprises had been set up by the eve of the signing of the Treaty of Shimonoseki, and nearly 30,000 workers were employed. The rise of China's national industries gave rise to another group of industrial workers.

With the development of China's modern industry, the Chinese working class began to emerge from the 1850s. Until the May Fourth Movement in 1919, its development can be roughly divided into three stages.

Stage 1: from the emergence of the Chinese working class to the signing of the Treaty of Shimonoseki in 1895. This was the starting period.

During this period of more than 40 years, the Chinese working class grew out of nothing, and emerged with modern industries run by foreign, bureaucratic, and national capital. China's modern industry was small in scale and slow to develop at that time. The working class was small in number, totaling only around 100,000 people.

Stage 2: from the signing of the Treaty of Shimonoseki in 1895 to the eve of the First World War in 1914. This was a period of initial development.

During these 19 years, the development of China's modern industry entered a new phase, mainly manifested in a rapid increase of imperialist investment in Chinese industry, and the development of a national capitalist industry. Meanwhile, world capitalism entered the stage of imperialism. While carrying out military aggression against China, the imperialists also stepped up the economic plunder of China, shifting from commodity-based export to capital-based export. In order to reap excessive profits, the Western powers concentrated a large amount of capital into China to further divide their spheres of influence economically, competing for rights and interests in building railroads, operating inland waterways, mining, and opening factories. This led to a substantial increase in industrial investment in China by the imperialists.

The growth of foreign capital can be clearly seen by comparing this stage with the first stage. In the 40 years before 1894, the total number of modern businesses operated by foreign capital in China was only about 100, with a total investment of about 28 million yuan. In the 19 years from 1895 to 1913, foreign capitalists set up 166 major factories and mines in China. The scale of the capital was greatly expanded over the previous period, and vast amounts of money were invested in large factories, with a total capital of 103 million yuan. With the heavy imperialist investment in China, the modern industries run by Chinese capitalists had also undergone initial development. According to incomplete statistics, from 1895 to 1913, 549 factories and mines with capital of over 10,000 yuan were set up by Chinese capitalists, with a total investment of 120.2 million yuan.

During these 19 years, the Chinese working class increased significantly with the sharp rise in foreign and domestic capital. According to incomplete statistics, there were 21,754 factories with at least seven workers in China. By 1913, the total number of workers in China was around 600,000.

Stage 3: from the outbreak of the First World War in 1914 to the eve of the May Fourth Movement in 1919. This was a period of rapid development.

During these five years, the Western powers were mainly focused on the First World War. Not only did they temporarily relax their economic aggression against China, but they also purchased a large number of military supplies from it. Chinese industries took advantage of this opportunity, and developed rapidly.

In these five years, 379 new factories and mines were set up, with a total investment of 85.8 million yuan. In terms of the total number of national endeavors, before the War there were 698 factories with capital of over 300 million yuan, and by 1919 there were 1,759 factories with capital of over 500 million yuan.

With the rapid development of domestic capital, the Chinese working class also increased significantly. By the eve of the May Fourth Movement, it had swelled to around two million people. Among them, there were around 700,000 factory workers, 160,000 railroad workers, 590,000 mineworkers, 150,000 seafarers, 40,000 post and telecommunications workers, and 320,000 staff at foreign-funded enterprises in China. This showed that the working class had become an important social force.

In addition, there were more than 10 million handicraft workers and shopkeepers, a rapidly growing student body at the new schools, a large number of new school teachers, and journalists for newspapers and magazines, creating a larger intellectual community with more advanced ideology than during the Xinhai Revolution. As Mao Zedong pointed out, "The growth and development of new social forces during that period led to the emergence of a growing camp for the anti-imperialist and anti-feudal bourgeois-democratic revolution in China. It was a camp formed by the working class, students, and the emerging national bourgeoisie."[1]

In a semi-colonial and semi-feudal Chinese society, capitalist wage labor inevitably took on a colonial and feudal character. The foreign capitalist-imperialists in China regarded themselves as conquerors, and saw Chinese workers as "yellow slaves." The foreign capitalists not only exploited Chinese workers but also practiced brutal national oppression. Racial discrimination played a part in employment relations. The foreign capitalists adopted barbaric labor systems in which workers were sold to factories within a regular period, or were bounded as "interns" without freedom or wages. The foreign capitalists also tried to retain and make use of the domestic feudal labor system, such as the butler system, to exploit and pressure the Chinese workers within feudal society.

1. *Selected Works of Mao Zedong, Vol. 2*, People's Publishing House, 1991, p. 558.

The Qing government-run enterprises imported a system and method of exploitation used by foreign capitalists, employing the exploitation methods of the original feudal government-run industries. They adopted military tactics to manage their enterprises. Although the Chinese capitalists had few political privileges, they still tried to use the systems and management of exploitation combined with modern capital and feudal guilds in their wage labor.

Thus, Chinese workers were subjected to triple exploitation and oppression by imperialism, feudal forces, and the bourgeoisie. They were in an even harsher and more difficult situation than workers in other countries, and lived miserable lives.

The working hours for Chinese laborers were exceptionally long and intense, which led to a general deterioration in their health. To strengthen their exploitation, both Chinese and foreign capitalists often used methods such as extending working hours, increasing the amount of work, and accelerating machine operation. Chinese workers generally worked more than 12 hours a day – sometimes up to 16 hours, and there were no statutory breaks. In June 1916, an article entitled 'An Investigation into the Life of Poor Women in Shanghai' was published in the *Women's Times*, describing the situation: "Before dawn, the steam whistle blows to instruct people to go to work. Those who have to travel far often get up around midnight. They start working before the sun comes up, and don't stop after it sets, going back and forth between the factory's furnace and machines all day long. They are not allowed to have a moment to enjoy the warmth of the sun. As a result, they are pale and depressed."

Working conditions were particularly harsh. There was little protection, and major accidents occurred from time to time. Chinese and foreign capitalists set up factories and mines to extract surplus value, and refused to spend money on improving working conditions, resulting in frequent casualties. An average of four workers died in the Kailuan coal mines each month. In the Fushun coal mine, there were 2,918 accidents in 1913, killing and injuring 3,184 workers, while 921 workers were killed in a gas explosion in 1917. At that time, it cost 180 yuan to buy a horse, but the family of a deceased worker only received 40 yuan for their pension. On 9 March 1919, Li Dazhao published an article called 'The Life of Workers in the Tangshan Coal Mines – Worse than Mules and Horses' in Issue 12 of the *Weekly Review*, demanding justice for the workers.

Wages for Chinese workers were particularly low. Adult men generally earned 20 to 40 cents a day (10 cents is about nine yuan in today's currency), which was only one seventh of the wages of the same type of worker in Great Britain at that time. For contract workers, adult women, and children, wages were halved. Girls earned even less than boys. In Shanghai in 1919, 10 cents would only buy two liters of rice, or a foot of cloth, or pay rent for a day or so. Even with such meager salaries, Chinese and foreign capitalists still deducted and extorted the workers' wages in various guises by using the combined forces of capitalism and feudalism. The most common tactic was the imposition of fines. For example, the Shanghai Deda and Housheng yarn mills imposed 92 penalties on workers across their factories. In addition, 42 penalties were imposed in each factory workshop, mainly for wage deductions and fines. The penalties ranged from three to 50 cents, or a half-day or one day of work.[1] With so many rules, the workers were blamed and punished at every turn, while bringing additional economic benefits to the capitalists. For example, from the foundation of the Shanghai Hongyuan Yarn Factory in 1890 until 1918, it accumulated up to 50,000 yuan in fines alone. There were other tricks to exploit workers, such as a depository system that required workers to deposit half a month's wages to prevent them from leaving, earning extra interest by paying wages in arrears, and taking advantage of the difference in the value of various currencies such as silver yuan, copper yuan, and coins. These exploitative tricks further reduced the pitiful wages of the workers, and made their lives even worse.

Thus, it was clear that the Chinese working class in a semi-colonial and semi-feudal society was under the triple oppression of imperialism, the bourgeoisie, and the feudal forces. With extremely low economic and political status, their working hours were long, their pay was low, and working conditions were poor. According to Mao Zedong, "The severity and cruelty of this triple oppression was rare among the peoples of the world."[2]

1. Liu, Mingkui and Tang, Yuliang. *A History of the Chinese Labor Movement, Vol. 1*, Guangdong People's Publishing House, 1998, p. 182.
2. *Selected Works of Mao Zedong, Vol. 2*, People's Publishing House, 1991, p. 644.

2

WORKERS' STRIKES ACROSS ALL SECTORS

FROM ITS BIRTH, THE CHINESE working class struggled heroically against exploitation and oppression. Even though this struggle was spontaneous in the early days of the labor movement, it demonstrated tremendous revolutionary spirit, and formed a tradition of anti-imperialism and anti-feudalism.

The early labor movement in China began with the Hong Kong Workers' Strike in 1858 against the occupation of Guangzhou by invading British and French forces. From this beginning, the struggle of the Chinese working class gradually developed and grew, moving from spontaneity to consciousness. About 60 years before the May Fourth Movement, the early Chinese labor movement could be divided into two broad periods.

The first period was from the late 1850s to the outbreak of the Xinhai Revolution in 1911. During this period, Chinese workers' strikes were mainly centered on opposition to foreign colonialist aggression, feudalist oppression, and specific economic purposes. Strikes were suspended once the limited demands had been met. The initiation and organization were scattered, small-scale, and disorderly – simply a spontaneous resistance of the working class against oppression and exploitation. According to incomplete statistics, in the 41 years from 1870 to 1911, there were 105 strikes – an average of 2.6 per year. In terms of the strikes' targets, as the Chinese working class was subjected to triple oppression, with exploitation by foreign capitalists being the harshest, the initial targets of the Chinese labor movement were mainly foreign invaders.

After the outbreak of the Second Opium War, more than 20,000 municipal and transport workers in Hong Kong and Macau went on strike in May 1858, to oppose the occupation of Guangzhou by the invading British and French forces. They returned to Guangzhou by resigning and taking leave. This was the first large-scale strike by Chinese workers against foreign aggression. In 1879, the workers of the British shipyard, S. C. Farnham & Co. in Shanghai went on strike against the withholding of wages by the feudal supervisor. The British managers of the shipyard took advantage of this situation, making up excuses to withhold the workers' wages, further provoking their anger. The workers persisted in their struggle, causing the shipyard to suffer financial losses and forcing the British managers and feudal supervisor to pay their wages in full. The strike finally succeeded.

During the Sino-French War, Hong Kong shipwrights refused to repair French warships, and transport workers refused to load and unload cargo for the French. The British colonial authorities colluded with the French to detain or fine the striking workers. The Hong Kong workers rose up in revolt and went on strike for 35 days, beginning on 2 September 1884 and lasing for 35 days. The British and Hong Kong authorities sent military and police to suppress the strike, and the striking workers started a tit-for-tat struggle. They forced the authorities to release the arrested workers, pay back the fines, and stop interfering with the Chinese workers' struggle against the French invasion.

The Qing government-run industrial feudal rule was extremely harsh, but it did not stop workers from fighting back. In 1882, some workers at the government-run coal mine in Kaiping, Zhili, went on strike to demand equal wages and benefits. In May 1883, workers at the Jiangnan General Administration of Machinery Manufacturing held a demonstration against the extension of working hours, but were eventually dispersed under the suppression of reactionary forces. In September 1890, Liu Linxiang – the new general manager of the bureau – decided to extend the working hours further, and the workers rose again in opposition. On the day when the new regulations were decided, despite the steam from the boilers and the sound of the whistle, the workers once again rose up against it and went on strike. This was the first demonstration of the workers' spirit of solidarity and struggle.

The defeat of the Sino-Japanese War and the deepening national crisis were a great stimulus to the Chinese people. Anti-imperialist and patriotic ideas continued to rise, prompting the gradual swell of patriotic movements led by the bourgeoisie. From 1903, people from all echelons of society opposed the control of Chinese railroads and mines by the imperialist powers. In 1905 there was a general boycott of American goods to protest against the mistreatment of Chinese workers and the persecution of overseas Chinese by the American imperialists, as well as their refusal to abolish the expired treaty that restricted Chinese workers. These anti-imperialist and patriotic actions had a great influence on the struggle of the Chinese working class.

The workers actively participated in the anti-imperialist and patriotic movement, and their struggle against the Chinese bourgeoisie also increased day by day. Within a year or so after 1898, workers at the Lunhua Silk Factory and the Huasheng Yarn Factory went on strikes of varying sizes against the factory's arrears and wage cuts. In 1904, 600 workers at the Chengdu Arsenal in Sichuan went on strike to protest against the foreman's arbitrary withholding of wages. In 1905, more than 400 workers at the Shanghai Qixin Yarn Factory broke the factory doors and windows and smashed the machinery in opposition to extra exploitation by the foremen. In 1906, more than 10,000 workers at the Anyuan Coal Mine went on strike against the foreman's oppression.[1]

At the beginning of the 20th century, bourgeois revolutionaries led by Sun Yat-sen were determined to pursue democratic revolution by violently overthrowing the rule of the Qing Dynasty. Under the influence and impetus of the bourgeoisie, the Chinese working class participated directly or indirectly in the old bourgeois democratic revolutionary movement, and became one of the important forces. When Sun Yat-sen established the Xingzhong Society overseas, Chinese workers joined. The total number of Xingzhong members was about 300, and there were 279 further candidates for membership. Among them were 54 workers, accounting for 19% of the total number of members. During the period of the Chinese United League, overseas Chinese workers actively supported a series of armed struggles launched by Sun Yat-sen in China. In December 1906, members of the Hunan Union Association went to

1. Sha, Jiansun. *History of the Communist Party of China (1921–1949), Vol. 1*, Central Literature Publishing House, 2006, p. 127.

the Pingxiang, Liuyang, and Liling areas at the junction of Hunan and Jiangxi to liaise with the Party and local revolutionary intellectuals, organizing groups, advocating revolution, and holding an armed uprising. The total number of workers, peasants, and soldiers who participated in the uprising reached more than 30,000, including more than 6,000 coal miners from Anyuan. In 1911, during the 'Road Protection Movement' that broke out in Hunan, Hubei, and Sichuan Provinces against the so-called 'state-owned railroad' policy of the Qing government, workers on the Chuan-Han Railroad held an uprising to support the struggle.[1]

In October 1911, the Wuchang Uprising broke out, and some workers in Wuhan joined it. On 18 October, when the revolutionary army attacked the Qing troops, workers at the Hanyang Arsenal stepped up production day and night to make weapons to support the front line. The capture of the Jiangnan General Administration of Machine-building the following day played a major role in the victory of the Shanghai Uprising.

The second period of the early Chinese labor movement was from the Xinhai Revolution in 1911 to the May Fourth Movement in 1919.

During this period, the ranks of the Chinese working class grew unprecedentedly, and the labor movement developed considerably. The self-consciousness of the struggle increased significantly, and it entered an organized state, increasingly taking on the nature of class struggle. At the same time, the number of workers' strikes and struggles increased dramatically, and their scale expanded. There were 180 strikes in these eight years – 22.5 strikes per year on average, which was a significant increase compared with the average of 2.6 strikes per year before the Xinhai Revolution.

The Xinhai Revolution overthrew the Qing Dynasty and put an end to the monarchical dictatorship that had ruled China for more than 2,000 years. However, the fruits of the revolution were usurped by Yuan Shikai – the head of the Northern Warlords. Yuan betrayed his country, surrendering to imperialism externally, and creating a dictatorship internally, while suppressing the revolutionary forces and attempting to restore the imperial system. Instead of seeing improvements in their living conditions, the workers were subjected

---

1. Sha, Jiansun. *History of the Communist Party of China (1921–1949), Vol. 1*, Central Literature Publishing House, 2006, p. 127.

to more cruel exploitation and oppression under the various reactionary bans of the Beiyang warlord government. However, the Chinese working class did not give in. They continued to struggle against imperialism and feudalism and for better living conditions.

In July 1912, soon after Yuan Shikai came to power, there was an uprising of kiln-burning workers in Jingdezhen, Jiangxi Province. The revolting workers besieged the gendarmerie barracks and seized guns and bullets. In the same year, more than 5,000 silk reeling workers in Shunde, Guangdong, held a large-scale strike against the capitalists' oppression of workers and the payment of wages with low-priced banknotes. In December, the general office of the Hanyang Arsenal attempted to detain 30 workers on the pretext that they were late. The workers went on strike against the factory's oppressive leadership and long working hours, demanding the dismissal of the general office. The struggle lasted for several days, and was later suppressed by a battalion of troops sent by the reactionary government.

In April 1913, there was another mass strike at the Hanyang Arsenal. At that time, paper currency was devalued. The workers objected to the payment of wages in this devalued paper money, and demanded silver dollars. These reasonable demands were rejected by the factory management, so the workers went on strike. The factory's general office collaborated with the garrison to suppress the strike, and the workers became even more indignant. They gathered more than 2,000 people and crossed the river to Wuchang to petition the then Vice President, Li Yuanhong. Li pretended to send someone to mediate the strike, but arrested the workers' representative, Liang Hansheng, and sentenced him to death. This strike failed because the reactionary authorities suppressed it by force.

After the outbreak of the First World War in 1914, Chinese capital-run industries developed further, and Japanese and American imperialist capital exports expanded once again. In 1915, due to the cruel exploitation of workers by the capitalists and foremen, and the beating of workers by foreign engineers, the workers at Anyuan Coal Mine went on strike under the leadership of the Brotherhood of the Secret Society. The strike was suppressed by the reactionary army, and the workers' leaders were killed. Next, the workers at the Dawangyan Coal Mine in Hubei were denied a wage increase, which provoked public anger. Two hundred miners went on strike and burned down the company, injuring many members of the mine's police.

In May 1916, workers at the Jardine and Swire shipping companies joined forces to demand a wage increase. As a result, the management was forced to recognize a 5%–10% increase in monthly wages. This strike was organized by the Shanghai General Association of Chinese Ship's Mates, reflecting the fact that the activities of Chinese trade unions had already begun. Although they were still influenced by the bourgeoisie and feudal forces, they began to play a role in the struggle.

After 1917, the labor movement in China developed further, and the number of workers' strikes and struggles increased significantly. The most strikes occurred in Shanghai, in addition to several strikes in Hangzhou, Wuxi, Suzhou, and Changning in Hunan. In March 1917, the printing workers at the Shanghai Commercial Press went on a general strike. Before this strike, spontaneous workers' organizations had sprung up. Workers from the Chinese typesetting department had formed the Integrated Comradeship Society, and members of the binding department had set up a trade association. Fearing that the workers would form a union, the capitalists ordered the dissolution of these two organizations and attempted to fire the leaders of the Chinese typesetters. This provoked the workers' anger, and pushed them to stage a strike. Within two days, the strike expanded from the Chinese typesetting and binding departments to the lead printing and foreign-language typesetting departments. Then, the typesetting workers at the Zhonghua Book Bureau and Wenming Book Bureau held a sympathy strike to support the workers at the Shanghai Commercial Press, bringing the total number of striking workers to more than 700. Later, due to a lack of strong leadership, the strike failed under the suppression of the military and police.

According to incomplete statistics, in the 50 years from 1870 to 1919, there were 235 spontaneous strikes by Chinese workers, with an average of three to four national strikes per year. From 1912 to May 1919, there were 130 strikes – an average of 16 per year. During this period, the outstanding feature of the Chinese labor movement was that the anti-imperialist and anti-feudal consciousness clearly increased, and the political nature of the struggle became more obvious. In the patriotic movement against Yuan Shikai's traitorous government and the Japanese imperialists' signing of the 'Twenty-one Demands', workers in many regions actively participated in the struggle.

On the whole, with the growing ranks of the working class and the gradual increase in class consciousness, the early labor movement in China progressed well. However, before the May Fourth Movement, regardless of the content of its struggles or the form of its organization, the Chinese labor movement still had not gone beyond the stage of spontaneous struggle, nor had it consciously realized its historical mission. It had not put forward its own political ideas and revolutionary program, and had not yet entered the political stage of Chinese society as an independent class force.

Historical facts show that only by accepting Marxism and establishing a revolutionary party representing the interests of the class could the Chinese working class take the political stage and play a leading role in the revolution.

3

THE POLITICAL AWAKENING OF THE WORKING CLASS

FROM ITS EARLIEST DAYS, THE Chinese working class had to struggle against heavy oppressors. In particular, it had to fight resolutely against the foreign capitalist forces of aggression and the feudal forces of the country. This determined the strong anti-imperialist and anti-feudal nature of the Chinese labor movement from the initial stage of its spontaneous development. It also determined that the Chinese working class had to be more resolutely and thoroughly revolutionary and rebellious than any other class in China.

In its long practice of production and struggle, the class characteristics of the Chinese working class determined that it was successful in organization and discipline, rich in the spirit of solidarity and cooperation, the least conservative and the most revolutionary, and the most progressive, revolutionary, and promising of all classes in Chinese society in the early 20th century.

Before the May Fourth Movement, two major anti-imperialist and anti-feudal political struggles took place in China.

One was a strike by more than 1,700 workers in the French Concession of Tianjin in 1916 against the French occupation of Old Xikai (present-day Xining Road in Heping District). Old Xikai was the place where the French Concession met the Chinese border of Tianjin. In October 1916, the French invaders tried after repeated activities and gradual encroachment to occupy Old Xikai, and the Beiyang warlord government acquiesced to this unreasonable demand. The people of Tianjin were outraged, and set up the 'Association for the Protection of National Rights and Land,' holding a citizens' meeting with thousands of people to denounce the aggressive acts of the French imperialists. Chinese workers in the French Concession and in French-owned enterprises decided to implement an allied general strike.

On 14 November, the Chinese workers at the French-owned Electric Light Company, an instrument company, a brick factory, the Yisan Industrial Iron Works, and the Huali Iron Works were the first to go on strike. Subsequently, workers in various types of jobs, as well as Chinese domestic workers employed by French shops and agencies, and Chinese domestic helpers in French families also went on strike – a total of more than 1,400 workers. The striking workers set up a trade union office that included a clerical department, an accounting department, an investigation department, an oratory department, and an inspection department to lead the workers in their struggle.

During the strike at the French Electric Light Company, the whole French Concession was plunged into darkness. Without electricity, the factories that were not on strike also stopped working. In order to sabotage the strike, the management of the Electric Light Company recruited scab workers to drive the machines that generated electricity for a heavy sum of 200 yuan per day. However, none of the workers would return to work. The Electric Light Company tried to borrow Chinese craftsmen from the British Concession Light Company, but the craftsmen refused. The management therefore had no choice but to ask French soldiers drive the machines to generate electricity. On 22 November, the trade union office organized a huge demonstration by workers from all industries. Workers in Beijing and Shandong also held strikes to support the workers in Tianjin, setting off a wave of anti-imperialist struggle.

This struggle lasted for almost six months, and finally forced the French imperialists to change the Old Xikai area into a Sino-French co-managed district. The strike was only partially won, but was unprecedented in its scale, its high degree of organization, and its far-reaching influence, indicating that the early labor movement in China reached a new height.

Another significant anti-imperialist and anti-feudal political struggle was the 1916 strike by workers at the Shanghai Jiangnan Shipyard against feudal rule.

The predecessor of the Jiangnan Shipbuilding Institute was the Jiangnan General Administration of Machine Building. It was bordered by the Huangpu River to the south, and had brick walls over 10 feet high on the north, east, and west sides, with trenches outside the wall. In front of the main gate, there were four large black lacquered pillars with a tiger-head sign that read: 'No entry to the manufacturing site'. On the tiger-head sign hung the 'water and fire stick,' which was used to torture the workers. Two stone lions squatted on both sides of the gate, and soldiers with guns stood next to them. From the outside, it looked like a feudal government office. Workers at the Jiangnan Shipbuilding Institute had to wear a waist tag indicating their lowly status, and had to be supervised at all times. If they resisted, they would be tied up and put on public display. When workers finished their shift each day, they had to be searched by the patrol before they could leave the factory. This humiliating system of body searches had already aroused the anger of the workers.

In the afternoon of 25 November 1916, several coppersmiths were ordered to repair warships along the Huangpu River. As they set off, the patrol commander Li Konglin came up to search them. He saw that they were carrying tools and materials out of the factory, so he accused them of stealing. When one of the coppersmiths came forward to explain the situation, Li Konglin did not say anything, but hit him in the mouth. Several other coppersmiths went up to reason with him, and were also slapped several times. Unwilling to accept such treatment, they fought back, wrestling with Li Konglin, who sounded a siren and summoned a dozen accomplices to beat the workers. The news spread, and more than 1,000 workers went on strike in protest. Liu Guannan (Director of the Jiangnan Shipbuilding Institute) and Lu Fagong (the captain of the patrol team) heard the news and rushed to intercede, telling the workers to return to their respective posts. The workers demanded that the body search system be abolished and that Li Konglin be investigated, otherwise they vowed not to go back to work. The next day, all of the workers continued to strike. The factory had to accept their demand, and announced that from now on, the body search system would be cancelled and Li Konglin would be investigated as a punishment. The strike was finally won.

From the above, it can be seen that the workers' struggle in this period developed gradually as the working class grew and class consciousness increased, and workers began to realize the significance of 'common resistance' in their struggles. However, workers' organizations were still largely under the influence of secret associations or feudal gangs, which was obviously not conducive to a united struggle.

As an emerging force in modern China, the Chinese working class represented the future direction of the nation's development. This trend was reflected in the May Fourth Movement three years later.

On 3 June 1919, the May Fourth Movement was in danger of being aborted when the Beijing government suppressed the students on a large scale. At a critical juncture in the movement's development, in the midst of China's growing national crisis, and under the influence of the October Revolution in Russia and new thinking in China, the Chinese working class quickly awakened. The May Fourth Movement broke out in Beijing, but it culminated under the initiative of Shanghai workers to participate. This was because Shanghai at that time was the largest industrial and commercial city in China, where modern industry and commerce run by foreign and Chinese capital were concentrated, and where the earliest, most concentrated and revolutionary faction of Chinese industrial workers arose. According to preliminary statistics, the Shanghai working class had grown to more than 500,000 people, accounting for about a quarter of the total number of industrial workers in China.

In the early days of the May Fourth Movement, the emerging labor force did not attract much attention from society. On 4 June, the Shanghai Federation of Students sent people to mobilize merchants to strike, but not workers, let alone kneeling down and begging for solidarity as they did with shopkeepers. Some students also persuaded the workers not to strike when the trolley workers and the telephone operators demanded it. They were afraid that after the strike, workers would have no income and would find it hard to get by, making it difficult to maintain the strike.

However, with the nation in peril, it was impossible to remain idle. The Shanghai working class took the lead in initiating the strike, with high and conscious patriotic zeal, in solidarity with the revolutionary struggle of the patriotic students. During the strike, many workers insisted that their actions were voluntary, saying, "We are all poor people, but we do not want our country to become the second Korea, where the situation is unbearable. The movement we are currently engaged in is one of the most incredible in the history of the world. It is a national movement that cannot be overpowered by any force."[1]

1. *North China Daily News*, June 10, 1919.

On 5 June, Chinese workers at the Japanese yarn factories came forward. Inspired by the slogan "No work for the enemy," they left their posts, launching the far-reaching 'June 5th' anti-imperialist patriotic political strike.

The *Shun Pao* newspaper reported: "At 11:30am, five or six thousand male and female workers of the third, fourth, and fifth yarn factories set up by the Japanese in and outside Caojiadu also went on strike. At 1:30pm, male and female workers at the Lujiawan Rihua Cotton Mill and Yangshupu Shanghai Cotton Mill also went on strike. The total number of workers in the factory was more than 20,000, which shows the patriotic fervor of our people."[1]

On the same day, workers at the Commercial Press and the China Bookstore were also among the first to strike.

From then on, the epicenter of the May Fourth Movement shifted from Beijing to Shanghai, and the main force of the movement moved from students to workers. A revolutionary storm of anti-imperialism and anti-feudalism soon formed in the country. It pushed the transformation of the Chinese working class from self-existing to self-acting, and inspired the transition of the Chinese labor movement from spontaneous struggle to a conscious fight.

On 6 June, the scope of the strike expanded rapidly, and workers across all sectors took action.

That day, all of the workers at the Chinese Tramway Company and some of the staff at the British, American, and French tramway companies started a strike. Workers at various factories also went on strike, including those from the Shanghai Qiuxin Machinery Factory, the Ruili Machinery Factory, the Yingshangxiang Pig Iron Factory, Customs Printing, and the Huajin Silk Factory.

An open letter from the workers at the Qiuxin Machine Factory expressed the voice of the Shanghai labor force: "Our country's diplomacy has failed, and the nation is in danger. The citizens are deeply indignant. The academic and business sectors are on strike, begging for salvation. We in the industrial sector share the same passion and conscience. At this time, we cannot sit back and watch. Therefore, from today (6 June), all of us will go on strike and act in unison with the business and academic circles."[2]

---

1. *Shun Pao*, June 6, 1919.
2. *News Press*, June 7, 1919.

According to the *News Press*, the workers from the machine factory made a collective donation to build an ironwood pagoda at the factory entrance. It was six feet high and five feet wide, and had four three-foot-high letters on it, saying 'Do not forget our national shame.' There was also a wind machine and a five-colored flag bearing the words 'Awaken the nation,' which rotated in the wind, and was designed to shock passersby.[1]

The local authorities hastily held an emergency meeting to discuss countermeasures, and mobilized the city's police and a division of the army in Shanghai in a vain attempt to suppress the anti-imperialist patriotic movement.

Britain, America, Japan, and Portugal planned to arm the 'Universal Merchant Corps' to assist the Shanghai authorities in suppressing the masses. The British force was located at the Laozha police station. The American force was located at the Hongkou police station, while the Portuguese and Japanese forces were based in Hongkou district.

However, the Shanghai working class was undaunted and fought bravely against the armed imperialist suppression. The angry masses injured the two inspectors from the suppressing forces. The unified action of the workers and patriotic masses completely disrupted the reactionary order in Shanghai.

On 7 June, workers at the General Machine Factory of the Shanghai-Nanjing and Shanghai-Hangzhou Railroads went on strike.

On 8 June, workers at the seventh, eighth, and ninth cotton yarn factories in and outside of Japan went on strike. Workers in the steel, machinery, shipbuilding, textiles, and transportation industries strengthened their interconnection and began to conceive a general strike.

On 9 June, Shanghai's car drivers, carpenters, assemblers, cleaners, and postal workers went on strike, along with workers at the Jiangnan Dockyard, the British-owned Yessong Old Dockyard, the American-owned Simsang Foreign Bank, and the British-American Tobacco Factory. The striking workers said, "We will not resume work until we have achieved the goal of punishing Cao, Zhang, and Lu."[2]

The Shanghai railroad workers' strike started at the Wusong General Engine Factory on 7 June. When the news spread, the workers on the Shanghai-

1. *Shun Pao*, June 8, 1919.
2. *Eastern Times*, June 9, 1919.

Nanjing and Shanghai-Hangzhou railroads decided to hold an allied strike starting on 9 June.

The director of the Shanghai Railroad Bureau and the British Chief Steward asked the workers to send their representatives to the Railroad Bureau to negotiate, in an attempt to stop them from striking.

The Chief Steward asked, "What are your demands? Why do you want to go on strike?" The workers' representatives replied, "The business and academic circles are on strike, demanding that the government punishes the traitors. We workers are part of the nation, so we should act in unison." After negotiations, the two sides reached an agreement.

On 9 June, the Shanghai-Nanjing and Shanghai-Hangzhou routes were opened to traffic as usual. The Railroad Bureau submitted the workers' demands to the Beijing government by telegram, limiting the answer to 48 hours, otherwise a strike would be called.

However, the Beijing government ignored the workers' demands. Therefore, at 8:00 am on 10 June, workers on the Shanghai-Nanjing and Shanghai-Hangzhou routes went on strike, and southeast railroad traffic was immediately interrupted.

The *Beijing* and *Ningshao*, which were ready to depart for Ningbo, were the first two ships to go on strike, on 10 June. Thereafter, the crew of the *Datong* and other ships bound for the ports on the Yangtze River also abandoned their vessels and went ashore. Around 5,000 crew members participated in what was the first Chinese seafarers' strike.

In just one week, more than 50 factories and enterprises participated in the strike, and around 60,000 workers were counted in all sectors of the city. A citywide strike of Shanghai workers had taken shape in conjunction with the heroic struggle of the patriotic masses, creating an unprecedented strike by workers, students, and merchants.

The wave of strikes in Shanghai quickly spread to the rest of the country. From 6 to 12 June, strikes broke out in Nanjing, Tianjin, Jinan, Wuhan, Tangshan, Hangzhou, Ningbo, Yangzhou, Anqing, Nanchang, Xiamen, and dozens of other large and medium-sized cities, rapidly forming a revolutionary wave on a national scale.

Urgent telegrams from all over the world flew to Beijing.

Under pressure from all sides, especially the united struggle of the anti-imperialist patriotic united front formed by Chinese workers, students, urban petty bourgeoisie, and national bourgeoisie, the Beijing government sensed that the foundation of its rule would be shaken, and had to make concessions to the people.

On the morning of 10 June, the Beijing government issued an order to remove Cao Rulin from office, but this was not enough to appease the people.

Beijing school students protested again, demanding the removal of the traitors Zhang Zongxiang and Lu Zongjiu, who had humiliated the country. The Beijing government was forced to issue orders to remove Lu and Zhang from their posts in the afternoon and evening respectively, and the May Fourth Movement achieved an initial victory.

The direct input of the Shanghai working class played a decisive role in this victory. It was deeply felt by the Shanghai Federation of Students, who spoke highly of the Shanghai workers' strike: "The students had been on strike for two weeks. The government ignored their demands, and treated them increasingly severely. The business strike lasted for less than a day, and the students arrested in Beijing were released; the labor strike went on for fewer than five days before Cao, Zhang, and Lu went."

The 'June 5th Strike' was a great feat for Chinese workers in creating their own history. After more than half a century of spontaneous struggle, the Chinese labor movement finally took on a new and unprecedented stance in the May Fourth Movement.

This shows that the Chinese working class has begun to get rid of its dependence on the bourgeoisie, and had entered the social and political arena for the first time as an independent political force, demonstrating its resolute and thorough political consciousness and revolutionary spirit. Because of this, Mao Zedong said that the Chinese working class had "rapidly become a conscious and independent force on the political stage." It had begun an incredible transformation from a self-existing class to a self-acting one.

In the great journey of the Chinese democratic revolution, a new leading class had emerged.

4

PROGRESSIVE ELEMENTS AND WORKERS UNITE

The Marxist materialist view holds that history is created by the people. The purpose of revolution is for the people, and the process of revolution must rely on the people to liberate themselves.

In his speeches and remarks written to celebrate the victory of the First World War, Li Dazhao repeatedly emphasized that the victory in Europe was "the victory of laborism and of the common people," that "in the future, everyone in the world will become a common person and a worker," and that "in the future, the world will become a world of labor."[1] "Red flags are flying everywhere, and labor unions are being set up... Such a huge and rolling tide cannot be held back by the present capitalist government."[2]

With the October Revolution and the spread of Marxism in China, Li Dazhao's understanding went one step further. He remarked, "Whoever is in charge should realize the greatness of the popular forces. The people themselves should be especially conscious of their authority, and use it resolutely. The power of the people is the only basis for all structures in modern society."

On 1 May 1919, under Li Dazhao's guidance, a special issue of the *Beijing Morning Post* was published to commemorate Labor Day – the first time a Chinese newspaper had done this. Li wrote that May Day was "the day when the only weapon of the workers of the world – direct action – was created."

---

1. *The Complete Works of Li Dazhao, Vol. 2*, People's Publishing House, 2006, pp. 255–256.
2. Ibid., p. 262.

During the May Fourth Movement, the patriotic workers' strike fully revealed the great power of the Chinese working class, demonstrated its anti-imperialist and anti-feudal resoluteness and thoroughness, and also began to establish the independent status of the working class in the political and economic life of Chinese society.

This led many revolutionary intellectuals to a raised awareness of the working class, and their worldview changed dramatically. Wu Yuzhang recalled his own ideological transformation with deep appreciation: "In the past, people who engaged in revolution always looked at the upper class officers, politicians, and legislators.... Today, in contrast to the 'May Fourth' mass movement, the social power of the upper class seems so insignificant that the power contained in the people, once liberated, is truly earth-shaking and indestructible."[1]

As a result, intellectuals began to seek contact with the working classes. As Deng Zhongxia said, "It was from here that some of the student leaders of the May Fourth Movement set out to 'go to the people,' and approached the workers to set up schools and trade unions for them."

This was a major historical event, and a turning point. From then on, revolutionary intellectuals who propagated Marxism with their writing took on the lofty mission of working for the interests of the people, stepping forward into real life, and approaching the working masses. With their physical actions they propagated, mobilized, and led people of all national ethnicities to unite, work together, and fight bravely. In this way, they promoted the wider spread of Marxism and its combination with the mass movement, and opened the way for the Party's future trajectory of close contact with the people.

From the practice of the October Revolution and the May Fourth Movement, Mao Zedong began to realize the tremendous power of the masses. His long article 'The Great Union of the People' was serialized in the *Xiangjiang Review* in July and August 1919, in the second, third, and fourth issues. He wrote, "The reason is that the people of a country are always more numerous than the aristocratic capitalists and other powerful figures, and movements in history, no matter what they are, are always the result of the union of people. The larger the movement, the larger the union." The basis for the unity of the

1. Liu, Mingkui and Tang, Yuliang, *A History of the Chinese Labor Movement, Vol. 1*, Guangdong People's Publishing House, 1998, p. 197.

people was the "common interest" of those who fought against the oppressors. For this reason, Mao called on the peasants (who made up the majority of China's population) to unite and fight for the reduction of land rent and taxes, and for the solution of the food problem. He called on students, teachers, and women to unite according to their own personal interests and demands, so as to realize the ultimate unity of the people.

On 10 October 1919, Peking University students mobilized more than 5,000 students from universities and high schools in Beijing to donate money to buy 170,000 loaves of bread decorated with the words 'The Sanctity of Labor', and distribute them to workers around the city. A total of 300,000 leaflets were distributed, and speeches were made. The event was a sensation throughout Beijing, and created a conducive atmosphere for revolutionary intellectuals to approach the workers.

In November of the same year, Li Dazhao wrote in his 'Message' in *Zhejiang Xinchao No. 1*, "What kind of people will be responsible for the transformation of society? What method will be used? The responsibility lies with the workers and peasants. The method lies in consciousness and unity. All those who are conscious within the intellectual class should break the very concept of the intellectual class and join the world of labor, uniting with the workers."

In the spring of 1920, at the founding meeting of the Federation of Shipping and Warehouse Workers initiated by the Shanghai dockers, Chen Duxiu asked, "Who are the most useful and valuable people in the world? There will surely be some who are confused, and say that it is the emperor, or those who study to be officials. I think they are wrong. I think that only those who work are useful and valuable. Of all the people in society, those who work are the pillars. So, how can we awaken the consciousness of these workers themselves?" According to Chen, the task could be divided into two steps. The first was to "demand improvements in treatment." The second was to "ask the workers themselves to rise up and manage politics, the military, and industry." The labor movement in China should not only strive to achieve the first step, but also define its second step. This leap in Chen Duxiu's ideological understanding represented a fundamental change in the position and worldview of intellectuals in that period.

In January 1920, Li Dazhao arranged for Deng Zhongxia to lead the members of the Civilian Education Lecture Group to the place where rickshaw drivers lived, to make an investigation. The poor and miserable lives of the drivers shocked them. The *Beijing Morning Post* reported, "When the delegation came back, they were looking at each other with sadness and dismay."[1] Given what the investigation had uncovered, Deng Zhongxia took a team to the streets to mobilize rickshaw drivers to strike *en masse*, with the aim of improving their treatment. To their surprise, only a few of the drivers responded, but when they went on strike, the police smashed their rickshaws. The effort was unsuccessful, and the rickshaw drivers were compensated for the damage. Some people sarcastically asked Deng Zhongxia, "How is the labor movement doing? Was your speech effective?"

In the face of this failure, how else could they 'go to the people'?

This sharp question was put to Deng Zhongxia and other advanced intellectuals who had just emerged from their 'ivory tower.' After a lot of thought, Deng came to the conclusion that rickshaw drivers were individual workers who were relatively scattered and easily influenced by gangs. 'Going to the people' should focus instead on reaching the organized industrial workers and the vast number of rural farmers.

On 14 March, the Civilian Education Lecture Group held its third executive meeting, and elected Deng Zhongxia and Yang Zhongjian as general officers, deciding that "in addition to urban lectures, emphasis would be placed on rural lectures and workshop talks."[2] Later, Deng Zhongxia and others suggested that members of the group should use the spring break to conduct "countryside lectures" in such places as Lugouqiao, Fengtai, Changxindian, Haidian, Luodaozhuang, and Tongxian.

From April, Deng Zhongxia led the Peking University Civilian Education Lecture Group to expand from lectures in the city to propagation among railroad workers in Changxindian. The 12 members of the Group were divided into two sections. They went to the countryside and factories, trying to establish contact with peasants and industrial workers and propagate revolutionary principles. This was a new attempt to bring the members of the Group and the content of their lectures closer to the workers and peasants. The key question was how the members of the delegation could instill their views into the hearts

1. *Beijing Morning Post*, January 26, 1920.
2. *Journal of Peking University*, March 16, 1920.

of their audience, and resonate with the workers and peasants in the face of the more universal masses.

The Civilian Education Lecture Group gave its first lecture in rural Changxindian. A phonograph – a fashionable but rare item – was played to attract a crowd. However, the audience dispersed even before the second speaker made his speech, and the lecture had to be stopped.[1] The main reason for the failure was that some of the students clearly had not yet set their pride aside, and did not empathize with the workers and farmers. The topics of the lectures were mostly vague, such as 'the difference between evening schools for the common people at Peking University and national schools in villages,' and 'women should study as much as men.' One student asked the workers at his lecture, "Is life rich?" The workers ignored him and walked away, feeling that they were not on the same page.

In response to this situation, some of the students – who saw themselves as "saviors" – blamed the masses for their "stupidity," and refused to visit the workers and peasants anymore. However, led by Deng Zhongxia, the activists persevered. They soon overcame the initial difficulties by learning from the workers, and got used to talking to them in common language. The topics of the lectures were also expanded from Marxist theories to the likes of 'What is the spirit of the Republican people?,' 'World and domestic events,' 'General knowledge of science,' and 'Why study?' The combination of spreading revolutionary principles and popularizing scientific knowledge received good results, thus gradually opening up Changxindian as an important stronghold of the early labor movement in the north.

In the 'Detailed Report on the Activities of the Fengtai Lecture Group,' it was written:

> "On the second of April at 8am, five of us took our flag and rode the Jingfeng bus to Fengtai. We walked more than three miles to a village called Qilizhuang. There were more than 50 families living there, with more than 200 people in total. We gave a lecture to them. Many of the old people listened to it, and all of them nodded their heads and said it was good. Only a young gentleman, who was smoking a dry cigarette and

1. *Journal of Peking University*, April 13, 1920.

had his eyes closed, looked a little disapproving. Later, we went to Dajing village, where there are more than 300 families and about a thousand people. This village is richer than Qilizhuang. More than 60 people came to listen. The Tong County Lecture Group reported that there were six lectures on the trip, and the total number of listeners was about 500. It was very successful."[1]

On 1 May 1920, Li Dazhao, Deng Zhongxia, He Mengxiong, Gao Junyu, and others organized the first large-scale public commemoration of International Labor Day in Beijing. In the morning of that day, a commemorative conference was held at Peking University with more than 500 students and workers in attendance. Li Dazhao attended, and delivered a speech promoting the significance of the eight-hour working day, and praising the achievements made after the October Revolution in Russia. He pointed out that their purpose was "to commemorate May Day as a beacon of light for us to follow – the light of the sanctity of labor." At 8:30am, eight students, including He Mengxiong, took two cars with red flags inscribed with the words 'The Sanctity of Labor,' 'Long Live May Day' and 'Down with Capitalism.' They distributed the 'May 1 Beijing Labor Manifesto' along the street, and called on workers to rise up to celebrate their own holiday, to "expel bureaucrats, politicians and soldiers who do not work," "return the fields, factories, and all production organs to public management," and create a society in which "everyone works, everyone does their best, and everyone gets what they need." However, their action was obstructed by the reactionary authorities, and the students and their drivers were detained at the police station. At 10am that day, a group of 50 people from the Peking University Civilian Lecture Group also set out from Peking University in five groups to speak to the masses in the streets and alleys. They publicized the historical significance of May Day, and shared their hopes for the future of society. Everywhere they went, they drew a large audience.

At the Changxindian Locomotive Factory, more than 1,000 workers held a grand rally to commemorate Labor Day. After the rally, a dozen people went to the street to put up slogans, some on coach cars. That morning, Deng Zhongxia and several others hurried to Changxindian on the Beijing-Hankou railroad

1. *Journal of Peking University*, April 13, 1920.

train, distributing leaflets and giving speeches inside and outside the factory, which were well received by the workers.

On 1 May, magazines such as *New Youth*, the *Peking University Student Weekly*, and the *Beijing Morning Post* published a special issue to commemorate International Labor Day. Among them, the 'Labor Day Commemorative Issue' of *New Youth* carried more than 20 articles – double the usual number – including an important piece by Li Dazhao called 'The History of the May Day Movement,' which began: "A day of commemoration is both a day of good fortune and a day of suffering, for all the victories that can be commemorated have come from the tragedy of struggle. The same is true of the 'May Day' anniversary." This was followed by a detailed account of how International Labor Day came about, and the struggles of the working class in various countries to commemorate it, as well as an expression of earnest hope for the Chinese labor movement. The article ended with an enthusiastic call: "Rise! Rise! Rise! Up! Today is the day of your awakening!" The special issue also published articles such as Chen Duxiu's 'The Workers' Awakening' and 'The Problem of Hunan Women Workers at the Shanghai Housheng Yarn Factory,' which analyzed and explained some important practical problems facing Chinese workers using Marxist views such as surplus value and how labor creates everything.

The 'Labor Day Commemorative Issue,' with more than 100,000 words, published the first survey report on the current situation of workers in a dozen cities and regions, including Shanghai, Beijing, Tianjin, Changsha, Wuhan, Nanjing, Tangshan, and Shanxi, with details about the labor conditions, wages, education, and family life of workers in various industries at that time. The special issue contained quotes not only by prominent figures such as Sun Yat-sen and Cai Yuanpei, but also by 12 workers. They wrote, "The clothes, food, and housing of those who do not work are all stolen goods," "The moral sanctities of those who do not work are all false," and "Only those who work have the spirit of equality and mutual assistance." These epithets directly expressed the voice of the workers, which was very valuable at that time.

It was clear from the commemorative activities in Beijing that Marxism had spread among workers through advanced elements, and that the union between intellectuals and the working class had become closer. However, as Li Dazhao pointed out back then, "At present, May Day in China is not a commemoration of the labor community, but of the news agencies. It is a movement initiated by a handful of intellectuals. It does not belong to laborers and workers, nor to the people in the street. It is merely a superficial movement. This is a huge regret for us!"[1] However, it is worth acknowledging that through the May Day commemoration in 1920, the class consciousness and the concept of political struggle of the workers in Beijing were significantly increased. It greatly inspired the working class to unite and organize groups, and moreover inspired the initial realization of the combination of Marxism and the labor movement.

In this way, within a relatively short period of time after the October Revolution sent Marxism to China, advanced Chinese intellectuals began to spread the truths of Marxism to the laboring masses in plain and simple language, to arm their minds and guide their work. It was in the process of contacting and communicating with the laboring masses and struggling together that the advanced intellectuals experienced the hardships of the laboring masses, deeply understood the excellent qualities of the working class, and were themselves trained. Their minds were transformed, their feelings were enhanced, and their sense of responsibility and mission was strengthened. Some rapidly changed from radical democrats to working-class intellectuals with communist consciousness. The changes and progress in these two aspects not only promoted the Sinicization and popularization of Marxism, but also promoted the combination of Marxism and the Chinese working class.

1. *The Complete Works of Li Dazhao, Vol. 3*, People's Publishing House, 2006, p. 195.

PART 5

Preparing to Build the Party:

From Planning to Founding

When the May Fourth Movement began, Sun Yat-sen and some Kuomintang members supported it, but were not its organizers and leaders. In his article 'Outline of The Development of the Communist Party of China,' Cai Hesen recalled that at that time, students in Beijing and Shanghai sent representatives to the Kuomintang, but its leaders "refused to participate on the grounds that they were unable to do so." This shows that the KMT was "no longer able to lead the revolution, and the objective development of revolutionary power had exceeded its subjective power."[1] Therefore, the establishment of a new revolutionary party to lead the struggle of the Chinese people had become an objective requirement for social progress and revolutionary development in modern China.

After the May Fourth Movement, the influence of Russia's October Revolution in China became increasingly profound. People's illusions about imperialism were shattered, and their aspirations for socialism grew stronger. More importantly, with the spread of Marxism in China and the influence of the labor movement during the May Fourth Movement, a group of advanced

1. The State Archives Administration of the People's Republic of China. *Selected Compilation of Reports on the History of the Communist Party of China*, Central Party School Press, 1982, p. 17–18.

elements aspiring to follow the path of the October Revolution emerged in China.

Once Marxism was accepted by the advanced elements, it developed a powerful spiritual power. Using Marxist theory as a tool to explore the future destiny of the country, they realized that to fundamentally transform Chinese society, it was necessary to establish a proletarian party like the Russian Bolsheviks. Thus began the great work of creating the Communist Party of China, which was epoch-making in modern Chinese history.

From the fall of 1920 to the spring of 1921, in addition to Shanghai, Beijing, and Changsha, early Chinese Communist Party organizations were established in Wuhan, Jinan, and Guangzhou, as well as overseas, in France and Japan. These early communist organizations studied and propagated Marxism, which not only enabled Marxist theory to be widely disseminated and to take root in China, but also cultivated a group of advanced elements with communist consciousness among intellectuals and workers, thus laying the organizational foundation for the formal establishment of the CPC.

Looking back today, the creation of the Communist Party of China in the early 20th century was a bold and groundbreaking idea. This is because, from the perspective of China's national conditions at that time, the country had long been under feudal autocracy, and party affiliation and sectarianism were strictly forbidden. As the saying goes, "A gentleman is a group, not a party." It was only after the successful Xinhai Revolution in 1911 that the concept of modern political parties was gradually established in China, with the emergence of parliamentary activities. At the same time, the number of industrial workers in China was relatively small. Marxism had been spread in China for only a short period of time, initially combining with the labor movement, so the class, ideological, and organizational bases for building the party were relatively weak.

The world's first socialist state was established only after the triumph of the October Revolution in Russia in 1917. Just over two years later, China – which had not yet completely freed itself from thousands of years of feudal dictatorship, and was experimenting with capitalist parliamentary politics – began to explore the creation of a Communist Party, with communism as its goal.

This was an incredibly bold and avant-garde vision at the time.

1

NORTH AND SOUTH UNITE UNDER LI AND CHEN

On a winter night in February 1920, a shabby mule cart covered with a canopy drove out of Chaoyang gate in Beijing, bumping slowly along the dirt road on its way to the city of Tianjin. On this typical northern two-wheel cart sat two people. One was around 40 years old, and looked very wealthy. Perched on the canopy, he was wearing a cotton vest over his robe, and a felt hat low on his head. The other, who was driving, was younger – tall and strong. He was carry a bag filled with piles of ledger-like documents, like a bookkeeper sent out to collect accounts before Spring Festival.

In fact, the 'rich' man was Chen Duxiu, who was an influential figure at that time. The 'bookkeeper' was Li Dazhao – Director of Peking University Library. Together, they formed the spearhead of the New Culture Movement and the May Fourth Movement. Legendary figures of the early 1920s, they were billed as two bright stars from the north and south of China. Their names were mentioned in a poem written at the time:

"In the library at Peking University
work Chen and Li –
two great men,
two bright stars.
Long live the pioneering spirit!"

Surely two such famous figures of the New Culture Movement should have been traveling in suits, in a dignified manner. Why did they have to disguise themselves and conceal their identities? There was a very good reason.

In early June 1919, at the height of the May Fourth Movement, Chen Duxiu had drafted a leaflet entitled 'Beijing Citizens' Manifesto', and was arrested by the Beiyang government police. As soon as the news of his arrest got out, it invoked huge shock throughout society. Social groups, scholars, and students rose up and took action, requesting that Chen be bailed out. Even Sun Yat-sen called on the government to release him. Under heavy pressure from the public, the government agreed to release Chen on bail after he had been imprisoned for three months, on the grounds of a stomach ailment. However, he was not allowed to leave Beijing, nor conduct political activities. He was placed under strict police supervision.

Time passed. In January 1920, the Guangdong military government decided to establish Southwest University, and wrote to Chen Duxiu for advice. After many invitations, Chen decided to leave Beijing for Shanghai. When he returned to Beijing, he got an invitation from Wuhan Student Association and Wenhua College (now Central China Normal University), so went to Wuhan in early February. In just a few days, he gave a series of influential lectures, such as 'The Method of Social Reform and Faith,' 'The Problem of Intellectual and Emotional Education,' and 'The Spirit of New Education.' The lectures were very popular among the students. Soon, newspapers in Wuhan and other parts of China published summaries of them. On the afternoon of 9 February, shortly after Chen Duxiu returned home, someone came knocking at his door. According to Hu Shi's recollection:

> "When Duxiu returned to Beijing, he was preparing to write a few invitations to meet with me and several other friends. Who was to know that just as he was writing the invitation, there was a knock at the front door? It turned out to be a police officer.
>
> 'Is Mr. Chen Duxiu home?' the policeman asked him.
>
> 'Yes. That's me.'
>
> This answer surprised the policeman. He said that some reactionary newspapers had reported that Chen Duxiu had been propagating 'anarchism' in Wuhan the previous day, so the police bureau sent him to see if he was at home.

> Duxiu said, 'I am at home!'
>
> The policeman said, 'Mr. Chen – you have just been released from prison on bail. According to the law, if you leave Beijing, you should at least tell the police about it.'
>
> 'I know! I know!' Duxiu said.
>
> 'Can you give me your business card?'
>
> Duxiu, of course, obeyed his orders. The policeman took the card and left. Duxiu knew something untoward was going on. The policeman would definitely be back to make trouble.
>
> Therefore, Duxiu didn't write his invitations. Instead, he came to my house in secret. Of course, the police department knew of our friendship, so he couldn't hide out at my house. He went to Li Dazhao's instead. The police didn't know where he'd fled to, so they had to patrol his door for two or three days in a row, waiting for him to return."[1]

At Li Dazhao's house, after discussing and analyzing the situation, both of them felt that because Chen Duxiu was already under police surveillance, could not stay in Beijing any longer. They would have to leave quickly. However, at that time, there were secret agents at Beijing's bus and train stations. Faced with this dangerous and urgent situation, and regardless of his personal safety, Li Dazhao stepped forward and decided to escort Chen Duxiu out of Beijing personally. The two of them went to the home of Wang Xinggong – a professor of chemistry at Peking University – in the dead of night. Wang was a native of Huaining in Anhui Province, and was an old friend of Chen Duxiu's. After discussing the matter, the three of them decided that Chen Duxiu and Li Dazhao would disguise themselves as businessmen collecting accounts at the end of the year, and sneak out of Beijing under the cover of darkness.

It was mid-February 1920, at the end of the lunar year. This was the time for businessmen in Beijing to collect debts from all over the country. So, the two of them hired a mule cart and left from Chaoyang Gate to the south. Chen Duxiu disguised himself, wearing a felt hat on his head and an undershirt belonging to Wang Xinggong's cook, which was shiny with oil. Chen sat inside

1. *Hu Shi's Oral Autobiography,* translated by Tang Degang, Huawen Publishing House, 1989, pp. 208–209.

the mule cart, while Li Dazhao straddled the handlebars. He carried a ledger book, printed on a red piece of paper from a store. Considering Chen's southern accent, Li alone settled things along the way.[1]

After safely escaping from Beijing and walking for an unknown period of time, Li Dazhao and Chen Duxiu felt a sense of relief. The cold air made them tired. Li decided to take this opportunity to exchange views with Chen on the establishment of a Communist Party in China. The two of them reviewed the May Fourth Movement, and concluded that the patriotic enthusiasm of the young students was very valuable, but that the youth movement had come and gone quickly, especially after the Chinese delegates refused to sign the Paris Peace Treaty. Most of the patriotic students thought that the goal of the May Fourth Movement had been achieved.

How could the hard-won spark of struggle ignite the blazing fire of the Chinese Revolution? Li Dazhao strongly believed that to completely transform China, a Bolshevik-style party had to be formed. So he said, "Comrade, do you think that we in China should also follow the path of Soviet Russia and form a Soviet-style political party?'"

Chen replied, "Yes. However, I used to oppose the establishment of a party to serve one class. If you had asked me to establish a new party at that time, I would not have done it."

Just a month previously, Chen Duxiu had written in his 'Manifesto of the New Youth' that he would never join "a political party that did not promote the wellbeing of society as a whole." Li Dazhao could not help but ask, "Oh? So what has changed?"

Chen Duxiu took a hard drag on his cigarette and said, "Nothing has changed. Soviet-style parties are parties that seek the wellbeing of society as a whole. Besides, when I declared that I would not join such a party, I didn't say that I wouldn't start a party based on my own beliefs!"

Li exclaimed, "Well said!"

As soon as the words left his mouth, the two men laughed in happy unison.

The journey from Beijing to Tianjin took three days, with an overnight stay at Li Dazhao's house in Laoting, Hebei Province. On the way, the two

---

1. *Memoirs of the May Fourth Movement (continued)*, China Social Science Press, 1979, p. 119.

men talked enthusiastically about building a party in China. They agreed that Chen would be in Shanghai and Li would be in Beijing, preparing to build the party in the south and the north. This led to a great story in the history of the Communist Party of China – 'Chen in the south and Li in the north, uniting to build the party.'

Upon arriving in Tianjin, Chen Duxiu took a boat to Shanghai, while Li Dazhao met with his Soviet friends in Tianjin's old Russian Concession to talk about the current situation in China and the revolution. On returning to Beijing, Li Dazhao and Deng Zhongxia established the Marxist Research Association in March 1920, and began to make ideological and cadre-related preparations for the establishment of the Party.

History is coincidental, and full of dramatic paradoxes. The Beiyang government intended to imprison Chen Duxiu in order to confine progressive ideas, but instead spread Chen's renown even more widely. He became a well-known leader of the May Fourth Movement, and the social impact of his new ideas grew even stronger. The Beiyang government wanted to force Chen Duxiu to give up his revolutionary ideas and stop participating in leading the student movement through prison and surveillance, but to their surprise, their actions caused Chen, Li Dazhao, and other advanced elements to see the true face of the warlord leadership. As a result, they felt a deep need to establish a new political party in China to completely overthrow the old system and forces. Thus, Chen and Li shifted their focus from mainly young students to workers and peasants, and from the study and dissemination of ideas and culture to the actual practice of Party building.

2

GUIDANCE FROM INTERNATIONAL REPRESENTATIVES

THE WEATHER WAS STILL COOL in Beijing in early April 1920, but the spring flowers were already in full bloom. One day, five people – three men and two women, all with Russian passports – arrived at a foreign apartment near Wangfujing Street. They were journalists from the Russian-language newspaper *Life*, and declared that they had come to China was to set up a Sino-Soviet news agency. In fact, they were a delegation from the Vladivostok branch of the Russian Communist Party's Far Eastern Bureau. The head of the delegation was a young Russian of medium build – fit, well-mannered, scholarly, and fluent in English. His name was Grigori Naumovich Voitinsky, and he was 27 years old – the same age as Mao Zedong.

Voitinsky was born in April 1893 in Nevel, in Russia's Vychebsk region, into a family of forest rangers. Due to his family's poverty, he began to earn an independent living as soon as he graduated from elementary school. At the age of 20, he went to the USA where he studied and worked as a laborer – an important change in his life. It was there that he became politically active, and joined the Socialist Party.

After the outbreak of the October Revolution in 1917, like thousands of other revolutionaries, Voitinsky was eager to return to his homeland. In the spring of 1918, he finally went. While passing through Vladivostok, he joined the Communist Party of Russia, and was soon sent to work at the workers' soviet in Krasnoyarsk. In May 1919, he was arrested in Vladivostok, sentenced to life imprisonment, and exiled to Sakhalin Island (one of the Kuril Islands) to serve hard labor. There, he showed his organizational skills, secretly uniting with the political prisoners on the island to stage a riot, which was a success and made him famous. After regaining his freedom, Voitinsky returned to Vladivostok in January 1920 and began working for the Comintern as Deputy Head of the Eastern Department of the Executive Committee, in charge of Far Eastern affairs.

How did he arrive in China?

Until 1920, the Comintern had not established direct contact with the revolutionaries in China. This was firstly because Soviet Russia was still engaged in a civil war, especially in the Siberian part of the Russian Far East, which was still under the rule of the British, American, French and Japanese imperialist interventionist forces and the White Russian bandits. It was also because the Beiyang warlord government had blocked the Russian-Chinese border and closed down Sino-Soviet transportation, leaving the Chinese and Russian populations in isolation.

The world revolutionary situation took a new turn in the 1920s. The revolutionary struggles in various European countries failed one after another, and the tide was at low ebb. Lenin and the Comintern then turned their attention to the East. At the beginning of 1920, Soviet Russia defeated domestic and foreign enemies in Siberia and the Far East, and consolidated Soviet power. The USA and Britain withdrew their troops, and the Japanese invasion forces returned to Primorsky Province and the Kuril Islands. The imperialist armed intervention was defeated. Under these circumstances, the pro-Japanese Duan Qirui government's policy of blockading the Russian-Chinese border ended, and Sino-Russian traffic was basically restored. In this way, the conditions were basically in place for the Communist International and Soviet Russia to establish direct contact with the Chinese revolutionaries.

In March 1920, the Central Committee of the Communist Party of Russia (CPR) decided to establish a special bureau to coordinate the revolution in the Far East. At the same time, the Vladivostok branch of the Far Eastern Bureau of the Communist Party of Russia was established. Then, in consultation with the Comintern, it was decided that a delegation would be sent to China immediately to carry out work.

Although he did not speak Chinese, Voitinsky had grown to be a loyal, courageous, and responsible revolutionary. He was trusted by the Communist Party of Russia and the Comintern, and was chosen as the first emissary to

China to take up the historic task of establishing direct contact among the CPR, the Comintern, and the Chinese revolutionary organizations.

To facilitate his work, Voitinsky gave himself a Chinese name – Wu Tingkang. Later, he wrote for *Guide* and *New Youth* under the names 'Wei Qin' and 'Wei Jin.' He was accompanied by his wife Kuznetsova, and Mamayev – a 25-year-old officer in the Soviet Red Army, who acted as his secretary – as well as Mamayev's wife, who joined the delegation as a typist. The delegation also had an interpreter, who spoke fluent Russian but was Chinese at first glance. His name was Yang Mingzhai, and he was a Russian expatriate and member of the Communist Party of Russia who had experienced the October Revolution.

Yang Mingzhai, formerly known as Yang Haode and nicknamed Mingzhai, was born in March 1882 into a peasant family in Xixiang Magozhuang, Pingdu County, Shandong Province. In his childhood, he attended a private school for several years. However, when he reached the age of 16, his family could no longer afford to support his study, so Yang had to go home to work on the farm. He quickly got married and took up the burden of the family, but his heart was broken by the untimely death of his new wife. In the spring of 1901, at the age of 19, Yang headed east to Vladivostok. In 1908, he went to remote Siberia to work as a miner. It was there that he came into contact with the Communist Party of Russia. Accepting its revolutionary ideas, he was placed in the Imperial Russian Diplomatic Office as a clerk, where he engaged in revolutionary work.

After the October Revolution, Yang Mingzhai became an active figure among the Chinese workers in Russia. The CPR sponsored him to attend the Moscow Oriental Workers' Communist University, where he studied Marxist-Leninist theory. On completion of his studies, he was dispatched by the Communist Party of Russia to Vladivostok, where he worked underground in the public capacity of 'Head of the Overseas Chinese Association,' promoting the October Revolution and spreading the seeds of revolution among the Chinese. It was thanks to his rich revolutionary experience that Yang Mingzhai became the main assistant to Vladimir Putinsky on his trip to China, taking on the important roles of interpreter, counselor, and guide. On learning about Yang's experience, Li Dazhao praised him as "a man of courage who had journeyed in the wilderness for 10,000 miles."

Since Voitinsky and his party were new to China, they ran into many difficulties working in Beijing, so planned to make contact with the Chinese communists through two Russian professors from Peking University – S. A. Polevoy and A. A. Ivanov. In order to avoid the attention of the reactionary military and police, contact was made by Yang Mingzhai in his capacity as a Russian-Chinese expatriate and journalist. Professor Polevoy was a China hand. He had grown up in Vladivostok, and spoke and read Chinese. He had a strong interest in *The Book of Songs*, and became an expert in Chinese. In his political stance, he supported reforms, so he maintained contact and friendships with many Russian communists. When he went to China, he also set up connections with people who advocated advanced culture in Beijing, Shanghai, and Tianjin. He read *New Youth* whenever there was a new issue, and knew Li Dazhao. Polevoy was connected with Li, and often sent him Marxist and Leninist pamphlets from Mexico. Li was grateful for this, and recommended Polevoy for a Russian teaching position at Peking University.

Because of this relationship, once they met, Polevoy naturally told Yang Mingzhai about Peking University, *New Youth*, Li Dazhao, Chen Duxiu, and other Chinese progressives. With a brief introduction, he sketched out the rough layout of the Chinese communist movement at that time. Galvanized into action, Yang Mingzhai decided to arrange for Voitinsky to meet Li Dazhao in the director's office in the library of Peking University. At that time, Li Dazhao was 31 years old – four years older than the Soviet Russian emissary.

Li, who had long been interested in the Russian October Revolution, naturally received Voitinsky and his party with great enthusiasm. Voitinsky said that the Far East Bureau of the Comintern had received a telegram from Vladivostok, and knew that the May Fourth Movement (in which millions of people had gone on strike in China) had taken place, so they had been sent to China to see if there was any possibility of starting a revolution and building a party.

After their meeting, at the request of Voitinsky, Li Dazhao invited Beijing progressives from all echelons of society to hold welcome parties, lectures, talks, and exchanges. At that time, the first declaration of the Soviet government to China (i.e. the abrogation of the unequal treaties made between the imperial Russian government and China) had just arrived in China, and many social groups there expressed warm welcome. As soon as they heard that the Soviet government had sent someone to Beijing, the mood was cordial. Many petty-bourgeois and bourgeois intellectuals also took part in the talks and discussions.

The details of the talks between Voitinsky and the main activists of the May Fourth Movement at the Peking University Library are described in detail in Luo Zhanglong's *The Records of Chun Yuan*:

> "Our meeting with Voitinsky was held in the library. At the meeting, he first explained the October Revolution, and brought out some books and magazines, such as *The International* and *Ten Days that Shook the World.* The latter was an English book by an American journalist about the October Revolution. In order to make it easier for people who did not speak Russian to read it, the books were available in English and German too. Voitinsky also gave a detailed explanation of the policies and decrees of Soviet Russia, such as the land decree; the policy of nationalization of industries, mines, and banks; the implementation of workers' supervision and management in factories; the system of the Supreme Council of the National Economy of Soviet Russia to manage the economic work of the country; and Lenin's ambitious plan for electrification. He also talked about the difficulties faced by Soviet Russia after the October Revolution, and the temporary introduction of military communism and a surplus collection system to solve them. The conversation was quite extensive. At that time, we were eager to learn about the October Revolution and post-revolutionary Russia. His talk was very refreshing and interesting to us, and gave us a clearer understanding of the Soviet system from political, economic, military, and cultural aspects, as well as the outline of a new socialist society."[1]

Voitinsky's talk was eloquent, emotional, cordial, and infectious. It showed participants the outline of a new socialist society, and strengthened their determination to follow the example of the October Revolution.

As the conversation progressed, based on the story of the Soviet Revolution and what he had learned about the actual situation in China, Voitinsky put forward a bold idea and proposal to Li Dazhao: China should have an organization like the Communist Party of Russia.

---

1. Luo, Zhanglong. *The Records of Chun Yuan,* Sanlian Publishing Company, 1984, pp. 74–75.

When Li heard this, his eyes lit up, thinking back to the long conversation he had with Chen Duxiu a month earlier about the establishment of the Chinese Communist Party. In this way, Voitinsky echoed the intentions of 'Li in the north and Chen in the south'.

However, Li Dazhao had always been a strict and steady man. In his view, after the May Fourth Movement, Chen Duxiu had become a nationally known figure. As the initiator and organizer of the Communist Party of China, no one would have more cohesive and rallying power than him. So Li Dazhao said to Voitinsky, "If you want to understand the communist movement in China, you must go to Shanghai and speak to Chen Duxiu, who was the founder and editor-in-chief of *New Youth* magazine."

Furthermore, Li Dazhao explained that Beijing was the center of the Beiyang warlord government. There was no industry there, and the working class was very small. Guangzhou was also underdeveloped in terms of industry, and was the focus of fighting among various factions. Shanghai was the largest industrial center in China, and had a huge proletariat. Since it was also a place where revolutionaries gathered, it was the best place to establish the party organization.

Voitinsky said, "Mr. Li, I've heard of Mr. Chen. Could you introduce him to me?"

So Li Dazhao wrote a personal letter to Chen Duxiu, and told Voitinsky that Chen would agree to an interview when he read it. Unfortunately, this historically significant letter has been lost.

The fact that representatives of the Comintern came to China in 1920 to give guidance shows that the creation of the Communist Party of China was closely linked to the world revolutionary movement from the very beginning, and was an open, innovative, and advanced cause.

3

LAUNCHING ON THE BANKS OF THE HUANGPU RIVER

IN 1920, LUNAR NEW YEAR fell in mid-February. Amid the celebrations, Chen Duxiu quietly arrived in Shanghai.

At that time, Shanghai was the largest city in China, with a population of 2.29 million, and many tall buildings and stores. The wide asphalt roads were home to yellow-skinned Chinese in long shirts, white-skinned Europeans and Americans in suits, and dark-skinned Indians wearing large turbans.

This noisy, bustling metropolis seemed no different from previous years. However, history tells us that Shanghai in the early 1920s was about to see the launch of the Communist Party of China. Chen Duxiu was a highly influential figure in Chinese intellectual and cultural circles at the time. In Beijing, his house in Arrowhead Hutong was often filled with New Culture figures such as Li Dazhao, Hu Shi, Liu Hanong, Shen Yinmo, Lu Xun, and Zhou Zuoren. When Chen arrived in Shanghai, No. 2 Old Yuyang Lane on Huanlong Road in the French Concession, which had been rather quiet before, was enlivened by his presence.

Frequent visitors included Dai Jitao, Shen Xuanlu, and Li Hanjun – editors-in-chief of the *Weekly Review*; Zhang Dongsun, editor-in-chief of the *New Journal of Current Affairs*; Shao Lizi, editor-in-chief of the *Shanghai Republican Daily*'s supplement *Juezhu*; and Chen Wangdao, Shi Cuntong, Chen Gongpei, Shen Yanbing, and Yu Xiusong. These people had studied in Japan, and spoke Japanese. Most of them had studied the Japanese versions of Marxist works, so they had a lot in common, and often discussed national issues.

At that time, there were three main forces propagating socialism in Shanghai.

One was the New Youth Society led by Chen Duxiu, and *New Youth* magazine, whose editors included Li Dazhao and Chen himself. This became the most influential publication in China in the wake of the May Fourth Movement, and Chen, Li, and their comrades were among the most popular leaders of the advanced elements with initial communist consciousness.

The second was the *Weekly Review*, which was run by Shen Xuanlu and Li Hanjun with the participation of Chen Wangdao, Shao Lizi, Yu Xiusong, Shi Cuntong, and Dai Jitao. In June 1920, when the *Weekly Review* ceased publication, most of its main members began to write for *Juezhu* – a supplement of the *Shanghai Republican Daily* edited by Shao Lizi of the Kuomintang left, to promote socialism.

The third was the Communist Society, run by Zhang Dongsun and members of the research department, which published the *New Journal of Current Affairs* in Shanghai. This newspaper had sympathized with and supported the May Fourth Movement together with the *Beijing Morning Post*. As Marxism spread after the May Fourth Movement, the *New Journal of Current Affairs* also talked about socialism. The Communist Society also published a bimonthly magazine called *Liberation and Reform* in the name of the New Society of Beiping, which was devoted to the study of socialism. It also published a large number of articles and translations on socialism. This gave the illusion that it supported socialism, or at least was "objectively" introducing socialist trends, and therefore *was* socialist. It was due to this particular historical background that the Party-building activities in Shanghai began with discussions on socialism. With the New Youth Society as the center, many talks were given on socialism and the transformation of Chinese society.

One day in late April, Chen Duxiu was in his study, writing for *New Youth*, when there was a sudden knock on the door. When he opened it, a young Russian man of medium build and strong physique appeared. It was none other than Voitinsky, who had come from Beijing to visit Chen on the advice of Li Dazhao.

After his meeting with Chen Duxiu in Shanghai, Voitinsky held several symposiums with him, as he had done in Beijing, inviting leading intellectuals.

Voitinsky enthusiastically explained the Russian Revolution and the post-revolutionary political and economic situation, and noted that the current surge of new ideas in China – anarchism, trade unionism, social democracy, and guild socialism – was too complicated. These ideas were diverse and disunified, causing chaos in intellectual circles. There was no organization. Many people were writing articles and using empty words, but there was a lack of practical action, meaning that the Chinese revolution would never happen. Therefore, Voitinsky proposed to combine *New Youth*, the *Weekly Review*, and the *New Journal of Current Affairs* in a revolutionary alliance, taking advantage of the fervor inspired by the May Fourth Movement. The main editors of these publications would unite and initiate the establishment of the Chinese Communist Party or the Chinese Socialist Party.

With the help of Voitinsky among others, Chen Duxiu sped up the process of Party-building. As the first step, in May 1920, he officially founded the Party with Li Hanjun, Chen Wangdao, Yu Xiusong, and Shen Yanshu. In the same month, the Marxist Research Association was set up by Chen Duxiu, Li Hanjun, Chen Wangdao, Yu Xiusong, Shen Yanbing, Shao Lizi, and Yang Mingzhai, to intensify the study, translation, and propagation of Marxism and, on this basis, to start preparations for Party-building through discussions about socialism.

As the discussion deepened, Chen Duxiu and his comrades came to believe that to fundamentally transform Chinese society, mere articles and a lack of organization would never advance the revolution. Chen therefore raised the issue of establishing a Communist Party, which was supported by most of the others. They unanimously felt that to fundamentally transform Chinese society, there was a need to study Marxism and set up a Chinese Communist Party.

However, Zhang Dongsun disagreed. After attending a symposium on the conception of a Party organization, he withdrew, revealing his true nature as a faux-socialist and anti-Marxist. Dai Jitao also agreed at first, but when it came to establishing a Communist Party organization, he withdrew on the pretext that he could not break off relations with Sun Yat-sen and the Kuomintang. Anarchists such as Shen Zhongjiu and Liu Dabai also withdrew shortly after participating in the initial events. The communists who remained, however, were determined to set up a Communist Party in China according to the principles of Party-building set forth by the Third International under Lenin.

In June, Chen Duxiu met with Li Hanjun, Yu Xiusong, Shi Cuntong, Chen Gongpei, and other comrades to begin preparations for the establishment of a Communist Party organization, tentatively named the Socialist Communist Party. Shortly thereafter, Chen Duxiu wrote to Li Dazhao to seek his opinion on whether to use the name 'Socialist Party' or 'Communist Party,' and Li Dazhao suggested the latter. On 19 July, Voitinsky held a meeting of the "most active Chinese comrades" in Shanghai. It was attended by Chen Duxiu, Li Hanjun, and Shen Xuanlu, who firmly advocated the establishment of the Communist Party of China.

In August, after some preparation, under Chen Duxiu's auspices, Yu Xiusong, Li Hanjun, Shi Cuntong, and Chen Gongpei met at the editorial office of *New Youth* at No. 2 Old Yuyang Lane in Shanghai's French Concession, and formally established the early organization of the Shanghai Communist Party, electing Chen Duxiu as its secretary. This was the first Communist Party organization in China, and lit the fire for the creation of the Communist Party on the Chinese mainland.

Soon, the early Communist Party organizations in Shanghai absorbed the likes of Chen Wangdao, Shen Xuanlu, Li Da, Shao Lizi, Shen Yanbing, Li Qihan, Zhao Shiyan, Lin Boqu, Zhou Fohai, and Liu Bochui. Some of them left Shanghai separately soon after. For example, Zhou Fohai and Shi Cuntong went to Japan; Chen Gongpei and Zhao Shiyan went to France; and Liu Bochui went to Wuhan. Most went on to become the initiators of the early Party organizations wherever they went.

The newly-established Shanghai Party organization carried out various revolutionary activities, and actively guided the establishment of Communist Party and Socialist Youth League organizations throughout the country.

In the process of developing the labor movement, the early Communist Party of Shanghai saw educating and introducing its ideology to workers as hugely important. On 15 August 1920, the weekly *Labor World* was launched – a popular publication designed to spread Marxism to workers. It used accessible language and vivid examples to explain some of the basic tenets of Marxism in a simple manner, and was well received by workers.

Through organized promotion and education, the class consciousness of the working masses continued to rise. A vast number of workers made urgent requests to the Party to help them establish trade unions that would truly represent the interests of the working class. The Party helped workers to set up organizations such as the Shanghai Machine Workers' Union, the Printing Workers' Union, and the Labor Movement Committee. This prompted workers to abandon the old-style line gangs and 'yellow' trade unions, and pushed the Shanghai labor movement into a new stage. This marked the shift of the Party's leadership of the Chinese labor movement from the promotional phase to the stage of organization.

In August 1920, almost simultaneously with the establishment of the CPC, Yu Xiusong (the youngest member of the Party) was sent to initiate the formation of the Socialist Youth League. Along with Yang Mingzhai and Li Zhenying, he went to the Foreign Language Institute to develop members among the advanced youth. The first cohort included Liu Shaoqi, Ren Bishi, and Xiao Jinguang. Yu Xiusong became the secretary of the Youth League, which was based at the Foreign Language Institute at No. 6 Yuyang Lane on Xiafei Road. The League met once a week, and each meeting had a political report, the content of which was mostly prescribed by the Party. After the Shanghai Socialist Youth League was launched, it sent out its constitution to advanced youths in many cities throughout the country, asking them to help build League branches everywhere. As a result, Socialist Youth League organizations were established in places such as Beijing, Changsha, Wuhan, Guangzhou, Tianjin, and Jinan.

In order to expand the promotion of Marxism, the early Communist Party in Shanghai decided to change *New Youth* into an open theoretical Party publication. On 1 September 1920, the first issue of the eighth volume of *New Youth* began to propagate Marxism-Leninism openly. On 7 November – the third anniversary of the October Revolution – a secret organ was launched, namely the monthly *Communist Party* magazine. It expounded the political ideas of the Chinese communists, and explained the process of Party building in other countries, which served as a universal guide.

In November, the early Communist Party of Shanghai drew up the 'Manifesto of the Communist Party of China', stating that "the aim of the communists is to create a new society in accordance with the communist ideal", and that to this end, the bourgeois regime should be overthrown and the dictatorship of the proletariat established through revolutionary class struggle.

Although the contents of the manifesto were not made available to the public, it was used as a criterion for absorbing new members, and became an important guide for the creation of early communist organizations in various regions. The establishment of early communist organizations in most regions was directly linked to Shanghai, and in some cases, Shanghai Party members went abroad to help create them.

After the launch of the Shanghai Party organization, Chen Duxiu asked Li Dazhao to set up a Beijing branch, and take charge of political work in the north. Chen helped to establish other Party organizations including in Guangzhou, Changsha, and Wuhan. In this way, the Shanghai Party organization was the initiator of the Communist Party of China, and the headquarters of its founding.

4

THE RED BUILDING AT PEKING UNIVERSITY

IN LATE SEPTEMBER 1920, ON a beautiful early fall day in Beijing, Zhang Shenfu – a young instructor who had just returned to Beijing from Shanghai at the age of 27 – came to Li Dazhao's office in the Red Building at Peking University, and told him the good news that the Shanghai Party had been officially established in August. He also conveyed a message from Chen Duxiu that the Party should be launched in the north as soon as possible, and that the Beijing branch should be set up first.

Hearing this news, Li Dazhao was both delighted and anxious, and immediately decided to step up preparations for the establishment of the Beijing Party organization.

On 1 May 1920, Li Dazhao, Deng Zhongxia, and other advanced members with communist consciousness arranged for a group of progressive youths in Beijing to commemorate May Day. That day, Li Dazhao hosted a commemorative meeting at Peking University, which was attended by more than 500 workers and students. Li delivered an impassioned speech, praising the achievements of the Soviet Union since the October Revolution, promoting the eight-hour work week, and emphasizing that "May Day should be a beacon of light to guide our way." He Mengxiong and eight other students drove two cars flying red flags with the words 'The Sanctity of Labor,' 'Long Live May Day', and 'Down with Capitalism,' and distributed the 'May 1 Beijing Labor Manifesto' along the streets. The Civilian Education Seminar Group went into the streets and alleys to explain the history and significance of May Day. The

Beijing Federation of Students also distributed a large number of leaflets such as 'The History of May Day.'

Meanwhile, at a locomotive factory in Changxindian, more than 1,000 workers held a grand rally to commemorate May Day. Deng Zhongxia and his comrades took the Beijing-Hankou railroad to Changxindian, where they distributed leaflets and gave speeches inside and outside the factory, which were well received by the workers. After the rally, a dozen people went out to put up slogans in the streets and on buses.

In addition, the 1 May issue of *New Youth* was a 'Labor Day Commemorative Issue' with an article by Li Dazhao titled 'The History of the May Day Movement,' which began: "A day of commemoration is both a day of good fortune and a day of suffering, for all the victories that can be commemorated have come from the tragedy of struggle. The same is true of the 'May Day' anniversary."[1] Interestingly, Sun Yat-sen – who had met and exchanged views with Chen Duxiu in Shanghai – gladly inscribed the four words 'The World is Public' for this issue of the magazine.

This commemoration of May Day in Beijing was unprecedented in the country, and played a catalytic role in promoting the union of intellectuals with the workers and peasants, and publicizing Marxism in the Chinese labor movement. It signified that the socialist-leaning intellectuals, who wished for an ideal society free from exploitation and oppression, were trying to find social strength in the working class. The working class demanded liberation from enslavement, and hoped to find the ideological weapon to liberate itself – i.e. Marxism-Leninism – as quickly as possible. It was clear from this commemoration that Marxism had spread among the workers through the advanced elements, and that intellectuals were becoming more closely united with the working class.

However, as Li Dazhao wrote, "At present, May Day in China is not a commemoration of the labor community, but of the news agencies. It is a movement initiated by a handful of intellectuals. It does not belong to laborers and workers, nor to the people in the street. It is merely a superficial movement. This is a huge regret for us!"[2]

---

1. *The Complete Works of Li Dazhao, Vol. 3*, People's Publishing House, 2006, p. 183.
2. Ibid., p. 195.

This proves that Li Dazhao had woken up to the urgency of creating a Chinese Communist Party.

Thus, in close communication with the early Communist Party organizations in Shanghai, their equivalents in Beijing started preparatory founding activities in parallel. In this process, Zhang Guotao and Zhang Shenfu acted as the contacts, passing messages and letters between Beijing and Shanghai, so that the plan of 'Chen in the south and Li in the north' could be promoted in concrete terms.

In July, Zhang Guotao (who was not yet 23 years old at the time) was sent by Li Dazhao to Shanghai, to stay at Chen Duxiu's house for two weeks. The central topic of discussion between them was Party building. They talked about Li Dazhao's intentions in this regard, and Chen Duxiu strongly advocated the establishment of the Chinese Communist Party as soon as possible. Li immediately wrote to Chen, expressing his support for the formation of a unified Chinese Communist Party.

At the same time, Zhang Shenfu also communicated with Li Dazhao and Chen Duxiu on the issue of creating the Communist Party of China. Zhang later recalled, "Chen Duxiu could not decide on a name – whether to call it the Socialist Party or the Communist Party, so he wrote to me and told me to ask Li Shouchang… Shouchang and I worked out that it would be called the Communist Party... We replied to the letter."[1] To this, Chen Duxiu expressed his full agreement.

In mid-September, Zhang Shenfu – a progressive intellectual – went to stay at Chen Duxiu's house at No. 2 Old Yuyang Lane, as he was hosting the famous scholar Russell in Shanghai. Zhang had attended a symposium when Grigori Voitinsky was active in Beijing, and had gained a deeper understanding of Marxism and the October Revolution. At this time, the early Party organization in Shanghai had just been established. Zhang talked with Chen Duxiu about the establishment of a Communist Party organization in Beijing. Chen asked him to tell Li Dazhao to "launch it in the north as soon as possible, and organize the Beijing group first," and then develop it in the vast areas of Shandong, Shanxi,

1. Selected and edited by the Modern History Research Office of the Chinese Academy of Social Sciences and the Party History Research Office of the Chinese Revolutionary Museum. *Before and After the First National Congress of the Communist Party of China, Vol. 2*, People's Publishing House, 1980, p. 220.

Henan, Tianjin, and Tangshan, as well as the northeast and northwest.

In late September, after returning to Beijing from Shanghai, Zhang Shenfu "told Li Dazhao all about his meeting with Chen Duxiu. Li was very happy, and agreed with Chen Duxiu on the issue of Party building."[1] They agreed on the need to develop Party members, and decided to carry out the Party building work at Peking University. A third Party member was developed in early October, when Zhang returned to Beijing from Nanyang to participate in a fund-raising campaign for the National Federation of Students.

In October 1920, Li Dazhao, Zhang Shenfu, and Zhang Guotao formally established an early Communist Party organization in Li Dazhao's office in the Red Building at Peking University. In November, Zhang Shenfu went to France to teach at the Sino-French University of Lyon, leaving only Li Dazhao and Zhang Guotao to set up the early Communist Party in Beijing. Huang Lingshuang was a university student in Beijing, and an anarchist, but believed strongly in communism and favored social revolution. Influenced by Huang, five more anarchists joined, namely Chen Derong, Yuan Mingxiong, Zhang Bogen, Hua Lin, and Wang Jinglin. They were followed by Liu Renjing and Luo Zhanglong, who were students from north China. In this way, the early Beijing Communist Party was expanded to 10 members, including six anarchists who made up the majority of the organization's members at that time.

After the expansion of the Party organization, a meeting was held at Li Dazhao's office in the library at Peking University to divide the work. Li presided over the whole project, and donated 80 yuan a month from his personal salary of 120 yuan for the Party's activities. Zhang Guotao was in charge of the labor movement, while Liu Renjing and Luo Zhanglong dealt with the Youth League. Huang Lingshuang and Chen Derong founded the popular workers' publication *Workers' Voice*, and were in charge of editing and distributing it.

As early as November, anarchists such as Huang Lingshuang began to lock horns with Marxists such as Li Dazhao, because they did not agree with the dictatorship of the proletariat as written in the provisional program. There were two main points of disagreement: first, the organizational question. In accordance with their view of free association, the anarchists did not favor strict

1. Wu, Tianyao (editor-in-chief). *The Chronicle of the Founding of the Party According to Those Who Experienced It*, PLA Press, 2011, p. 11.

organization and unified leadership of the Party, and opposed the division of labor and discipline within it; the second was the question of the dictatorship of the proletariat. This disagreement made it impossible for the Party to carry out its work.

Li Dazhao wrote a series of articles to refute the anarchists' views. He emphasized that freedom and order were inseparable, as were the individual and society. Society and social groups needed order and discipline, because "there is no truly rational individualism that disregards social order, and no truly rational socialism that disregards individual freedom."[1] Unlike the bourgeois parties and politicians, political parties had to build a red state for "thorough reform," and therefore had to "establish a strong and precise organization, and pay attention to promoting the training of its elements as a group."[2] After some argument, all of the anarchists except Chen Derong withdrew from the Party, and the weekly *Workers' Voice* was taken over by Luo Zhanglong.

After the anarchists withdrew, the early Beijing Communist Party developed Deng Zhongxia, Gao Junyu, He Mengxiong, and Miao Boying – the backbone of the Beijing Socialist Youth League –as Party members. They unanimously elected Li Dazhao as secretary, Zhang Guotao as organizer, and Luo Zhanglong as publicist.

After the founding of the Beijing branch, the organization rapidly expanded. By July 1921, before the First National Congress of the Communist Party of China was held, it had 16 members, namely Li Dazhao, Zhang Guotao, Deng Zhongxia, Gao Junyu, He Mengxiong, Luo Zhanglong, Liu Renjing, Fan Hongjie, Miao Boying, Zhang Tailei, Li Meigeng, Zhu Wushan, Song Jie, Jiang Hao, Wu Yuming, and Chen Derong – the largest number of members among early Communist Party organizations around the world.

As a result, the early Communist Party organization in Beijing not only had a complete organizational system and a growing team, but also became more ideologically pure. Its work was carried out with strength and dedication, placing it as the northern center of the early Communist Party of China (echoing Shanghai), and playing a vital role in the process of building the Party.

1. *The Complete Works of Li Dazhao, Vol. 3*, People's Publishing House, 2006, p. 253.
2. Ibid., p. 271.

5

THE ESTABLISHMENT OF PARTY ORGANIZATIONS AROUND THE COUNTRY

IN OCTOBER 1920, WITH BEIJING (the seat of the Beiyang warlord government and political center) as the main front in the north, and Shanghai (then the largest industrial city and economic center in the country) as the main front in the south, the north and south echoed one another, liaising extensively, working actively, and guiding Party-building activities across the nation.

The early Communist Party organization in Wuhan was initiated by Dong Biwu, Zhang Guoen, and Liu Bochui under the direct guidance of the early Communist Party organization in Shanghai.

In the summer of 1920, Li Hanjun wrote to Dong Biwu and Zhang Guoen from Shanghai, and later made a special trip to Wuhan to discuss Party building with Dong Biwu in person. At the same time, Chen Duxiu sent Liu Bochui to Wuhan to help Dong Biwu prepare for the establishment of the Communist Party. At that time, Liu Bochui brought back from Shanghai a handwritten draft of the CPC platform, and some series of books published by the New Youth Society. Dong Biwu, Liu Bochui, and Zhang Guoen had all studied in Japan. They were members of the League of Nations, and had participated in revolutionary activities led by Sun Yat-sen.

Dong Biwu (then aged 34) and Zhang Guoen (then aged 40) had lived next door to Li Hanjun in Shanghai, and had gained their initial communist consciousness under his influence as well as the example of the October Revolution. On returning to Wuhan, they founded Wuhan High School in early 1920, to propagate Marxism and develop revolutionary talents.

Liu Bochui (then aged 33) met Li Hanjun while studying in Japan. He later embraced Marxism during the May Fourth Movement, returning to Wuhan from Guangzhou in 1920. He ran into Li Hanjun while passing through Shanghai, and was encouraged by Chen Duxiu to join the early Communist Party in Shanghai.

These experiences gave them a common ideological basis for the establishment of the Party in Wuhan. After repeated discussions, they finally reached a consensus.

In August 1920, a meeting was held at Dong Biwu's apartment on Fuyuan Street in Wuchang, chaired by Liu Bochui. At this meeting, the early Wuhan Communist Party was established as the 'Wuhan Branch of the Communist Party.' The attendees included Liu Bochui, Dong Biwu, Zhang Guoen, Chen Tanqiu, Zheng Kaiqing, and Bao Huiseng. The proceedings began with the circulation of the draft Party Program, which had been drafted by the Shanghai Party Organization and brought from Shanghai by Liu Bochui, explaining the situation of the Shanghai Party, and noting the work arrangements of the Wuhan branch after its establishment. Liu Bochui proposed that Bao Huiseng be elected as secretary of the branch, and everyone agreed. In order to avoid the attention of the enemy, the early Wuhan Communist Party decided to rent a house behind the Hubei Police Department, at No. 5 Duogongzhi in Wuchang, as the Party's organ, and put up a sign saying 'Liu Fen (i.e. Liu Bochui) Law Office' at the entrance as a cover for secret Party activities.

Bao Huiseng – the secretary of the Wuhan branch of the early Communist Party – was a graduate of Hubei First Division and a student of Zhang Guoen. Aged 26 at the time, he was working as a journalist in Wuhan. Zheng Kaiqing (then aged 32) was fortunate enough to become the first worker member of the Communist Party of China. A janitor at Wenhua College, he had met Chen Duxiu when Chen was invited to Wuhan to give a lecture in February 1920.

The early Communist Party organization in Changsha was established under the planning of Mao Zedong. During the preparation for the establishment of the Party, Mao had direct contact with Li Dazhao and Chen Duxiu in Beijing and Shanghai around 1920.

Mao Zedong came to Beijing for the second time in 18 December 1919, and stayed until 11 April 1920. During that time, he arranged for members of the New People's Society to go to France to work and study, and had organized the movement to expel Zhang Jingyao. He also read many articles about what was happening in Russia, as well as the few Chinese translations of communist literature that could be found at that time, thus establishing his faith in Marxism.

In early May, Mao went to Shanghai to send the second group of New People's Society members to France to work and study. During that time, he met Chen Duxiu several times, exchanged knowledge of Marxism, and learned that a Marxist Research Association and a Communist Party organization were in the making in Shanghai. This had a significant impact on the establishment of Mao's Marxist beliefs. He said, "When I went to Shanghai for the second time, I talked with Chen Duxiu about the Marxist books I had read. Chen's expounding his own beliefs made a deep impression on me in what was probably a critical period in my life."[1]

In July, when Mao returned to Changsha from Shanghai, he set up groups such as the Cultural Book Club and the Russian Studies Society, and talked with the stalwarts of the New People's Society about the issue of Party building. By the fall, the New People's Society already had more than 100 members, and was a progressive group with considerable influence. Some of these advanced elements had already accepted Marxism and advocated the path of the October Revolution.

In November, Mao received a letter from Chen Duxiu and Li Da, asking him to initiate the establishment of a Communist Party organization in Hunan. He accepted their request. Around the same time, after careful preparations, Mao and He Shuheng secretly founded the early Communist Party organization in Changsha.[2]

The process of establishing the early Communist Party in Guangzhou was somewhat convoluted. First, a Communist Party organization was established in September 1920, but most of its members were anarchists. It was only when Chen Duxiu arrived in Guangzhou in early 1921 and helped to reorganize the Party that it was gradually freed from anarchist influence.

In the summer of 1920, Tan Pingshan, Tan Zhitang, and Chen Gongbo – recent graduates of Peking University – went to teach at Guangdong

1. Snow, Edgar. *A Journey to the West*, translated by Dong Leshan, Sanlian Publishing Company, 1979, pp. 132–133.
2. Pang, Xianzhi and Jin, Chonghe. *Mao Zedong*, Central Literature Publishing House, 2010, p. 76.

Higher Normal School, the Public School of Law and Political Science, and the Provincial Industrial College respectively. These three schools were greatly influenced by the May Fourth Movement, and had a strong revolutionary atmosphere. So, Chen Duxiu wrote to them, telling them that Guangdong was the fountainhead of the revolution and could not lag behind, and asking them to organize and establish a communist organization in Guangzhou. On receiving the letter, the three of them openly launched the Guangzhou Socialist Youth League in August, which attracted a large number of teachers and students as members. However, due to the complicated composition and ideological situation of the members, there was no strict organizational program and no indication of what kind of doctrine they believed in. Therefore, they could only be considered a peripheral organization of the Communist Party.

Also in the summer of 1920, the Comintern representative Grigori Voitinsky sent Russian Communists Minol and Beslin to Guangzhou to carry out their activities. They were accompanied by the anarchist Huang Lingshuang, who had joined the early Communist Party in Beijing. As soon as they arrived in Guangzhou, they were "surrounded by anarchists." At the end of the year, after a period of contact and discussion, seven anarchists (including Minol, Beslin, and Ou Shengbai) began Party-building activities. Due to their differing views, Tan Pingshan, Tan Zhitang, and Chen Gongbo refused to join the organization. At the end of the year, Chen Duxiu arrived in Guangzhou from Shanghai. Soon after, he called a meeting and brought the Party Program he had drafted out for discussion. Among other things, it emphasized the need for strict organizational discipline of the Party, and adherence to the dictatorship of the proletariat. The anarchists were reluctant to accept it. There were many heated arguments, and it was difficult to reconcile the opposing views. Finally, the anarchists withdrew from the Guangzhou Party organization.

In March 1921, after careful consideration, Chen Duxiu, Chen Gongbo, Tan Pingshan, Tan Zhitang, Minol, and Beslin formed a new early organization of the Communist Party of Guangdong. Known as the Communist Party of Guangzhou, it had Chen Duxiu and then Tan Pingshan as secretaries, Chen Gongbo in charge of organizational work, and Tan Zhitang in charge of publicity, putting Party building in this area on the right track.

The early Communist Party of Jinan was established with the help and guidance of the early Communist Party of Beijing. In April 1920, Voitinsky came to China with his fellow Comintern representatives. When Li Dazhao brought him to Shanghai to meet Chen Duxiu, they passed through Jinan, because their interpreter Yang Mingzhai was from Shandong. In Jinan, Voitinsky and his party spoke with Wang Guomei and Deng Enming about the spread of Marxism and the establishment of the Communist Party.

In the fall of 1920, a Marxist Research Association was founded in Jinan by Wang Jinmei, Deng Enming, and other comrades. This organization started as an open academic research group, but was soon banned by the reactionary government on the charge of "propagating radical ideas," and was semi-openly active for some time afterwards. Through the study and propagation of Marxism, the Association united a group of revolutionaries with strong beliefs and a willingness to die for communism. It gradually formed a nucleus, thus making ideological and organizational preparations for the establishment of the Party.

After the establishment of the early Communist Party in Beijing, Li Dazhao sent Chen Weiren to Jinan to help establish a branch there. In the spring of 1921, at a welcome tea party, Chen Weiren explained the activities of the Beijing Marxist Research Association, and took the opportunity to establish the early Communist Party in Jinan, with the likes of Wang Jinmei, Deng Enming, and Wang Xiangqian as members.

Shanghai, Beijing, Wuhan, Changsha, Guangzhou, and Jinan were mostly central cities that were deeply influenced by the New Culture Movement and the May Fourth Movement, with a high concentration of industrial workers, and groups of intellectuals who believed in Marxism. While many early Communist Party organizations were established in China, they were set up by advanced elements among foreign students and overseas Chinese in Japan and France.

The Party-building activities of foreign students in Japan were initiated under the influence of the Party back home. The first two members – Shi Cuntong and Zhou Fohai, who both went to Japan after joining the early Communist Party organization in Shanghai – logically formed a group, with Shi Cuntong as leader. Since there were only two of them, it was the smallest early Communist Party organization at that time.

The early organization of the Communist Party in France, mainly formed among the Chinese work-study community, was founded in 1921 by Zhang Shenfu and Zhao Shiyan, with Chen Gongpei, Liu Qingyang, and Zhou Enlai as members. Zhang Shenfu was a lecturer at Peking University, and was a member of the early Communist Party in Beijing. He was not a diligent student, but was hired by Wu Zhihui – President of the Sino-French University of Lyon – to be a professor of logic in France. Zhao Shiyan was introduced to the Party by Chen Duxiu when he arrived in Shanghai from Beijing in May 1920. Chen Gongpei went to France in July 1920 after attending the preparatory meeting for the establishment of the Party in Shanghai, and already had Party connections by the time he arrived in Paris. Liu Qingyang and Zhou Enlai were introduced to the Party by Zhang Shenfu.

Notably, the names of the early communist organizations were not uniform throughout the world. For example, the early Communist Party organization in Shanghai was called the Communist Party of China from the beginning, while the one in Beijing was called the Beijing Branch of the Communist Party of China. These local organizations soon formed the unified Communist Party of China.

After the early Communist Party organizations had been established in the various locations, they studied and propagated Marxism in a systematic and organized manner, and waged resolute polemics against anti-Marxist trends. They carried out publicity and organizational work among workers, and established socialist youth organizations. All of this laid a solid foundation for the formal establishment of the Communist Party of China.

PART 6

A New Dawn:

From the Shanghai Shikumen *to the 'Red Boat' of Jiaxing*

In the early 1920s, against the backdrop of internal and external troubles and the unprecedented social crisis facing the Chinese nation, in the process of combining Marxism-Leninism with the Chinese labor movement, and with the efforts of the early Communist Party organizations in various regions, the conditions for the formal establishment of the CPC were becoming increasingly ripe, and the preparation for the convening of the Party's National Congress was on the Party organization's agenda.

In July 1921, the First National Congress of the Communist Party of China was held, announcing the formal establishment of the CPC.

The birth of the Communist Party of China was a historical necessity and the choice of the people.

History is harsh. In a large semi-colonial and semi-feudal Eastern country that was facing the powerful forces of imperialism and feudalism, the task of the Chinese revolution was extremely difficult and complex. The setbacks and failures of the previous democratic revolution showed that the path of peasant revolt was not possible, the path of reformism was not feasible, and the path of bourgeois democratic revolution was not viable. Neither the Chinese peasant class nor the bourgeoisie was capable of taking up the important task of leading the Chinese revolution, so it was impossible to lead the Chinese people to accomplish the task of anti-imperialist and anti-feudal democratic revolution.

History is fair. However, in the face of powerful Chinese and foreign reactionary forces, parties were weak and compromised, including the Kuomintang. They could not put forward a correct program or mobilize the people extensively, and were unable to take up the historical responsibility of anti-imperialism and anti-feudalism. The revolutionary process was like a great wave washing away the sands of China's political arena, and many political parties were eliminated one after another by history. The Chinese people and the Chinese revolution called for a new leadership class and a new political party to solve the urgent problems facing China's modern society.

It was against this historical background that advanced elements in China finally chose Marxism as the theoretical weapon to transform Chinese society. They elected to follow the example of Russia's October Revolution, and formed a Chinese proletarian party based on Lenin's doctrine of Party building. From this, it is clear that the creation of the Communist Party of China met the objective needs that China had for social progress and revolutionary development since the dawn of the modern era, and was the inevitable result of the historical choice of modern China and the Chinese people.

The birth of the Communist Party of China was like a red sun rising, shining in the darkness of the night and bringing hope to the Chinese people. From then on, the Chinese revolution was able to move forward in the right direction. The Chinese people had a strong cohesive force, and China's future had bright prospects for development. Because of this, the First National Congress of the Communist Party of China went down in history for its great achievements.

The formal founding of the CPC was an epoch-making milestone in the history of Chinese revolution, and a major event in the international communist movement. This groundbreaking event profoundly changed the direction and course of the development of the Chinese nation in modern times. It inexorably altered the future and fate of the Chinese people and nation, and transformed the trend and pattern of global development.

1
PLANS AND PREPARATIONS

On 3 June 1921, in the warm and humid sea breeze of early summer, a cruise ship from Italy sailed slowly up the Huangpu River and docked at the bustling Shanghai Bund. The passengers – who had travelled thousands of miles across several oceans – were finally able to stretch their weary bodies after many weeks at sea, before quickly disembarking with their luggage.

In the midst of that bustling crowd stood a tall, well-built man with a high forehead, wide eyes, and sideburns, wearing a pair of gold-rimmed glasses. He looked around 40 years of age. He was wearing a tie, but his suit was in no way elaborate. He had the look of a manual laborer, yet the air of a learned man.

This person was none other than Maring – the first official delegate of the Comintern who was sent to China. Maring was born Hendricus Josephus Franciscus Marie (Henk) Sneevliet in 1883 in the Dutch city of Rotterdam, into a poor working-class family. His desire to pursue justice and equality for all led him to join the socialist movement in the Netherlands at an early age. In 1902, he joined the Dutch Social Democratic Workers' Party (SDAP) and the Dutch Association of Railroad and Tramway Employees (NV). He was keen to make his mark in the revolutionary struggle against colonial rule, and displayed extraordinary ability in organizing and canvassing. In December 1913, Maring moved to the Indonesian island of Java, which was colonized by the Dutch at the time. There, he worked as a reporter for the Semarang Business Daily, before becoming the chairman of the Surabaya Chamber of Commerce, and meeting many others who were active in the socialist movement. After witnessing first-hand the depravity of colonial oppression, Maring began to participate actively in the Indonesian people's struggle against the suzerain. He was particularly active in the founding activities of the Communist Party of Indonesia. When the October Revolution broke out in Russia, Maring and his compatriots stepped up their efforts, and called on people to follow in the footsteps of the Russians. This led to their being charged by the authorities. After a trial that lasted several grueling months, Maring was eventually acquitted, but he was deported and had to return to the Netherlands in January 1919. Nevertheless, he remained active in promoting the cause of the revolution in Soviet Russia.[1]

In May 1920, the Indische Sociaal-Democratische Vereeniging (ISDV, or Social Democratic Association of the Indies) held its seventh party congress, and made the decision to change its name to the Communist Party of Indonesia (PKI). In the same month, under the auspices of the Social Democratic Workers' Party of the Netherlands, Maring was deployed to Soviet Russia as a representative of the PKI to attend the second congress of the Comintern, held in July. From then on, Hendricus Sneevliet came to be known as 'Maring,' and is fondly remembered in history by this name.[2]

On the eve of this congress, when a series of revolutionary activities in Europe had been defeated, Lenin's gaze turned from the West to the East. He placed increasing hope in the national liberation movements in the colonial and semi-colonial countries, putting forward the idea of actively fighting for the peoples of the East (who made up the majority of the world's population) to join the war against international imperialism. During the congress sessions, Maring talked about his efforts in uniting the different factions in order to oppose colonial rule in Indonesia, and made suggestions for strengthening the revolutions in the Far Eastern colonies. He caught the attention of Lenin, and was elected as a member of the Executive Committee of the Comintern. With Lenin's backing, Maring was appointed as the Comintern representative for China in August 1920, and was deployed to Shanghai.

The core objectives of Maring's trip to Shanghai were to study, and to serve as the contact for revolutionary movements in various countries in the Far East,

1. *The Pictorial Biography of Maring,* edited by Li Yuzhen of the Memorial Hall of the First National Congress of the Communist Party of China. Shanghai People's Publishing House, 2018, pp. 2–3 of the preface.
2. Huang, Xiurong and Huang, Li, *History of the Founding of the Communist Party of China*, China Youth Press, 2014, p. 486.

as well as to ascertain whether an outpost for the Comintern could be feasibly established in Shanghai.

Arriving in Shanghai at the same time as Maring was Nikolski, who was sent by the Far East Bureau of the Comintern to replace Voitinsky, carrying much-needed funds. Nikolski, who was born Vladimir Neiman Abramovich in Russia in 1898, served in the People's Revolutionary Army of the Far East Republic from 1919 to 1920. He joined the Bolsheviks in 1921 as a staff member of the administrative branch of the Comintern. In June the same year, he was deployed to China by the Far East Bureau of the Comintern.

At the time, Nikolski was barely 23 years old, and had little practical work experience. He had no knowledge of English, and found it difficult to communicate with his Chinese comrades. This unfortunately gave the impression that he was merely Maring's assistant. This was not the case. In fact, Nikolski was handpicked and sent by the Far East Bureau of the Comintern in Irkutsk to succeed Voitinsky in his role. Nikolski concurrently represented three organizations, the other two being the Military Intelligence Service of the People's Revolutionary Army of the Far East Republic, and the Far East Bureau of the International Federation of Trade Unions.

When discussing the founding of the Party, two central figures of the movement cannot be neglected, namely Chen from the south and Li from the north. Regrettably, six months prior to Maring and the others arriving in Shanghai, Chen Duxiu had gone to Guangzhou to take on the role of Chairman of the Education Committee of the Guangdong Government, while Li Dazhao was in Beijing leading the teaching staff of the city's eight universities to secure their hard-earned income from the Beiyang warlord government, which controlled the northern part of China. As such, Maring was not fated to meet either of the much-celebrated duo.

Maring and Nikolski therefore had to meet with Li Da and Li Hanjun, who were presiding over the Shanghai Communist Party apparatus at the time. After several in-depth discussions, they agreed that a National Congress should be convened as soon as possible, to formally establish the Communist Party of China. Li Da and Li Hanjun discussed the details with Chen Duxiu in Guangzhou and Li Dazhao in Beijing by post, and decided that Shanghai would be the location for the first National Congress of the Communist Party of China.

As such, the man who presided over the Shanghai Communist Party in its early days – 31-year-old Li Da – undertook the bulk of the preparatory work for the Congress alongside his 23-year-old wife Wang Huiwu.

Li Da was born in October 1890 in Hunan Province, in what was then the town of Caijiabu in Lingling County, into a typical agricultural family (this area is now part of Lanjiaoshan Town in the Lengshuitan District of Yongzhou City). In the fall of 1909, Li Da was admitted to Peking Normal University (now Beijing Normal University). While studying in Beijing, he had an awakening, and came to realize the main reason why China was being bullied by the imperial powers. It all boiled down to the fact that China's educational landscape was behind the rest of the world, and that its scientific methods were underdeveloped. This prompted him to come up with the idea of saving the country through education. In the aftermath of the Xinhai Revolution of 1911, and influenced by Sun Yat-sen's philosophy of promoting enterprises to benefit the country and strengthen livelihoods, Li Da responded to Sun's 'Industrial Salvation' school of thought and switched to studying science and engineering. In 1913, he placed second in his cohort, and attained a full-ride scholarship sponsored by his home province to study in Japan. He was also admitted to Tokyo First Normal University to study mathematics and science.

Li Da was deeply encouraged when he learned of the success of the October Revolution, and saw that there was a new path forward to save his country and people. He began to learn more about Marxism from Japanese newspapers and books, and actively sought out the most influential Marxists in Japan at that time, such as the economist Hajime Kawakami. He pored over Marxist-Leninist works such as *the Communist Manifesto*, *Capital*, and *The State and Revolution*, and gradually became a fervent believer and enthusiastic promoter of Marxism. The success of the May Fourth Movement encouraged Li Da even further. He promptly launched a rally among Chinese students in Japan, and organized a demonstration in front of the Chinese Embassy. He was an active participant in this great anti-imperialist patriotic movement, writing a letter to the Japanese Cabinet as a form of protest, and penning progressive articles that were published in Chinese newspapers and magazines.

From 1918 to the summer of 1920 when he returned to China, Li Da also translated three easy-to-digest books about Marxism, namely *An Explanation of Historical Materialism*, *Marxist Economics*, and *An Overview of Social Issues*, and sent them back to China to be published for readers there. In particular, *An Explanation of Historical Materialism* made Li Da a pioneer in popularizing Marxist philosophy among the masses in China in the 1930s. Even Mao Zedong praised him for producing materials that were easy to understand.

In August 1920, Li Da returned to Shanghai from Tokyo with fire in his belly, seeking like-minded comrades to partake in the social revolution. Once he returned home, Li joined the predecessor of the Shanghai Communist Party, and participated in the editing of *New Youth* magazine. Soon after, he became acquainted with a girl in Shanghai who was blessed with both beauty and brains. This girl was Wang Huiwu, who worked as a secretary for Xu Zonghan – President of the Chinese Women's Federation in Shanghai, and wife of Huang Xing.

Wang Huiwu was born in 1898 in the town of Wuzhen, within the county of Tongxiang and the prefecture-level city of Jiaxing in Zhejiang Province. This area is commonly known as China's 'Land of Fish and Rice' and the 'House of Silk.' In 1911, 13-year-old Wang Huiwu, who was a pupil at Jiaxing Normal School, returned to her hometown after the death of father due to ill health. She took on her father's previous role, and set up the first elementary school for girls in Tongxiang County. After the May Fourth Movement, Wang Huiwu arrived in Shanghai and joined the Chinese Women's Federation. Whilst she was living in Shanghai, *New Youth* became her favorite magazine, and she began to write fervent letters to Chen Duxiu and Li Da, expressing her support for their revolutionary ideas, as well as for the use of vernacular Chinese in written texts (as opposed to Classical Chinese, which had been predominantly used in imperial China). At that time, as a representative of the General Association of Students in Japan, Li Da often had dealings with the Chinese Women's Federation, so he met Wang Huiwu in the course of his work. During this contact, their common revolutionary beliefs attracted them to each other, and they soon fell in love.

On one particular day in April 1921, No. 2 Old Yuyang Lane could be described as a place bursting with happiness and jubilation. Li Da and Wang Huiwu became husband and wife. The wedding ceremony was simple, but the atmosphere was as warm as one could imagine it to be. Chen Duxiu's wife Gao Junman was present as a witness. Once married, Wang Huiwu became Li Da's indispensable helper, and actively engaged in the work of the Party.

At the beginning of June that year, it was decided that the first National Congress of the Communist Party of China would be held on the 20th of that month.[1]

Judging by the letters written by the key personnel at that time, the preparations for the Congress must have been carried out at superhuman speed.

Li Da immediately wrote a letter to the Party branches in Beijing, Changsha, Wuhan, Guangzhou, and Jinan, as well as to the Party members among the Chinese students in Japan. They were told to send two representatives each to Shanghai to attend the Party's National Congress. Shanghai was selected as the location of the Congress, as it had become the central point of contact for communists scattered all over China. The city was also blessed with a unique geographical location, and was well connected to all other parts of the country. It also had a relatively relaxed political environment.

After the notice of the meeting was issued, Li Da promptly drafted the 'Declaration of the Communist Party of China' and other documents for the meeting. He entrusted his wife, Wang Huiwu, to arrange accommodation for their out-of-town delegates, and to find a location for the Congress. The ideal venue would have to accommodate more than a dozen people, and allow them to convene safely without attracting unwanted outside attention. Where could such a location be found?

At the time, Wang Huiwu was working as a secretary for Xu Zonghan, President of the Chinese Women's Federation in Shanghai, and was also the editor of the *Women's Voice* magazine. As such, she was well-acquainted with Huang Shaolan – the principal of Bowen Girls' School. Huang Shaolan had worked under Huang Xing in her early years. In 1917, she had moved to Shanghai to take on the role at Bowen, and hired Xu Zonghan as the chair. Huang Shaolan and her husband Huang Kan hailed from Hubei Province, as did brothers Li Hanjun and Li Shucheng, so they naturally shared a close bond. In fact, Li Shucheng's wife was still a student at Bowen Girls' School at the time. Such relationships meant that they got along very well, and it was thus easy for them to trust one another. As the summer vacation drew closer, Bowen Girls' School – which was located in the French Concession at No. 389 Bai'er Road

1. *Ninety Years of the Communist Party of China*. Party History Research Office of the CPC Central Committee, CPC History Publishing House and Party Building Readers' Publishing House, 2016, p. 35.

(later renamed Pubai Road, and again re-designated as No. 127 Taicang Road) – would be empty of students, thus rendering the premises safe and quiet.

Therefore, in the name of the 'Peking University Summer Term Tour Group' visiting Shanghai for an "academic conference," Wang Huiwu put forward her request to Huang Shaolan to house her guests. Something amusing arose in their discussions. Because of their close relationship, and the fact that Huang Shaolan's husband was also a professor at Peking University, Huang Shaolan casually asked, "These people aren't a bunch of radicals, are they?" Wang Huiwu was no doubt shocked to hear this, but she managed to reply in a tactful manner. "Let's put it this way: judging from the way things are going, the two of us can be considered radicals too." Huang Shaolan laughed, and immediately agreed to provide the much-needed lodgings.

With the accommodation settled, it was just a question of finding a place for the meeting itself.

The Li Mansion, which was a stone's throw from Bowen Girls' School, was owned by Li Hanjun's brother Li Shucheng. Li Shucheng – a veteran of the United League – was coincidentally out of town, and the mansion was unoccupied. After talking with Li Hanjun, Wang Huiwu arranged to hold the Congress at Li Mansion, which was located in the French Concession at No. 106 Wangzhi Road (now No. 76 Xingye Road).

With the June temperatures rising in Shanghai, preparations were in place, and the Congress was starting to take shape. All that was left was to wait for the representatives from afar to gather to witness the historic moment that would soon unfold.

2

A SECRET MEETING OF NATIONAL REPRESENTATIVES

Many great endeavors often seem unremarkable in the beginning, but with the passage of time, the years of hard work will eventually be validated and made known to the world, and their significance in global history will be recognized.

In June 1921, China was still in dire straits. However, in an otherwise typical early summer, there seemed to be something simmering below the surface. Communists scattered all over China had received notice of the Congress that was to be held in Shanghai. Back then, few would have thought that this would eventually be recognized as one of the most profound and monumental meetings in the world, and that every representative who attended would eventually earn a permanent place in the history books.

Understandably, those who missed out on the golden opportunity to attend this historical Congress would have certainly carried a huge pang of regret through the rest of their lives. Meanwhile, there were others who, by fate or sheer coincidence, became some of the lucky few to have witnessed the great birth of the Communist Party of China.

When the various branches received their letters from Shanghai informing them to convene for the Party's First National Congress, it led to a flurry of excitement among the members, who were enthused by the swift development of the preparatory work for the official establishment of the Party. Without any hesitation, all branches began to make plans to send their representatives to the Congress.

On receiving the notice, the early Communist Party of Beijing convened a special meeting to elect representatives for the National Congress. The early members in Beijing were mainly students from Peking University. When the letter was received, it was the middle of the summer vacation. The young members were renting a house in the Xicheng district of Beijing, and they had set up an enrichment center to conduct preparatory classes for high school students who were planning to take college entrance examinations. Many Party members were teaching at this center. Deng Zhongxia taught Chinese, Liu Renjing taught English, and Zhang Guotao taught mathematics and physics, to name but a few. As such, it was the ideal location for the meeting to elect delegates for the Congress.

Who would be the best candidates to attend?

On the basis of his contribution to the founding of the Party, Li Dazhao was certainly the most qualified to attend the inaugural Congress. However, at the time, he had been leading the staff of the eight universities in Beijing to lobby the Beiyang warlord government for several months regarding the non-payment of salaries. He was undoubtedly a busy man. Moreover, on 3 June, when Li was leading a group to petition in front of the Presidential Palace's Xinhua Gate, he was severely beaten by the military police, causing him to lose consciousness and be hospitalized. Therefore, the other members in Beijing felt that it was most prudent to not elect Li Dazhao as the Beijing representative, out of consideration for his health. They all agreed that a younger member stepping to the fore and ensuring that the operations continued as per normal was the responsible thing to do.

Zhang Guotao was one of the three founding Party members in Beijing, and was one of the most critical when it came to day-to-day operations. He was outstanding at performing outreach, and was extremely active. During the preparations for the official establishment of the Party, he frequently shuttled between Beijing and Shanghai, faithfully passing letters and organizational blueprints between Li Dazhao and Chen Duxiu. Given the fact that Li Dazhao was not physically well enough to attend the Congress, Zhang Guotao was a natural and unanimous choice for the Beijing representative.

Deng Zhongxia was the backbone of the early Party apparatus in Beijing, and the main person in charge of leading the Beijing Labor Movement. As such, it was only logical and natural that he be elected as a representative for the Congress. However, Deng was already scheduled to attend the annual meeting of the Young China Association in Nanjing in early July, and had to leave for Chongqing directly after that to give a series of lectures. Therefore, he "very humbly and politely declined on the grounds that he was too busy with work."[1]

When the communists in Beijing were debating the representatives they wanted to elect, another name that was floated was Luo Zhanglong. However, as he was presiding over the preparations and publication of the *Workers' Weekly* newspaper, it was not practical for him to go. Given that Deng Zhongxia and Luo Zhanglong were both unable to attend, Liu Renjing was elected as the second Beijing representative for the Congress.

After a thorough discussion and debate, it was finally decided that Zhang Guotao and Liu Renjing would go to Shanghai for the First National Congress of the Communist Party of China on behalf of the communists in Beijing.

In the latter half of June, Zhang Guotao traveled by train to Beijing, and got to Shanghai early. He recalled that "he was the first delegate to arrive in Shanghai because he had to attend to some of the preparatory work for the Congress."[2] On arriving in Shanghai, Zhang met up with Maring (the representative sent by the Comintern) and brought him up to speed on the accomplishments made by the communists in Beijing and the general situation in the north of China.

Maring made use of his status as a Comintern representative to assume control, even though he was new to China and lacked an in-depth understanding of the situation that the communists there were facing. Li Da – who was innately outspoken – and Li Hanjun – who would never blindly follow orders from others – naturally resented Maring's attitude, and the three of them did not get along. Although Zhang Guotao was seven years younger than both Li Da and Li Hanjun, he was more sociable, and had good interpersonal skills. He was able to maintain a cordial relationship with Maring, and thus served as a mediator to sooth the tense relationships among the three.[3]

---

1. Liu, Renjing. *Miscellaneous Notes from the First National People's Congress, Recollections from the First National People's Congress,* Knowledge Publishing House, 1980, p. 47.
2. Zhang, Guotao. *My Recollections, Vol. 1,* Modern Archives Publishing House, 1980, p. 131.
3. *The Beginning: An Account of the Founding of the Communist Party of China (Part 2)*, p. 542.

Liu Renjing, Deng Zhongxia, and several others traveled south by train on 28 June, and went to Nanjing to attend the annual meeting of the Youth League. On 4 July, after the conclusion of the meeting, Liu Renjing immediately headed to Bowen Girls' School in the French Concession of Shanghai.

Although the members in Beijing had only organized themselves into a group mere months earlier, amazingly, within a short period of time after receiving the letter from Shanghai, they were able to hold a vote to decide on their representatives, even though not all of the members were in Beijing during the summer vacation. Even with all the difficulties in arranging the meetup, they still managed to conduct several rounds of democratic talks to elect their representatives, and the branch in Beijing was the only one out of the six to conduct a vote.

Given that the operations of the communists were shrouded in secrecy at that time, in the initial stages there were no unified regulations, and there was no strict organizational system. Moreover, given that the political environment of each city and the activities each group was focusing on differed greatly, the method of determining and electing representatives for the inaugural Congress also differed by location. Some held votes during their meetings, some were appointed by their leaders, and in some cases, the initiator of the branch naturally felt that he needed to be the one to attend.

Representing the communists in Changsha were the founders of the local operations – Mao Zedong and He Shuheng. In the afternoon of 29 June, the pair boarded a small steam-powered boat in the twilight at Xiaoximen Wharf in Changsha. They departed very secretively, and did not even let their families and friends know about their trip.

Xie Juezai, who was working alongside He Shuheng at the Hunan People's Press at the time, wrote in his diary, "At 6pm, Shuheng headed off Shanghai, and the traveler answered the call to attend the National ○○○○." Regarding these circles, Xie Juezai's wife Wang Dingguo mentioned them in an article recounting the events of that fateful day. "Dark clouds were looming over the Xiang River [the longest river in Hunan Province, and a main tributary of the Yangtze] and the reactionaries were out in full force. He could sense that what was about to happen would be a major historical event. While he did not want to forget the minute details of that day, he also could not afford to record too much, so he had to draw a series of large circles in that particular day's diary entry."[1] Xie Juezai himself recounted, "One night, dark clouds covered the sky, and it was raining relentlessly. From out of nowhere, I heard that Comrade Mao Zedong and Comrade He Shuheng needed to leave for Shanghai immediately. I felt that their sudden actions were very strange. They forbade us to board the ship. It was only much later that I learned that this would be the First National Congress of the Communist Party of China – the Congress at which the great and glorious Communist Party of China would be announced."[2]

When the communists in Wuhan received the notice from Shanghai, Dong Biwu and Chen Tanqiu were elected as representatives to attend the Congress. The summer vacation was about to begin. After Dong and Chen had finished their teaching duties in early July, the duo travelled downstream on a steamship to Shanghai. They arrived earlier than the representatives from other areas, so decided to stay at the Hubei Rehabilitation Association. It was not far from Li Hanjun's residence, and was thus extremely convenient for all of them.

In Jinan, the capital of Shandong Province, communists Wang Jinmei and Deng Enming both received letters from Shanghai, and subsequently travel expenses. In the latter half of June, Zhang Guotao made a brief stopover in Jinan for a day, en route from Beijing to Shanghai. Wang Jinmei, Deng Enming, and the other communists in Jinan arranged to meet up with him, and the group spent a leisurely day boating on Daming Lake. Shortly after Zhang Guotao left, Wang Jinmei and Deng Enming also travelled south by rail to Shanghai, arriving in the bustling metropolis some time at the end of June or the beginning of July.

Chen Duxiu was the head of the communists in Guangzhou at that time. On receiving the letter from Shanghai, he realized that Moscow had sent another representative, but it was not Voitinsky as he had expected. In the letter, Chen was urged to return to Shanghai swiftly, and to elect representatives from Guangzhou to attend the Congress.

Unfortunately, at the time, Chen Duxiu did not realize the profound historical significance and implications that would arise from attending this Congress. Therefore, during a meeting at the residence of fellow member Tan

1. Wang, Dingguo. 'Eternal Clouds Spinning Intently over the Skies' *Workers' Daily*, December 23, 1978.
2. See Xie, Juezai. 'The First Meeting with Comrade Mao Zedong' in *New Observation*, No. 11, 1952.

Zhitang, he made it clear that he would not be able to return to Shanghai, at least not in the short term. He was trying to secure a sum of money to help build a wing at the university, and it would be difficult to do this if he were to leave. So, in accordance with his prestigious position and customary style, he assigned Chen Gongbo and Bao Huiseng to attend the Congress.

Although he was originally from Wuhan, Bao Huiseng attended using the quota reserved for members from Guangzhou. This caused some controversy between representatives at the time, and later party historians have disputed whether Bao was even qualified to be a representative in the Congress.

Bao had joined the Wuhan Communist Party in September 1920. In January 1921, he travelled from Wuhan to Shanghai with several young members who were planning to further their education in the Soviet Union. They stayed at a Party office at No. 6 Xinyuyang Lane, on Avenue Joffre (now Huaihai Middle Road) in the French Concession. However, due to later financial difficulties and an interruption in the sea route to Vladivostok, it was deemed impossible for them to make the trip. Therefore, Bao Huiseng stayed in Shanghai to participate in Party education and promotional outreach. In May, Li Da – who was in charge of the operations in Shanghai – arranged for Bao Huiseng to go to Guangzhou to find Chen Duxiu and ask him to return to Shanghai to preside over the operations. Instead, Chen Duxiu ended up extending an invitation to Bao Huiseng to remain in Guangzhou for a while longer, and even arranged for him to work at a news agency for around two months. When the letter from Shanghai arrived, Chen Duxiu appointed Bao Huiseng to attend the Congress, as it would also allow him to meet Li Da and provide the updates. So Bao Huiseng left for Shanghai by ship on 15 July, and arrived around five days later. Newlywed Chen Gongbo had set out a day earlier with his wife, making a stopover in Hong Kong before traveling by ship to Shanghai.[1]

There were only two Chinese communists in Japan in the early days, namely Zhou Fohai and Shi Cuntong. When he received the letter from Shanghai, Zhou Fohai – who was studying at the No. 7 High School in Kagoshima in

1. This recollection by Bao Huiseng was dictated to the author. In numerous occasions in his memoirs, Bao mentioned that the First National Congress was held in July, but he did not specify a date, nor did he indicate the time that he arrived in Shanghai. On 20 June 1979, in an interview with Bao Huiseng, Professor Shao Weizheng pressed him on this issue. After much recollection, this was the reply that he provided.

western Japan – just so happened to be preparing for a trip back home during the summer vacation, so was designated as a representative. In his book, he recounted, "Through the letter from comrades in Shanghai, I knew that the Congress would be held in July. Very coincidentally, I was planning to return to Shanghai during the summer vacation."[1]

In 1936, Chen Tanqiu wrote 'Memories of the First Congress' for the fourth and fifth issues of the seventh volume of the Comintern magazine, which included the following:

> "Towards the end of July 1921, nine guests appeared out of the blue on the ground floor of the private Bowen Girls' School on Pubai Road in Shanghai's French Concession. As it was the middle of the summer vacation, all the students and teachers had gone back to their hometowns, so the compound was very quiet. The only staff member there was the cook, who doubled up as a janitor. He was entrusted to cook for the guests upstairs every day, and to guard the front door. No unauthorized personnel were allowed to enter. If it hadn't been for the organizer making introductions, the cook would have had no idea who the guests were. He was unable to understand them, as none of them could speak the Shanghai dialect. Some had thick Hunan and Hubei accents, while a few of the others were conversing in northern dialects. It turned out that they were representatives from communist groups from many different locations. Their sole purpose in Shanghai was to attend a Congress to formally establish the Communist Party of China."[2]

These nine guests were Mao Zedong, He Shuheng, Dong Biwu, Chen Tanqiu, Wang Jinmei, Deng Enming, Liu Renjing, Bao Huiseng, and Zhou Fohai, and they stayed in the teaching staff dormitories in the west wing of the building. The rooms had simple wooden beds, but there weren't enough, so Wang Huiwu bought some sleeping mats and laid them on the wooden floor. The summer heat was punishing, so sleeping on the ground was much cooler.

---

1. See Zhou, Fohai. *The Past and the Future*, Shanghai Ancient and Modern Press, August, R.O.C. 33, 10th revised edition.
2. *The Biography of Dong Biwu* (1886–1975), Central Literature Publishing House, 2006, p. 103.

As Chen Gongbo had brought his new wife, they had decided to stay in the Dadong Hotel. Zhang Guotao often visited Bowen Girls' School and would sometimes even sleep there, but he had another residence in Shanghai. Li Da and Li Hanjun were, of course, in their own homes in the city.[1]

All 13 representatives sent by the Communist Party branches all over China arrived in Shanghai safely and soundly.

The fact that both Li Dazhao and Chen Duxiu – founders of the Party – were unable to attend the Congress is certainly one of the greatest strokes of misfortune in human history. However, from another point of view, both were social and cultural celebrities in China at that time, especially Chen Duxiu – a famous 'radical' who had escaped the Beiyang warlord government. They wielded great social influence, and the entire country was watching their every move. Had they both participated as representatives, it is difficult to predict whether the Congress could have been held in secret, and whether its business could have been completed safely.

Events in history cannot be assumed, nor can they be repeated or changed.

What we do know is that in the latter half of July 1921, everything was in place, ready for the day the Reds would make their mark.

---

1. Ye, Yonglie. *The Red Beginning: How The Communist Party of China Was Created*, Sichuan People's Publishing House, 2016, pp. 246–247.

3

THE FIRST NATIONAL CONGRESS TAKES PLACE IN THE FRENCH CONCESSION

In his essay 'The French Civil War,' Marx pointed out that "if 'chance' did not play any role, then world history would be of a very mysterious nature" and would be incomprehensible.[1]

The day of 23 July 1921 is a prime example in world history when serendipity certainly played a dramatic role, and thus became a key juncture in the eventual development of Chinese revolutionary history.

According to a document hailing from that era, "the Congress was scheduled to be held on 20 June, but delegates from Beijing, Hankou, Guangzhou, Changsha, Jinan, and Japan did not arrive in Shanghai until 23 July, and so the Congress began then."[2]

If one were to start tracking the passage of time from 1840, when China first plunged into a long era of suffering and humiliation, this meant that the Chinese people had waited a full 81 years for this important day to arrive.

The day was destined to be extraordinary. It would be a day like no other.

---

1. Yang, Kuisong. *The Revolution of the 'Middle Ground' – Understanding the Success of the Communist Party of China in the Context of World Events*, Shanxi People's Publishing House, 2010, p. 5.
2. Party Literature Research Office of the CPC Central Committee, National Archives Administration of China. 'Selected Important Documents since the Founding of the Party (1921–1949),' Vol. 1, Central Party Literature Press, 2011, p. 21.

On this day, in faraway Moscow – the capital of Soviet Russia – the Second Congress of the Young Communist International (affiliated with the Comintern) concluded successfully.

On this day, Shanghai – popularly known as the Pearl of the Orient – was experiencing a brutal heat wave. In the dimness of an early summer night, representatives from all over, including teachers, students, and men with long beards resembling the scholars of yesteryear, converged there, ready to turn their Marxist hopes and dreams into something more concrete. They gathered at No.106 Wangzhi Road (now No.76 Xingye Road) in the French Concession, in a *shikumen* house.

This was the residence of Li Shucheng, the brother of Li Hanjun. The building was modelled in the *shikumen* style – a popular form of architecture that incorporated both Western and Chinese elements. It was a two-story building made of brick and wood that contained a courtyard, with an outer wall made of cyan bricks inlaid with red ones. Guarding the courtyard were large black doors with brass knockers. There were alum reliefs on the lintel, and floral decorations laced the upper part. Beige stone bars went around the perimeter of the doorframe, with a simple yet elegant effect.

The 18-square-meter dining room on the first floor had been repurposed as a conference room, with a long dining table in the middle and small stools placed around it. A simple tea set and two purple brass tobacco cylinders had been placed on the table. A coffee table and two chairs were arranged along the east and west walls, and a small table was positioned next to the red panel wall on the north side. Although simple in decoration, the room had a stately look. The only brightly-colored item was a wide-mouthed glass vase on the dining table, which contained rose-red lotus leaf trimmings and numerous stems of fresh flowers.

The 13 representatives gathered around the large dining table for the inaugural Congress. They were:

Li Da, born in 1890, aged 31, from Lingling (now known as Yongzhou) in Hunan Province – an editor from the Commercial Press, and a representative from Shanghai.

Li Hanjun, born in 1890, aged 31, from Qianjiang in Hubei Province – an editor at the Commercial Press, and a representative from Shanghai.

Zhang Guotao, born in 1897, aged 24, from Pingxiang in Jiangxi Province – a student at Peking University, and a representative from Beijing.

Liu Renjing, born in 1902, aged 19, from Yingcheng in Hubei Province – a student from Peking University, and a representative from Beijing.

Mao Zedong, born in 1893, aged 28, from Xiangtan in Hunan Province – Principal of the No. 1 Primary School affiliated to the No. 1 Hunan Normal University, and a representative from Changsha.

He Shuheng, born in 1876, aged 45, from Ningxiang in Hunan Province – a teacher at the No. 1 Primary School affiliated to the No. 1 Hunan Normal University, and a representative from Changsha.

Dong Biwu, born in 1886, aged 35, from Huang'an (now known as Hong'an) in Hubei Province – Principal of Wuhan High School, and a representative from Wuhan.

Chen Tanqiu, born in 1896, aged 25, from Huanggang in Hubei Province – an English teacher at Wuhan High School, and a representative from Wuhan.

Wang Jinmei, born in 1898, aged 23, from Zhucheng in Shandong Province – a student at the High School affiliated to Jinan Normal Normal, and a representative from Jinan.

Deng Enming, born in 1901, aged 20, from Libo in Guizhou Province – a student at Jinan's No. 1 High School in Shandong Province, and a representative from Jinan.

Chen Gongbo, born in 1890, aged 31, from Nanhai (now part of the city of Foshan) in Guangdong Province – a lecturer at Guangdong College of Political Science and Law, and a representative from Guangzhou.

Zhou Fohai, born in 1897, aged 24, from Yuanling County in Hunan Province – a student at Japan's No. 7 Institute of Higher Learning (equivalent to a preparatory school for Chinese universities), and a representative of overseas students in Japan.

Bao Huiseng, born in 1894, aged 27, from Huanggang in Hubei Province. While he did not have a permanent job, he was working temporarily at a printing press after being introduced by Chen Duxiu to Su Xinfu, who published *New Youth* magazine. He was appointed as a representative by Chen Duxiu.

Editors, journalists, students, and teachers made up the majority of the 13 representatives, as well as the majority of the 50-odd Party members in China at that time. The oldest representative was 45-year-old He Shuheng, and the youngest was 19-year-old Liu Renjing. The average age of the representatives was 28 years, which coincidentally was Mao Zedong's age.

In addition, two representatives from the Comintern were present at the First National Congress. They were:

Maring, born in 1883, aged 38 – a Dutchman, and a Comintern representative.

Nikolski, born in 1898, aged 23 – Russian, secretary of the Far East Bureau of the Comintern and a representative of the Red International of Labor Unions (RILU, also known as the Profintern).

The First National Congress of the Communist Party of China on 23 July 1921 was presided over by Zhang Guotao, who had been elected at the preparatory meeting the day before, with Mao Zedong and Zhou Fohai taking the minutes and Li Hanjun and Liu Renjing as English translators.

After Zhang Guotao had announced the commencement of the Congress, he started off by briefly reporting on the preparatory work that had been done to organize the meeting, before stating the agenda. He also read out the letter that Chen Duxiu had entrusted Chen Gongbo to bring along. Zhang was followed by the Comintern representatives Maring and Nikolski, who both delivered rousing speeches.

In a commanding and booming voice, Maring declared, "The formal establishment of the Communist Party of China will have a profound impact on the world. The Communist International now has a new branch in the East, and the Soviet Bolsheviks now have a new comrade here." Maring explained the nature, organization, mission, and other matters relating to the Third International, and said, "I hope our Chinese comrades will work hard, and under the guidance of the Communist International, will make their due contribution by uniting the proletariat all around the world." Maring went on to talk about his experience of forming the Communist Party of Indonesia in Java. He spoke for three or four hours, in English, and seemed very much to be a world revolutionary as he expounded on his bold vision. His speech left a very deep impression on Mao Zedong, who described the Dutchman as being "full of energy and blessed with the gift of eloquence," while Bao Huiseng commented that he was "eloquent, and had the talent to artfully maneuver through difficult political situations."

When Nikolski tried to speak, he faced a huge roadblock. None of the 13 Chinese representatives present understood Russian. Fortunately, he spoke a little English, while Maring knew some Russian, so Nikolski could still attempt to make a very brief speech. He congratulated everyone on the formal establishment of the Communist Party of China, and briefly explained the work done so far by the RILU and the Far East Bureau of the Comintern. He expressed his belief that the Chinese Communist Party needed to pay attention to developing the labor movement. He also suggested that the proceedings of the Congress should be swiftly reported to the Far East Bureau by telegraph.

It was midnight by the time Nikolski finished speaking. The meeting was then declared over for the day. The representatives left in groups via the back door of the Li Mansion, and returned quietly to their homes under the cover of darkness.

On 24 July – the second day of the Congress – representatives reported the status and progress of the members in their respective regions. On this day, Mao Zedong made a speech, primarily to explain the efforts of the communists in Changsha thus far. This was Mao's only official speech at the Party Congress. Other than that, he was remembered as a man of few words, who listened attentively to what others had to say.

No sessions were held on 25 or 26 July. The main objective of these two days was to draft the Party's guiding principles as well as future plans. The drafting team included Li Da, Li Hanjun, Zhang Guotao, Dong Biwu, and Liu Renjing. After two days of intense work, the team produced the first drafts of the 'First Program of the Communist Party of China' and the 'First Resolution of the Communist Party of China,' which were presented to the representatives for discussion.

Three consecutive days of talks were held from 27 to 29 July.

The three days of discussion were fruitful. The representatives reached a basic agreement on the main issues of the Party's name, nature, program, and organizational principles. They decided that the name of the party would be the Communist Party of China. It would be the party of the working class, and the nerve center of the proletarian revolution. The basic task of the Party was to lead the proletariat in revolutionary struggle to overthrow the bourgeois state apparatus, implement the dictatorship of the proletariat, and eliminate private ownership, with the ultimate aim of installing socialism and communism.

However, the representatives had their differences and even disputes when it came to issues such as whether Party members could take official posts in the current administration, how to tackle the northern Beiyang and southern Nationalist governments, the Party's current goals and tactics, and the relationship between the CPC and the Comintern.

During the discussion of the conditions of Party membership, there was a debate as to whether Party members could be 'officials' in the present government. Chen Gongbo argued that it was possible, because he was serving as Director of the Promotional Training Institute in Guangdong, while Chen Duxiu was serving as Chairman of the Guangdong Provincial Education Committee – a not insignificant 'official.' Li Hanjun agreed with him. However, the majority of the representatives believed that the CPC was a proletarian party, and therefore its members should not be officials in a bourgeois government. The two sides argued endlessly, and in the end the issue was consciously avoided. Ultimately, the article written on the Party's program adopted at this meeting read: "Party members shall not serve as government officials or members of Congress unless compelled by law to do so and without the Party's charter. Soldiers, police officers, and clerks are not subject to this restriction." This article was again hotly debated at the Second Congress in 1922.

When discussing their views and attitudes toward the northern and southern governments and other political parties of the time, the representatives believed that the Beiyang warlord government in Beijing was reactionary, and that it must be opposed and defeated from the standpoint of the people. However, the representatives' attitudes diverged with regard to the Kuomintang led by Sun Yat-sen, and its southern government in Guangzhou.

According to Bao Huiseng and others, Guangzhou was full of "soldierless commanders," casinos, tobacco shops, and brothels, and there was no flavor of revolution. The southern government was also engaged in military dictatorship, just like its northern counterpart. The Party could not be associated with the southern government, let alone compromise with Sun Yat-sen. Most delegates disagreed with this view, including Dong Biwu and Li Hanjun. They believed that the revolution carried out by Sun Yat-sen since the founding of the League should still be affirmed, that Sun's doctrine was also progressive, and that Sun must not be compared with Xu Shichang. Others said that the leader of the Party (Chen Duxiu) was still serving in the Guangdong government, meaning that the southern government was clearly better than its northern counterpart, and that the two should be treated differently and not be generalized. Failing to reach a consensus, they decided not to dwell further on the subject of the southern Government, but expressed a clear attitude of exclusionary non-cooperation towards other political parties.

When discussing the current goals of the Party's struggle and the means that they wished to employ, two completely different paradigms emerged. The most active and controversial speakers were Li Hanjun – who had read and researched Marx's works the most deeply – and Liu Renjing – who was politically inexperienced but daring.

Given the October Revolution in Soviet Russia and the revolution started by the German Socialist Party (DSP), Li Hanjun pondered over the kind of party and political platform that the CPC should adopt. They would have to send representatives to Soviet Russia and Germany to do on-the-ground research, then set up a research institute in China to conduct more in-depth analysis before arriving at a final decision. As it stood, the Chinese communists were to focus on their publicity and outreach, and support the revolutionary movement led by Sun Yat-sen. If the revolution turned out to be successful, they could participate in the parliamentary sessions.

On this particular subject, the youngest and most impetuous representative – Liu Renjing from Beijing – spoke with vigor and passion, and crossed swords with Li Hanjun. Liu resolutely decried the parliamentary model of democratic socialist parties in Western Europe, and all their reformist ideas. He felt that the Communist Party of China ought not only be a Marxist research group, but should also not have too many illusions regarding collaborating with the Kuomintang and other parliamentary bodies. They should actively engage in the labor movement and ready themselves for the communist revolution. He advocated that the CPC should be rooted in revolutionary Marxism, and not shy away from using arms to secure political power, in order to establish a dictatorship of the proletariat and realize communism as the supreme principle. He suggested that the Party platform clearly stipulate that only proletariat-led leadership could save China from the depths of the abyss. His impassioned speech certainly made its mark on the representatives, and the majority present agreed with this view.

On the topic of the dynamics between the Communist Party of China and the Comintern, the representatives also differed slightly in their stances. Maring had made clear his position on behalf of the Comintern during his address at the opening ceremony. Nikolski also received clear instructions from Irkutsk's Far East Bureau of the Comintern, saying that the CPC's Congress "needed to include him."

On this matter, the representatives were more inclined to agree with Li Hanjun's opinion that the CPC could accept the theoretical guidance of the Comintern and be concerted in their actions, but it was not necessary to explicitly make the CPC a branch of the Comintern. The representatives also advocated using the term 'United Communist International' in the Party Program. As such, the following was written in the resolution: "The Party's Central Committee should report to the Third International monthly. If necessary, an official representative should be sent to the Far East Bureau of the Third International in Irkutsk. In addition, representatives could also be sent to other countries in the Far East to discuss plans for mutual cooperation in the class struggle."

Evidently, the representatives all agreed that the Communist Party of China should be in regular contact with the Comintern and other fraternal parties, in order to strengthen their support and cooperation in the proletarian revolutionary struggle. However, it is worth noting that the word "union" used in the Party Program did not explicitly spell out a clear link in the relationship, with the Comintern in the leadership position. It was not until a year later that the 'Resolution of the Communist Party of China Joining the Communist International' was passed at the Second National People's Congress, which clarified, "The Communist Party of China is the Chinese branch of the Communist International."

Topics such as the relationship that the CPC should have with the current government, and determining whether the goals of the struggle and the direction of the actions taken were in line with their own expectations, were brand-new for the youthful Chinese communists. It was very normal for there to be differences of opinion and even the occasional dispute.

After much debate, the drafts of the Party Program and Resolution were filled with many scribbled revisions before being finalized.

On the evening of 29 July, Maring had proposed that the proceedings for the following day be moved to a different location, so as not to attract the attention of the police patrols. No one paid much heed to his suggestion. Moreover, as there was only one evening left of the Congress, and given the fact that it would have been difficult to find another suitable location nearby in such a short span of time, they decided to hold the meeting on 30 July in the same location, as per the original plan.

4

SPIES DISRUPT THE MEETING AT SOUTH LAKE

The evening of 30 July was quite stuffy. The First National People's Congress had been going on for seven days, and would have concluded that night if everything had gone according to plan. As night fell, the representatives converged in small groups on the Li Mansion with a slightly more relaxed pace, along with Maring and Nikolski. Only Zhou Fohai was unable to attend due to sudden and severe stomach troubles. He had to lie down and rest in his lodgings at the Bowen Girls' School, so that he missed the meeting.

That evening, the Congress held its sixth day of talks. According to the original plan, the session would begin with a speech by a Comintern representative, before discussing and adopting the 'First Program of the Communist Party of China' and the 'First Resolution of the Communist Party of China,' electing the central organization, and declaring the formal establishment of the CPC.

At around 8pm, the representatives were sitting round the long table. Just as the meeting was about to begin, a middle-aged man clad in gray, whom none of them recognized, suddenly barged through the back door of the Li Mansion, which had been left ajar. He took a good look at all the people in the room. The sudden appearance of this uninvited guest immediately aroused suspicion.

Li Hanjun asked him, "Who are you looking for?"

The man replied casually and vaguely, "I'm looking for Chairman Wang of the Social Council." Then, he bowed slightly and said, "I'm sorry. I must be in the wrong place," before rushing out.

There was indeed a social council near the premises, but there was no chairman, and no one with the last name Wang. Their suspicion grew. Comintern representative Maring, who had a lot of experience in intelligence and espionage, declared without hesitation, "He must have been a secret agent! I suggest that the meeting be stopped immediately. Everyone needs to leave quickly!"

In a flash, most of the representatives evacuated the Li Mansion and fled in all directions.

Of course, Li Hanjun could not leave, as he lived there. Chen Gongbo stayed with him. Chen explained his reasoning in his personal memoir *The Cold Wind Collection*, "By nature, I am a person who is upright and uncompromising. The good-for-nothing [Zhang] Guotao was oblivious to the danger that his comrade was in. I sympathized with [Li] Hanjun for the predicament he suddenly found himself in after everyone had fled. I was very upset, but surprisingly I also found the situation preposterously funny. Everyone else had left, but here I was, refusing to leave. I just carried on chatting with Hanjun, to learn more about him, and to understand why there was so much animosity between him and Guotao."[1]

Less than a quarter of an hour after the delegates had left the meeting, two police cars from the French Concession Police stopped at the entrance of Wangzhi Road. Out came a French chief inspector with four detectives, one heavily armed French soldier, and three interpreters. In the blink of an eye, the Li Mansion was plunged into a state of danger, and the atmosphere suddenly became tense.

The French chief inspector entered the house with several secret agents. Li Hanjun and Chen Gongbo were first separated into different rooms before the agents began searching the house from top to bottom. After much effort, they found no evidence that was of value, except for a few books about introducing and promoting socialism. Perhaps the most dangerous item in the house was the draft of the Party Program in a drawer, but it went unnoticed by the spies who searched the room. This was because it had been discussed and revised over the course of many days, and the handwriting was very messy and unclear.

---

1. Ye, Yonglie. *The Red Beginning: How The Communist Party of China Was Created*, Sichuan People's Publishing House, 2016, p. 267–268.

The search yielded nothing, so the French chief inspector turned to interrogation. The first question was who owned the house. Li Hanjun answered in French.

The French chief inspector asked, "Why was there a meeting here?"

Li replied, "There was no meeting. Just a few professors and students catching up on old times and having a chat."

The French chief inspector asked, "What were two foreigners doing here? Why are there socialist books in the house?"

Li Hanjun replied calmly, "They were British professors from Peking University. They're in Shanghai as part of an academic exchange during the summer vacation. As for these books, I'm a teacher and also an editor at the Commercial Press, so I need to have a lot of books at home to do my research."

Chen Gongbo was kept in another room for questioning. The detective mistakenly thought he was Japanese, so he asked him when he arrived in China. Chen explained, "I'm Chinese, and I'm a newlywed on my honeymoon. I took my wife from Guangzhou to Hangzhou for a visit. We passed through Shanghai, so we decided to stay for a few days."

As the chief inspector found no evidence of political activities, and after learning that this was the residence of General Li Shucheng (Li Hanjun's elder brother, and a former military undersecretary in the Office of the Presidential Palace), the tense atmosphere eased considerably. The French chief inspector spoke to Li Hanjun and Chen Gongbo, as if to warn them: "Today, we could have sealed the entire house off and arrested you all. However, as you are intellectuals, I've decided to make an exception." Finally, the French chief inspector left with his secret agents. Although no arrests were made, spies were still deployed in the area, and the authorities continued their monitoring.

The representatives were very fortunate to have fled the scene so quickly. Otherwise, the loss to the establishment of the Party would have been incalculable. This false alarm, however, presented its own unsolved "mystery" for a long time. Who was the secret agent who barged into the premises?

Later, Party historians got to the bottom of the "mystery" after much research. The man was Cheng Ziqing. He was born in Zhenjiang in Jiangsu Province in 1882, and attended a private school for three years. While working as an assistant at a rice shop for several years, he trained intensely, and thus was known for his extraordinarily strong arms. This caught the attention of Huang Jinrong – an influential man in Shanghainese circles, who recommended him for a job with the police in the French Concession. Cheng started out patrolling, before being promoted as an inspector. During his employment there, he performed his duties in an exemplary fashion. After the birth of the PRC in 1949, Song Qingling (wife of Sun Yat-sen) put a good word in for him to the authorities, considering that his actions in 1921 would have made him liable to be punished. Fortunately, Cheng Ziqing did not suffer too much censure, and managed to spend the rest of his days peacefully, passing away from ill health in Shanghai in 1961. Thus, the curtain fell on this "mystery."

During the night of 30 July, the evacuated delegates dispersed and took cover.

The two foreigners, Maring and Nikolski, looked very conspicuous, and would most certainly be followed, so they left the French Concession quickly, moving between locations around the city, before heading back to their own lodgings.

Some of the representatives who were staying at Bowen Girls' School dared not return to the premises straight away, for fear that the place would already be full of spies monitoring their every move. They decided to traverse the lanes and alleys, before quietly making their way to No. 2 Old Yuyang Lane, where the couple Li Da and Wang Huiwu were residing, as well as Chen Duxiu's wife Gao Junman.

Mao Zedong was brave enough to sneak back to Bowen Girls' School alone to check on the situation. Zhou Fohai – who did not attend the meeting at Li Mansion that night because of stomach troubles – was fast asleep. He was awoken from his slumber by someone making his way up the stairs. In a whisper, Mao asked him if anyone had been searching the premises. Zhou Fohai was shocked to hear this, and realized that the meeting had been plunged into jeopardy. The two felt that it would be better to head over to Li Da's house to discuss their next course of action, and made their way there as quietly as possible.

Many of the representatives ended up gathering at Li Da's house by sheer coincidence. After much discussion, they all agreed that the Congress should not continue in Shanghai. They would need to change locations.

So where could they go to conduct their meeting safely?

A few suggested Hangzhou, the capital of Zhejiang Province. While everyone agreed that it had its merits, it was far too bustling a metropolis, and they would run the risk of being noticed if they gathered there. At that critical moment, Wang Huiwu had a brainwave: "Here's an idea. I'm from Tongxiang County in Zhejiang Province, and I went to school in nearby Jiaxing. Jiaxing isn't as busy as Hangzhou, and it is closer to Shanghai, so it's more convenient. South Lake is close to the railroad station, but it doesn't attract many tourists. There are boats on the lake. We can pretend to be tourists, and rent them for our meetings." This suggestion sat well with everyone, and they immediately made plans to move to Jiaxing's South Lake.

Just to be on the safe side, the representatives travelled south by rail in two groups, each buying tickets at different sections and pretending not to know one another. The two international representatives, Maring and Nikolski, were worried that their foreign looks would make them conspicuous targets and thus expose them, so they did not attend the meeting in Jiaxing. Chen Gongbo, who had already had a brush of bad luck on the night of 30 July, found himself in another harrowing situation at the crack of dawn the next day. There was a fatal shooting at the hotel he was staying at. After these two back-to-back incidents, he decided he could not stay any longer in Shanghai. He forwent the opportunity to attend the meeting at South Lake, and hurriedly made his way to Hangzhou with his new wife.

Jiaxing is an ancient city rich in culture that stretches back millennia. During the Qin Dynasty (221–206 BCE), it was known as Youquan County. During the Three Kingdoms era (220–280 CE), the State of Wu called it Jiaxing County. South Lake is a scenic spot there, named after its location in the south of city. Along with the charming West Lake in Hangzhou and the elegant East Lake in Shaoxing, these bodies of water in Zhejiang Province are collectively known as the 'Three Famous Lakes.' South Lake has an island where the famous Misty Rain Tower is located. It also features prominently in a poem by one of most famous Tang dynasty poets, Du Mu (803–852 CE). "There are 480 temples of the Southern Dynasty. How many of them are obscured by the misty rain?"

Wang Huiwu booked two rooms at the Yuan Lake Hotel near South Lake, and asked the hotel's accountant to help them rent a traditional pleasure boat. After the safe arrival of both groups of representatives in Jiaxing, they hopped on a little vessel that took them to the pleasure boat in the middle of the lake.

The boat they took was one of the well-furnished pleasure craft that plied the lake. The broad, flat bow was sheltered by an arbor, which protected passengers from the sun and rain as they enjoyed the scenery. The middle cabin was decked with tables and chairs where passengers could eat and have a cup of tea. The rear cabin allowed passengers to rest, and provided accommodation for the crew. To ensure that the final day of the Congress proceeded safely, the representatives brought along musical instruments and *mahjong* sets, and prepared tables full of food in order to pass as regular tourists. Wang Huiwu even dressed up as a singer, although in reality she sat in the bow of the boat and kept watch, like a soldier on sentry duty.

In her capacity as a staff member making arrangements for the Congress, Wang became the only non-representative participant at the First National Congress of the Communist Party of China.

At about 11am, the closing meeting of the Congress took place on board the vessel. In the course of the meeting, the representatives debated and adopted the 'First Program of the Communist Party of China.' Although short, with 15 articles and about 700 words, it was the first official document of the Party. The name of the Party was henceforth formalized as the 'Communist Party of China.' Next, the 'First Resolution of the Communist Party of China' was discussed and adopted, which aligned with the goals stipulated in the Party Program. It proposed that the Party should concentrate its efforts on leading the labor movement, and made specific provisions for its organization and publicization.

The Congress progressed smoothly into the afternoon. Suddenly, a loud 'tuk-tuk-tuk' sound came out of nowhere. A motorboat was coming towards them. All the representatives could think was that it must have been a patrol boat from the local police force. All the documents were put away, and they began to play *mahjong*. The motorboat swept by the side of their boat, but fortunately they were not on the lookout for any signs of trouble. Later, it emerged that it was merely a boat carrying a large local family who were just throwing a celebration for a one-month-old baby. On realizing that it had nothing to do with the police, the representatives heaved a sigh of relief.

The meeting then discussed and adopted the 'Declaration of the First National Congress of the Communist Party of China.' Since the Party was still operating in secrecy, the Declaration was not announced publicly until much later. The Congress also elected the Central Politburo of the Party. Due to the small number of Party members and the fact that local operations were ill-equipped, the Congress decided not to set up a Central Executive Committee in the interim, and establish a Central Bureau first. Chen Duxiu was unanimously elected as the Secretary of the Central Bureau, Li Da as the Director of Publicity, and Zhang Guotao as the Director of the Organization.

At about 6pm, the First National Congress of the Communist Party of China was officially concluded. "Let's shout the slogan again! But remember to keep your voice down." The representatives called out softly in unison, "Long live the Communist Party of China!"

It was a low cry, but it was powerful nonetheless, and to this day its echoes reverberate around the world.

The little red boat on Jiaxing's South Lake bore the weight of history, and witnessed the birth of the Communist Party of China. It sowed the seeds for the Chinese revolution, and was the starting point of the cross-century voyage of the CPC.

Thirty-five years later, in 1956, Dong Biwu returned to the site of the inaugural Congress at No. 106 Wangzhi Road (re-designated in 1943 as No. 76 Xingye Road) and was deeply touched. He borrowed a few lines from *Man in The World* by renowned philosopher Zhuang Zi (c. 369 BCE – c. 286 BCE) and wrote this inscription: "It may have started off very humbly, but it ended with a strong finish." Indeed, what is miniscule, inconspicuous, and not worthy of attention at the start, may turn into a force that is so impactful and consequential that it cannot be ignored.

Forty-two years later, in 1963, when Dong Biwu revisited South Lake and recounted that fateful day, he wrote the following words: "The revolution was born right here at the Misty Rain Tower. The spark that ignited here became as fiery as the stars. While the volatile world turns dormant every spring, the thunder of the revolution can still be heard everywhere."

The secret gathering of 13 representatives was a landmark event that changed the future and destiny of one fifth of the world's population. It was a milestone in the rewriting of the fate of modern China.

China produced the Communist Party, which was a monumental event in the history of the country.

With the CPC, the Chinese people's revolutionary struggle gained a scientific and methodical guiding ideology, and set off on a clear path towards the goal of realizing socialism and communism.

With the CPC, the Chinese people's revolutionary struggle gained a strong leadership core, and the distressed and suffering Chinese people gained reliable leaders and organizers.

With the CPC, the movement to liberate the Chinese nation became a significant part of the global socialist revolutionary movement, and the people began to see that a brighter future would be within reach in the struggle for freedom and independence.

5

THE ORIGINAL MISSION SPURS A GREAT UNDERTAKING

HEROIC PEOPLE ALWAYS SHOW THEIR mettle in troubled times.

After the First National Congress of the Communist Party of China, the 13 representatives who attended embarked on a new journey.

In the turbulence and fervor of revolutionary times, choosing a belief is akin to selecting a life pathway. The power of the resolution of a belief determines the direction of life, and affects the progress of revolutionary development. The 13 Congress representatives experienced many trials and tribulations along the way, and ended up leading very different lives. Some devoted themselves to ideals, while others made sacrifices. Some made mistakes, and some turned back from the wrong path. Some betrayed the cause, and others were completely discredited.

Such differentiation is inevitable in the progress of history, the philosophy of which is both illuminating and thought-provoking. In summary, the life paths of the 13 representatives can be divided into five general types:

Type 1: Representatives who remained devoted to their original aspiration, and fought for it their whole lives.

An original aspiration is the initial wish of an individual or a party. It requires the pursuit of dreams through action, and necessitates potential at the beginning of a life and career. An original aspiration is the most pure, the most passionate, and the most beautiful because it indicates that an individual can proceed without hesitation, full of hope, and at peace with themselves. An original aspiration directly influences ideals and paths on the way forward. However, original aspiration alone is not enough. One needs resolution, determination, confidence, and ambition in order to persist with revolution. Among the 13 representatives, Mao Zedong, Dong Biwu, and Wang Jinmei faced challenging revolutionary struggles. They experienced a variety of failures and tests, yet rose up and devoted the best years of their lives to their revolutionary careers. Their initial aspirations and beliefs when joining the Communist Party of China never changed.

Mao Zedong was only 28 years old when he joined the CPC. Immediately after the First Congress, he went back to Changsha and established a Party organization there. As one of the founding members of the CPC, Mao demonstrated the indomitable will of a revolutionary leader in terms of both his pursuits and his beliefs. This involved addressing the question "how long can we persevere?" in the revolutionary dilemma, and risking being underestimated under Wang Ming's leadership. It included achieving revolutionary goals at Zunyi, leading the army north, and uniting with enemies in the Anti-Japanese War to take control of the situation and liberate China. Mao's determination led him to found the People's Republic of China from scratch, and allowed him to feed and clothe the entire nation. His revolutionary work included changing the world's image of China as weak in the Korean War to making it an influential country through the invention of two types of bombs and one satellite. All of these deeds were embedded with the belief, determination, and responsibilities of the generation of communists that Mao Zedong represented as a core founder of the Communist Party of China, the Chinese People's Liberation Army, and the People's Republic of China. On 9 September 1976, Mao died of ill health at 83 years old. He had lived up to his promises and adhered to his initial aspiration with high virtue and unceasing struggle.

Dong Biwu was seven years older than Mao Zedong, and was a *xiucai* (one who passed the imperial examination at the county level during the Ming and Qing eras) during the Qing Dynasty. He was one of only two *xiucai* among the 13 representatives, the other being He Shuheng. There is a proverb that states "a *xiucai* will not rebel even after 10 years." However, Dong Biwu contributed to the great revolutionary cause through many decades of fighting. The Central Committee wrote to him on his 60th birthday: "Your revolutionary battle has witnessed every period of fighting from the Revolution of 1911, the May Fourth Movement, and the Northern Expedition, to China's War of Liberation, and represents the glorious history of the liberation of the Chinese nation." This is an ideal summary of this great man's persistent pursuit of his initial aspiration. After the founding of New China, Dong Biwu was an important leader of the Party and the nation. He died of ill health on 2 April 1975 in Beijing, at the age of 89.

Wang Jinmei was still a student when he attended the First National Congress. During the Congress, he changed the characters in his name from 烬梅 (jìn méi) to 尽美 (jìn měi, meaning 'perfection'), in order to display his willingness to dedicate his life to the fight for a perfect world. After the Congress, he acted as a representative of the CPC, attending the first congresses of national revolutionary groups and communists in Far Eastern countries held by the Comintern in Moscow. From 1923 until May 1925, he worked as Secretary of the Provincial Party Committee in Shandong Province, and devoted himself to his revolutionary career. Soon after, he collapsed from overwork, and died at the young age of 27 on 19 August 1925. He was the first Party representative to pass away.

Type 2: Representatives who devoted themselves to the pursuit of truth.

Revolution is fierce, and the battle is cruel. Sacrifice is inevitable in the process. Revolutionaries must have guts and courage. They must not be afraid to make sacrifices, and must always face up to their responsibilities with passion. These characteristics are perfectly reflected in Party representatives He Shuheng, Deng Enming, and Chen Tanqiu, who dedicated their whole careers to the pursuit of truth, and gave their lives to protect it.

He Shuheng was 45 years old when he attended the First Congress, and was the oldest of the 13 representatives. After the Congress, he went back to Changsha with Mao Zedong, where they re-established Party organizations and carried out revolutionary work. In the Central Soviet Area, he stood firmly against the "leftist" ideology of Wang Ming, and was removed from office. After the failure of the fifth counter-campaign against encirclement and suppression, the Red Army was forced to withdraw from the central revolutionary base. He Shuheng's fellow communist elders Lin Boqu, Dong Biwu, Xu Teli, and Xie Juezai were all ratified to transfer with the main force of the Red Army, but he was not. On 24 February 1935, He Shuheng met with enemy aggression and was killed. He was 58 years old.

Deng Enming was the only member of an ethnic minority in the First Congress, born into a family of the Shui nationality in Libo County, Guizhou Province. After the Congress, the organization appointed him to lead the labor movement in Shandong Province. He was arrested In 1925, and was rescued by the organization and released on medical parole. In 1928 he was re-arrested, and tried unsuccessfully to escape from prison twice. In the farewell poem he penned for his mother, he wrote, "I shall die first. As long as the next generations can inherit our revolutionary careers, I will be comfortable in the afterlife." He was killed by Kuomintang reactionaries in Jinan on 5 April 1931, at the age of 30.

At the time of the First Congress, Chen Tanqiu was the person in charge of the early organization of the Communist Party in Wuhan. After the Congress, he was put in charge of the Party organization there, and went on to lead a mass movement. In May 1939, Chen stopped in Xinjiang on his way back to Yan'an after attending the Seventh National Congress of the Comintern, and was appointed to form a united front with Sheng Shicai – the so-called 'King of Xinjiang.' In 1942, Sheng Shicai blamed a fabricated communist rebellion conspiracy on Chen Tanqiu and others, and arrested them. He then tried to persuade Chen to sign a "statement of secession," but Chen declined. In the middle of the night on 27 September 1943, Chen Tanqiu was secretly murdered. He was 47 years old. The news of his death never reached Beijing, and when the Seventh National Congress of the Party was held two years later, he was elected as a member of the Central Committee.

Type 3: Representatives who held too stubbornly to their initial aspirations.

Outstanding members of the Communist Party of China must always put the interests of the Party and the people first. They should pay attention to the interests of the whole, and be open and aboveboard. Mature members of the CPC must have backbone, and be upright and resilient. They must weather difficulties and misunderstandings, and should not judge matters from their own perspectives. They should handle contradictions within the Party properly, avoid interference, and move forward with determination. However, First National Congress representatives Li Da and Li Hanjun failed to realize these things and handle these matters correctly, leading to lifetimes of regret.

After Li Da joined the revolution, he began to study Marxism extensively, and won renown as a remarkable promotional activist. He spent a lot of time preparing for the First Congress, and was elected as Publicity Director of the Central Bureau. With his stubborn and forthright personality, Li was a typical Marxist scholar. While working at government offices in Shanghai, he ran into a series of conflicts with Chen Duxiu and Zhang Guotao. In the fall of 1923, he had a serious argument with Chen Duxiu about the cooperation between the KMT and CPC. Chen threatened to expel him from CPC, and Li was so angry that he quit the Party of his own accord. This was the biggest mistake of his life. Nevertheless, he never gave up on his ideals, and carried on studying and disseminating Marxism. Notably, he remained friends with Mao Zedong for decades. Before Mao's revolutionary victory over the Nationalists, he sent Li a coded telegram: "You were also a founder of this company. Now that the company's business is booming, I would like you to join us and work with us again." On receiving this telegram, Li Da gladly accepted the offer, and arrived in Peiping on 14 May 1949. In December that year, with Mao Zedong serving as a historical witness and Liu Shaoqi as a facilitator, Li Da rejoined the Communist Party of China. After the founding of the PRC, he held successive posts as President of Hunan University and Wuhan University. On 24 August 1966, at the age of 76, Li Da was purged to death in the 'Cultural Revolution.'

Another of the representatives present at the First National Congress suffered a tragic demise. However, at the time of his death, he was no longer a member of the CPC. This was Li Hanjun, who was once the Acting Secretary of the Shanghai Party organization, and used his brother's residence as the venue for the First National Congress. After the Congress, Li continued to devote himself to Marxist publicity and revolutionary activities. On the eve of the Second National Congress of the CPC in 1922, Chen Duxiu telegrammed Li Hanjun to invite him to attend the meeting, but Li did not show up. Instead he sent a letter of opinion, mainly stating his opposition to joining the Communist International. For this reason, the Party had done his work, but at this time there was a grievance between Li Hanjun, Zhang Guotao, and Chen Duxiu. What's more, his proposal was not adopted, so he began to distance himself from the Party's activities. When the CPC expelled him due to his self-secession, he wrote, "I can't be a member of the Communist

Party, but I can still be a communist. This puts my heart at ease." Although Li Hanjun did not participate in any Party activities thereafter, he never gave up his belief in Marxism, and did a lot of work for the revolution. During Chiang Kai-shek's Nationalist rebellion against the revolution, Li Hanjun was killed on 17 December 1927 by the Guangxi Clique as a 'communist ringleader.' He was 37 years old. Fortunately, Mao Zedong did not forget this martyr, even though Li had left the Party. In 1952, Mao wrote a 'Memorial Certificate for the Family Members of Revolutionary Martyrs' for Li's family: "Comrade Li made a glorious sacrifice in the great revolution, and his great achievements will be immortal!"

Type 4: Representatives who realized the error of their ways after their faith was challenged.

Revolution overthrows old systems and breaks old orders, then establishes a new system and a new order. Its process is bound to be hindered and resisted by old ideologies and reactionary forces. The resulting hardships can be severe. On the long revolutionary journey, it is inevitable that some people will waver when faced with difficulties and obstacles. They may even lose their way and go astray.

Liu Renjing was just 19 years old when he attended the First National Congress, and was the youngest of the Party representatives. Despite his young age, Liu spoke many times at the Congress, and later went on to work for the Youth League. In 1926, he went to the Soviet Union to study, but ended up going astray due to his stubbornness. On his way back to China in 1929, he visited Trotsky in Turkey. On returning home, he was expelled from the CPC for participating in Trotskyist activities, and went on to serve in the Kuomintang government. After the founding of the PRC, he realized the error of his ways, and went to Beijing in 1950. He was later employed as a counselor at the Counselor's Office of the State Council. He died in a car accident on 5 August 1987 at the age of 85.

Like Liu Renjing, Bao Huiseng left the Party and later returned. He was appointed by Chen Duxiu to attend the First National Congress, and afterwards did a lot of work for the revolution. After the failure of the Nanchang Uprising in 1927, Bao lost contact with the organization. Facing a revolutionary dilemma, he decided to quit the Party. He said, "I didn't make a statement in a newspaper. I didn't betray the organization or any Party members." He later worked at the Ministry of the Interior of the National Government, and went to live in Macao in 1948. In November 1949, with the approval of the Central Government, he returned to Beijing and was appointed as a counselor at the Counselor's Office of the State Council. He died of ill health on 2 July 1979 at the age of 85.

Type 5: Representatives who abandoned their ideals and left the Party.

A good beginning does not necessarily lead to a positive ending. On the path of revolution, it is inevitable that there will be mud and sand, dangerous shoals, undercurrents and whirlpools, and even some who rebel, such as Chen Gongbo, Zhou Fohai, and Zhang Guotao. However, their actions did not damage the positive image of the Communist Party of China. The Party organization became all the purer through distancing itself from these defectors.

Chen Gongbo was the first of the representatives at the First National Congress to leave the Party. In the summer of 1921, Chen was elected as a representative of the Party in Guangzhou, and traveled to Shanghai with his new wife. In the evening of 30 July, the Congress venue was attacked by spies, and a murder was committed at the Dadong Hotel where Chen Gongbo was staying. This terrified him. He did not attend the re-arranged Congress meetings at Jiaxing's South Lake the following day, going instead to Hangzhou with his wife. After spending several days there, Chen returned to Shanghai and realized that the Congress had ended. After meeting with Zhang Guotao, Li Da, and Zhou Fohai, Chen Gongbo took a copy of the conference proceedings to Guangzhou for Chen Duxiu – the newly elected Secretary of the Central Committee of the CPC. By the time Chen Gongbo returned to Guangzhou, the warlord Chen Jiongming had defected. The Party organization decided to unite with Sun Yat-sen to fight Chen Jiongming, but Chen Gongbo refused to go along with it. He wrote to Chen Duxiu: "Hereafter, I will go my own way and no longer be subject to Party discipline." He later made it clear at a Party meeting that he would no longer perform Party duties. During the Anti-Japanese War, Chen Gongbo followed Wang Jingwei, betraying his country and seeking glory, and thus becoming the second traitor among the Congress representatives. After the defeat and surrender of the Japanese, Chen escaped to Japan but was escorted back to Nanjing. On 3 June 1946, he was executed by a firing squad at the Shizikou No. 3 Prison in Suzhou, Jiangsu Province. He was 56 years old.

The story of Zhou Fohai, another Party rebel, is also steeped in crime. In July 1921, Zhou was the only representative who came from abroad to attend the First National Congress of the Communist Party of China. After the Congress, he continued his studies in Japan, but developed a misunderstanding of Marxist theory, believing that it was too early for China to carry out a communist revolution. In his outlook on life, he upheld the vulgar philosophy that "ambition cannot satisfy hunger, and ideals cannot keep out the cold." On returning to China, Zhou Fohai broke three major Party rules: he did not pay Party fees, did not participate in Party activities, and spread discontent. In September 1924, he withdrew from the Party and turned away from communism, holding an important position in the Kuomintang government for many years. During the Anti-Japanese War, he took refuge with Wang Jingwei and became a traitor. After the surrender of Japan, Zhou was sentenced to death for the crime of conspiring with an enemy country and plotting to rebel against his homeland. His sentence was later reduced to life imprisonment. On 28 February 1948, at the age of 51, he died of ill health at Nanjing Prison.

Another notorious figure among the First National Congress representatives who eventually turned traitor was Zhang Guotao. Zhang was very active at the Congress, and was elected as Organization Director of the Central Bureau. Afterwards, he served as the Director of the Secretariat of the Chinese Labor Union. As a representative of the CPC, he traveled to Moscow to attend the first congresses of the communist parties and national revolutionary groups of Far Eastern countries, where he was cordially received by Lenin. This gave him special political capital. He later held an important position in the Party for many years. In 1935 during the Long March, after the First and Fourth Front battalions of the Red Army joined forces, Zhang led the Left Route army south to the Sichuan-Tibet border without authorization. There, he set up another 'Central Committee' and appointed himself chairman. In this capacity he carried out activities that split the Party and the Red Army, which caused great losses to the Fourth Front battalion. Zhang was forced to abolish this pseudo 'Central Committee' in 1936. In April 1938, he absconded from the border area on the pretext of visiting the mausoleum of the Yellow Emperor. He passed through Xi'an on his way to Wuhan, took refuge in the Kuomintang, and later became a military spy. He fled to Hong Kong in 1949, and died in Canada at the age of 82 in 1979.

Only when there is comparison can there be identification; only where there is identification can there be consensus.

The various life outcomes of the representatives of the First National Congress of the Communist Party of China show that only by keeping our original aspiration in mind can we guarantee a bright future.

Firm ideals and beliefs are the spiritual support of the Communist Party of China. Only by persisting with the tenets of communism, abiding by the pledge made when joining the Party, persevering in the spirit of struggle, and never slacking off can we move in the right direction, keeping the revolutionary passion alive, not being afraid in the face of difficulties, resisting temptation, and never avoiding sacrifice. If we neglect these things, we risk becoming traitors and spies, betraying the Party and country, and degenerating into the dregs of society.

Lu Xun, who lived in the era of the First National Congress and could resonate with its themes, wrote in his essay 'A Radical Revolutionary Who is Not Revolutionary':

> "Because of different ultimate goals, there will always be soldiers who leave the battle along the way. Some will abandon it completely, some will become decadent, and some will rebel. However, as long as there is no obstacle in the way ahead, the army will move onwards, becoming purer and more elite as time goes by."[1]

Engels wrote, "Where history starts, the ideological process should also start." The great cause of the Communist Party of China, the many contributions of its pioneers, and the heroic sacrifices of the early revolutionaries gave birth to the great spirit of Party building. In 2005, Xi Jinping – who was then Secretary of the Zhejiang Provincial Party Committee – summed up the great course of the founding of the Communist Party of China, describing the so-called 'Red Boat Spirit' for the first time. It consists of:

1. *My Second Social Class: Collected Essays*, People's Literature Publishing House, 1973, p. 29.

The spirit of creativity: To initiate and take the lead.

The spirit of striving: To be firm in one's ideals and never yield.

The spirit of dedication: To found the Party for the interests of the people, and be loyal to them.

This 'Red Boat Spirit' embodies the Party-building impetus of the CPC, depicting its original "why start?" mission, and answers the historical question "where did the Communist Party of China come from?" It is the source of the Chinese revolutionary spirit, offering valuable spiritual wealth for the prosperity of the Party and nation, as well as strong support for the promotion of socialism with Chinese characteristics in the new era.

PART 7

A New Chapter:

From the Labor Movement to the Launch of the Peasant Movement, the Youth Movement, and the Women's Movement

As Mao Zedong so incisively wrote in his *On Practice*, "Marxism values theory precisely and only because it can guide action. If we have a theory, and simply talk about, leaving it on the shelf instead of utilizing it in practice, then no matter how good the theory is, it will be meaningless."[1]

The guiding principle and resolution adopted by the First National Congress of the Communist Party of China was that Party members should successfully mobilize workers, peasants, soldiers, and students, emphasizing the importance of an effective labor movement. The 'Resolution on the Constitution of the Communist Party' that was adopted at the Second National Congress of the Communist Party of China in July of the following year stressed that the CPC was not "a Marxist society organized by intellectuals," nor a "revolutionary group through which a handful of communists were cutting themselves off from the masses." Instead, "it should be a party organized by the masses with the most revolutionary proletarian spirit, to fight for the interests of the proletariat and be the vanguard of the proletariat revolutionary movement." To this end, it would have to "go to the people" and form a large "mass party."

1. *Selected Works of Mao Zedong, Vol. 1*, People's Publishing House, 1991, p. 292

Thus, since its founding, the Communist Party of China has used Marxism-Leninism as its guiding theory in the work of liberating all of mankind and realizing communism, maintaining close contact with the masses, and launching and publicizing the struggle for the welfare and wellbeing of the people.

The founders of the Communist Party of China were all revolutionary intellectuals, and the original Party members were mainly advanced elements such as Li Dazhao and Chen Duxiu (who were already famous), as well as Mao Zedong and Deng Zhongxia (who were relatively new to the political world). Regardless of their backgrounds, they all threw themselves into their work alongside peasants and laborers, using mobilization and reliance on the masses as the fundamental and most basic method of realizing the Party's goals.

As a result, shortly after the successful First National Congress of the Communist Party of China, and with the efforts of local Party organizations, a new chapter in the Chinese revolution was begun with the launch of a new labor movement, peasant movement, youth movement, and women's movement.

1

THE FIRST CLIMAX OF THE LABOR MOVEMENT

On 11 August 1921, at No. 19 North Chengdu Road in Shanghai's International Settlement (now No. 899 North Chengdu Road), there stood a two-story east-facing *shikumen*-style house. A wooden sign hung on the front of it, which read 'Secretariat of the Chinese Labor Union.'

The walls of the house were made of green and red brick. There were dormer windows in the sloped roof, and black lacquered doors with Western-style relief decorations on both sides. Left idle for many years, it was covered with dust, not unlike many of the other *shikumen*-style houses nearby.[1] However, many of the people who passed by that day were puzzled when they saw the wooden sign, wondering what went on in this strangely-named organization.

In fact, it was the original head office from which the Communist Party of China openly led the national labor movement, and the predecessor of the All-China Federation of Trade Unions.

There are historical reasons for its name. At that time, there were many trade unions in Shanghai, most of which were controlled by gang leaders. Under the guise of representing the workers, they deceived and cheated them instead. During labor disputes and conflicts, these so-called unions made trouble for the workers, profiting from their plight and secretly protecting the interests of

1. Shanghai Writers' Association. *The Red Secret in the* Shikumen*: Stories from the Birthplace of the Party – Shanghai Revolutionary Sites Series*, Shanghai People's Publishing House, 2019, pp. 105–106.

the managers. This not only seriously damaged the reputation of genuine trade unions, but also placed a huge obstacle in the way of workers' ability to organize properly.[1]

In response to this situation, Chen Duxiu published the article 'The Reality of Workers' Unions' in the second issue of *Labor World* in August 1920. He wrote bitterly, "If workers want to improve their situation, there is no other way but to form unions. However, even another 10,000 workers' organizations in Shanghai will make no difference. Most of the new trade unions have been run by unscrupulous politicians, and most of the old guilds have been operated by gang leaders. Enlightened workers! Let's join together and form a real workers' union!"

As well as publishing this article, Chen Duxiu took urgent action. The Shanghai Machine Workers' Union held a meeting at the public school at No. 207 Baike Road on 21 November, announcing its formal establishment. In just over two months from its initiation to its founding meeting, its membership rapidly grew from dozens to 370 people. The magazine *Machine Workers* was published, and the union became one of the most influential in Shanghai at the time. It was the first union to be led directly by the Party, indicating the CPC's shift from the propagation phase to the organizational stage in regard to empowering the workforce.

Thereafter, in places where the early Communist Party organizations were active, they began to explore and establish new trade unions that were different from the old, gang-led ones. The new groups included the Beijing Changxindian Trade Union, the Hong Kong Chinese Seafarers' Industrial Federation, and the Hunan Labor Association.

The newly founded Communist Party of China decided to concentrate on leading the labor movement, and put the establishment of trade unions on the agenda. At the beginning of the 'First Resolution of the Communist Party of China' adopted at the First National Congress, it was pointed out that "the basic task of our Party is to set up industrial trade unions," specifically stipulating that "where there is more than one industrial department, trade

1. Shanghai Writers' Association. *The Red Secret in the* Shikumen*: Stories from the Birthplace of the Party – Shanghai Revolutionary Sites Series*, Shanghai People's Publishing House, 2019, p. 109.

unions should be organized; where there is no large industry but only one or two factories, factory trade unions can be set up that are more suitable for local conditions."[1]

Following the guidelines and arrangements put forward at the First National Congress, Party organizations all over the country began to establish trade unions of various kinds. In order to strengthen the centralized leadership of the labor movement, unite the local trade unions, and launch the movement on a broader scale, the CPC decided to set up a national trade union organization as its "public head office for the labor movement."[2]

As for the name of this head office, Zhang Guotao (who was in charge of the labor movement in the Central Committee at the time) thought that in order to distinguish it from the old trade unions of the time, it was better not to call it "trade union." Neither could it be called a "general trade union," because it was not an institution created by trade unions in various places. The Comintern representative Maring suggested following the example of the labor movements in other countries, and calling it the 'Secretariat of the Chinese Labor Union.'[3] This long, awkward name came from the English 'Trade Union Secretariat.' A labor union is a 'labor association,' which had been translated into Japanese as 'labor combination'; secretariat means 'secretarial department' or 'agency.' At that time, many new Western terms and concepts were introduced to China from Japanese.

In this way, the Secretariat of the Chinese Labor Union was officially established on 11 August 1921. Its director was Zhang Guotao, and its secretaries included Li Qihan, Li Zhenying, and Bao Huiseng. From the outset, great emphasis was placed on publicity and the mobilization of workers. On 20 August, in order to expand publicity and facilitate contacts, the Secretariat of the Chinese Labor Union founded its official publication, *Labor Weekly*. This was the first national workers' newspaper in China, and was a source of ideas

1. Central Archives: *Selected Documents of the Central Committee of the Communist Party of China, Vol. 1 (1921–1925)*, Party School of the Central Committee of the Communist Party of China Press, 1989, p. 6.
2. *The Collected Works of Deng Zhongxia*, People's Publishing House, 1980, p. 437.
3. Zhang, Guotao. *My Recollections, Vol. 1*, Modern Archives Publishing House, 1980, p. 151.

and inspiration for many workers, spurring their participation in trade union activities.[1]

In order to strengthen the guidance of the labor movement in various regions, the Secretariat of the Chinese Labor Union set up local branches in Beijing, Wuhan, Changsha, Guangzhou, and Jinan. All branches established night schools for workers, founded workers' magazines, and raised class consciousness among workers. They also established trade union organizations according to the principle of industrial combination, and led strikes, all of which played a positive role in promoting the development of the labor movement.

The dynamic development of the national labor movement even attracted the attention of Sun Yat-Sen. He sent people to Shanghai to contact Chen Duxiu, and asked the Secretariat of the Chinese Labor Union to convene a National Labor Congress. The Kuomintang was willing to give full support. After deliberation, Chen Duxiu agreed to the KMT's proposal. In May 1922, the Secretariat of the Chinese Labor Union held the first National Labor Conference in Guangzhou, and passed a bill that stated, "before the establishment of the All-China Federation of Trade Unions, the Secretariat of the Chinese Labor Union is the country's chief communication authority." This recognized the leading position of the Communist Party of China in the labor movement, and guided the working class towards national unity.

With the leadership of the CPC, the Chinese labor movement developed rapidly and healthily.

In January 1922, Hong Kong seafarers went on strike for more pay. Under the leadership of Su Zhaozheng – head of the Hong Kong Chinese Seafarers' Industrial Federation – plus Lin Weimin and other authority figures, they overcame all kinds of obstructions and sabotage by the Hong Kong and British establishments. The strike lasted for 56 days. The British and Hong Kong authorities were forced to cancel the closure of seafarers' unions, and promised to increase seafarers' wages by 15 to 30%. This was the first time that the Chinese working class engaged directly in a tit-for-tat struggle against imperialism. The victory of the strike greatly enhanced the labor force's courage and confidence in the struggle.

---

1. Shanghai Writers' Association. *The Red Secret in the* Shikumen*: Stories from the Birthplace of the Party – Shanghai Revolutionary Sites Series*, Shanghai People's Publishing House, 2019, p. 108

In the 13 months after the strike in January 1922 until February 1923, there were more than 100 strikes across the country, including the Anyuan Road Miners' Strike, the Kailuan Minmetals Strike, and the Beijing-Hankou Railroad Strike. More than 300,000 workers took part, setting off the first climax of the Chinese labor movement, and showing the power of the Chinese working class.

The Anyuan Road Miners' Strike led by Mao Zedong, Liu Shaoqi, and Li Lisan was the first time that the Communist Party of China had independently led and won a complete victory in the workers' struggle. It was a great feat in the history of the Chinese labor movement.

The Anyuan Road Mine was the collective term for the Anyuan Coal Mine in Pingxiang, Jiangxi Province, and the Zhuzhou-Pingxiang Railroad from Zhuzhou in Hunan Province to Pingxiang. The mine was founded in 1898, and was one of the largest in China at that time. It could produce more than 2,000 tons of coal, mainly as industrial fuel for Daye and Hanyang. In order to facilitate the transportation of coal, the Railroad and Mining Bureau built a special rail line from Anyuan to Zhuzhou to connect with the Yuehan road. Therefore, although Anyuan is located in Pingxiang in Jiangxi, it has close political and economic ties with Hunan Province. In 1907, Hanyang, Daye, and Anyuan established the Hanyeping company. The real power of the company belonged to the Japanese. The engineering was controlled by a German foreman, and the enterprise was administrated by a feudal leader. The miners at the Anyuan Road Mine were exploited and oppressed by Chinese and foreign capitalists and feudal contractors. Their lives were very difficult, and their working conditions were extremely bad. Corporal punishment and casualties often occurred. Anyuan road miners had fought back many times in the past, but had been brutally suppressed.

The newly-established Hunan Branch of the Communist Party and the Secretariat of the Chinese Labor Union saw the great importance of the Anyuan labor movement. In the fall and winter of 1921, Mao Zedong – then Secretary of the Hunan branch of the CPC – went to Anyuan twice to investigate and mobilize the workers. In February 1922, the Anyuan branch of the CPC was established, with Li Lisan as Secretary. In May, the Anyuan Road Mine Workers' Association was established, and Li Lisan was elected as the director. In July, the workers at the Hanyang Iron and steel plant (part of the Hanyeping company) went on strike, demanding higher wages and better treatment. After several days of struggle, they won. This greatly encouraged the Anyuan workers. At the same time, they were even more dissatisfied with the wage arrears from the Railroad and Mining Bureau, and began to plan a strike.

At the beginning of September, Mao Zedong went to Anyuan again. After investigating the situation, he felt that the conditions for a strike were ripe, so he arranged for Li Lisan to lead it. He then sent Liu Shaoqi to Anyuan to help Li launch and lead the strike. On 12 September, Li Lisan presided over the Anyuan branch meeting and established a strike headquarters, with himself as the commander-in-chief and Liu Shaoqi as the plenipotentiary representative of the association.

After hearing the news of the impending strike, the Anyuan Railroad and Mining Bureau threatened to dissolve the workers' association, expel its leaders, and dispatch the army to suppress it. The workers' association decided to fight back, and put forward conditions to the Railroad and Mining Bureau, such as protecting and subsidizing the association, and paying wage arrears, with a reply expected within two days or a strike would be held. The authorities refused on the grounds of financial difficulties.

On 14 September, more than 17,000 workers from the Anyuan Road Mine went on strike, proposing 17 conditions of negotiation. The main contents included: changing the association into a trade union; recognizing that the trade union had the right to negotiate on behalf of the workers; dismissing the staff of the Railroad and Mining Bureau with the consent of the trade union; paying wage arrears; abolishing the feudal contract system; and improving working and living conditions. To prevent damage, workers organized pickets to maintain order and protect equipment.

The Railroad and Mining Bureau was very shaken by the strike. They sent representatives to negotiate with the association, but also colluded with the warlords to send troops from a brigade in an attempt to suppress the strike and kill the commander-in-chief, Li Lisan. The workers were very angry, and immediately organized for thousands of people to protect the association and the strike leaders, launching face-to-face combat with the military police. On 16 September, Liu Shaoqi ventured to the martial law headquarters for negotiations along with the representative of the striking workers and others. In order to ensure the safety of the representative, thousands of strikers surrounded the headquarters and shouted, "If anyone dares to touch our representative, we will die at the hands of the authorities!" The Railroad and Mining Bureau still refused to accept the strike conditions. That night, strike commander Li Lisan stated that if the authorities did not agree to the terms of negotiation, he would leave Anyuan immediately and let the workers riot. The Railroad and Mining Bureau was afraid that the workers would destroy the mine if Li wasn't there, so it was forced to agree to continue the negotiations.

In the afternoon of 17 September, Li Lisan and the representative of the workers' association negotiated the conditions for the resumption of work with Li Yihuan (the representative of the Railroad Bureau), Shu Jihuan (the representative of the mine), and four businessmen who acted as mediators. Li Lisan stressed that the strike conditions should no longer be compromised. If they accepted it, the workers would return to work; if not, he would leave Anyuan. After five days of fierce struggle, the Railroad and Mining Bureau's conspiracy to sabotage the strike failed. Under great pressure, they had to give in, and basically accepted the strike conditions proposed by the workers. They merged the 17 conditions into 13, and signed them on the morning of 18 September. The Anyuan Road Miners' Strike achieved a major victory with no injuries – a unique event in the fledgling Chinese labor movement. The victory raised the prestige of the Communist Party of China among the workers, and expanded its influence.

Railroad workers were a major force in the first climax of the labor movement led by the CPC. In December 1922, the Central Committee of the Communist Party of China formulated the 'Plan for the Current Practical Problems,' which pointed out that among the Chinese working class, railroad workers, seafarers, and miners were "three powerful elements". Before the establishment of the All-China Federation of Trade Unions, it was necessary to establish a joint organization for these three industries as the backbone of the trade union movement. Among the railroad workers' uprisings organized by the Party, the most influential was the Beijing-Hankou Railroad Strike.

The Beijing-Hankou Railroad ran through the provinces of Zhili, Henan, and Hubei, and was the transportation lifeline that connected northern and central China. Its operating income was one of the main sources of pay and provision for warlord Wu Peifu's soldiers, and therefore had important economic, political, and military significance. The large-scale strike was triggered by the establishment of the All-Railroad Federation of Trade Unions.

By the end of 1922, trade unions had been set up at 16 major stations along the Beijing-Hankou Railroad, and the majority of workers were eager to establish a unified trade union organization for the entire line. In response, the preparatory committee of the Federation of Beijing-Hankou Railroad Trade Unions decided to hold its founding meeting in Zhengzhou on 1 February 1923. At that time, the establishment of a federation of trade unions did not involve specific economic issues between labor and capital, so it could be carried out in public. The committee submitted a report to Zhao Jixian – Director of the Beijing-Hankou Railroad Bureau – and published the news in various newspapers. However, fearing that the rising labor movement was a threat to his dictatorship, the warlord Wu Peifu prohibited the establishment of the Federation of Beijing-Hankou Railroad Trade Unions in Zhengzhou on the pretext that a meeting should not be held in a military region.

On 1 February 1923, in the depths of a cold winter, the city of Zhengzhou came under emergency martial law, with armed military police. More than 300 delegates and guests arrived at the venue – the Zhengzhou Puleyuan Theater – at 10am, including Zhang Guotao, Chen Tanqiu, and Luo Zhanglong from the Communist Party of China, representatives from the trade union branches of the Beijing-Hankou Railroad, delegates from the local trade unions, student representatives, and journalists. With red flags in their hands, and regardless of danger, the delegates and the vast contingent of workers broke through the heavy encirclement of the military police. They entered the venue, held their meeting, and announced the establishment of the Federation of Beijing-Hankou Railroad Trade Unions. The participants were in high spirits, chanting, "Long live the Federation!" and "Long live the victory of the working class!" Armed police had surrounded the venue, but delegates broke through the siege and left. On returning to the Wuzhou Hotel, they were surrounded again. Reactionary military police forcibly destroyed the clubhouse of the Federation of Trade Unions' Zhengzhou branch, and ordered all representatives to leave Zhengzhou immediately.

The delegates were very angry at this insult. In the evening of 1 February, the Executive Committee of the Federation of Beijing-Hankou Railroad Trade

Unions held a secret meeting, and decided to hold a general strike along the entire railroad. The strike resolution called on railroad workers to "fight for freedom and human rights – only to advance, never to retreat."[1] Meanwhile, a decision was made to move the Federation of Trade Unions to the Hankou river bank, and a temporary office was set up on 3 February.

On 4 February, the Beijing-Hankou railroad workers went on strike, sending shockwaves around the world. On the 1,200-kilometer long railroad line, 30,000 workers organized a general strike in just three hours, paralyzing the whole system. This example of discipline and organization was unprecedented in the history of the Chinese labor movement.

The outbreak of the Beijing-Hankou Railroad Workers' Strike caused foreign powers to panic and attempt to intervene. Envoys of the imperialist countries in Beijing held an emergency meeting to demand that the Beiyang warlord government use force to suppress the strike as soon as possible. On 7 February, with the support of the imperialist forces, Wu Peifu mobilized more than 20,000 military police officers in Jiangan, Changxindian, Zhengzhou, and other main stations along the Beijing-Hankou Railroad, and began to massacre the striking workers. There were 52 killed and over 300 injured. More than 40 people were arrested and imprisoned, and more than 1,000 were expelled and exiled, resulting in the February 7th Massacre, which shocked the nation and the rest of the world.

The railroad workers showed brave and indomitable spirit in the face of this warlord violence. Some fought the reactionary army and police with their bare hands, and some sacrificed their lives to protect the trade union. Lin Xiangqian, aged 31 – the chairman of the Jiang'an branch – was tied to a telegraph pole by the reactionaries and forced to give an order to resume work. He replied firmly, "The resumption order has to be given by the Federation of Trade Unions. My head can be split open, my blood can spill, but work cannot be resumed." The angry reactionary cut off his head and hung it at the station. Unfortunately, Shi Yang – a member of the CPC and legal adviser to the Federation of Beijing-Hankou Railroad Trade Unions – was arrested. Before he died, he chanted "Long live the workers!" and was shot three bullets. He was 34 years old.

1. 'A Brief History of the Chinese Labor Movement (1919–1926)', *The Collected Works of Deng Zhongxia,* People's Publishing House, 1983, p. 502.

After this tragedy, the Central Committee of the Communist Party of China immediately published a document titled 'Comforting the Working Class and the People after Wu Peifu's Massacre of Beijing-Hankou Railroad Workers,' calling on the people and the working class of the entire nation to unite, overthrow the warlords who had oppressed and killed the workers, and strive for freedom. The country quickly launched a huge movement of support for the Beijing-Hankou Railroad workers. The Comintern and the Profintern also issued manifestos to support the heroic struggle of the Chinese working class. In order to preserve the revolutionary forces, the Federation of Beijing-Hankou Railroad Trade Unions and the Hubei Provincial Federation of Trade Unions reluctantly ordered the resumption of work on 9 February.

Although the strike failed, it fully demonstrated the strength of the Chinese working class, marking the beginning of a shift of the Chinese labor movement from an economic struggle aimed at improving living conditions to a political struggle aimed at fighting for freedom. It further awakened the masses, and made them realize more clearly that imperialism and feudal warlords were the enemies of the Chinese people of all ethnic groups, and must be fought to the end.

The first climax of the labor movement showed the firm revolutionary spirit and strong fighting capacity of the Chinese working class. It expanded the political influence of the Communist Party of China as the vanguard of the working class throughout the country, and prepared the Party to establish cooperation with other revolutionary forces and launch a nationwide revolution. It was from these struggles that Sun Yat-sen realized that the CPC was a new and vigorous revolutionary force, and decided to cooperate with it.

What was particularly important about the strike was that it provided a bloody lesson for the young Communist Party of China: the enemy of the Chinese revolution was extremely strong. To overthrow imperialism and feudal warlords, it was far from enough to rely on the working class fighting alone. It was necessary to have mass allies, to unite the broad masses of peasants, the petty bourgeoisie, and bourgeois democrats, and to form a broad revolutionary united front. It was based on this understanding that the Party realized its first cooperation with the Kuomintang, and set off the climax of the great revolution.

2

THE RISE OF THE PEASANT MOVEMENT

"This year is an inauspicious year,
After the great drought came a plague of locusts.
There is no grain to harvest and no rice to pound.
It is the same in the entire village.
My neighbor's family had no food for the night.
My own rice bucket is empty.
The poor man with white hair in the hall –
He can hardly survive the winter with his single coat.
The little children at his knees…
I don't have enough to eat each day.
The mountains are exhausted and the water is poor."[1]

THIS IS PART OF A song titled 'The Old Peasant Collecting Rent,' which was published in the *Yueduo Daily* in 1921, and reflects the poverty of farmers in Xiaoshan.

Xiaoshan is located on the south bank of the Qiantang River – a densely populated and well-developed area on the north Zhejiang plain. Yaqian is a small rural market town on the edge of the East Zhejiang Canal in Xiaoshan County, 14 kilometers west of the county town. The rivers and harbors here are crisscrossed, the land is fertile, and rice is plentiful, so it is known as the 'Land

1. *The Peasant Movement in Yaqian*, edited by the office of the Party History Collection and Research Committee of Xiaoshan County (CPC Committee), December 1985, pp. 131–132.

of Fish and Rice.' However, under the rule of the Beiyang warlord government, the peasants in Yaqian suffered not only from the exploitation of high land rents and the extortion of exorbitant taxes, but also directly experienced the economic aggression of imperialism, which intensified class conflicts in rural Xiaoshan.

Xiaoshan was only a river away from Hangzhou, the capital of the province, and not far from Shanghai. Both before and after the May Fourth Movement, Shanghai and Hangzhou were two of the key areas for the propagation of socialism and the spread of new ideas in China. Thanks to Xiaoshan's superior geographical conditions, its peasants were influenced by the new ideas earlier.

After the founding of the Communist Party of China, while concentrating on leading the labor movement, some Party members also began to nurture a peasant movement in rural areas. The Xiaoshan Peasant Movement started in Yaqian. Its initiator was Shen Xuanlu, who was an early Communist Party member.

Shen Xuanlu studied in Japan in his early years, and participated in the League of Nations in Tokyo. When he returned to China, he edited the *Weekly Review* in Shanghai. In 1920, he co-sponsored the establishment of the early Communist Party there, with Chen Duxiu and others. The fathers and grandfathers of the Shen family were all well-known landlords in Xiaoshan. After he joined the Party, Shen Xuanlu took the side of the peasants instead, with great revolutionary enthusiasm. He centered his efforts to develop and organize peasants on Yaqian.

In April 1921, a poor peasant named Li Chenghu and his brothers asked Shen Xuanlu to help them seek justice after the rapeseed they had planted was stolen. Shen Xuanlu immediately proposed the organization of a peasant association to protect the interests of the farmers, and the Li brothers were extremely supportive. With Shen's inspiration and guidance, Li Chenghu began to prepare for the establishment of such an association.

One day in August, on the stage at the Temple of the Earth in Shanbei, Shen Xuanlu made a speech titled 'Peasant Self-Determination' to peasants from more than 20 nearby villages. He was wearing a straw peasant hat and a rustic cloth shirt, and spoke in the local dialect. He said, "The country belongs to you, the workers… The sovereignty of the country belongs to you… You're asking me to express my fundamental proposition, and this is to abolish private property and 'public ownership of land.' In the future, this proposition will certainly be realized, but it depends on the strength of your unity and organizational efforts." In conclusion, Shen Xuanlu called on the peasants to "Unite quickly! Organize yourselves with precision! The landlords will one day surrender to you." Easy to understand and with a distinctive point of view, Shen's words spread widely among the peasants in Xiaoshan, and had strong repercussions.

In order to encourage the establishment of peasant organizations, Shen Xuanlu borrowed from the Party's practice of launching the labor movement in cities, starting with night schools for workers. He established rural primary schools in Yaqian to spread the revolutionary principles of the peasants' struggle for emancipation and liberation in various ways, which in fact became the center of activity for mobilization and unity. After a series of preparatory projects, the conditions were basically ripe for the establishment of a peasant association.

On 27 September 1921, the Yaqian Farmers' Congress was held in front of Dongyue Temple in Yaqian Town, announcing the formal establishment of the Yaqian Peasant Association. At the meeting, the declaration and constitution of the Association were adopted. This was the first written record of the peasants' struggle in the history of modern Chinese revolution. It put forward the motions that the land belonged to the peasants, reflected the peasants' urgent requirements, and stipulated the purpose, nature, and organization of the Peasant Association. In accordance with regulations, the Congress voted six members into the Association, and elected Li Chenghu to take overall responsibility.

News of the pioneering work of the Yaqian peasants spread quickly to the surrounding countryside. Farmers in dozens of villages in the Xiaoshan area took the Yaqian Peasant Association as an example, taking action and setting up similar groups. In the winter of 1921, dozens of villages in Shaoxing, Cao'e, and other counties within a radius of 300 miles established 80 peasant associations.

The new Peasant Association extensively mobilized farmers, and liaised with various progressive groups. It undertook a lot of useful work, and fought in many ways to protect the peasants' interests. It encouraged villagers to destroy several rice stores, including that of Zhou Heji. The Association also formulated slogans about breaking superstition, eradicating illiteracy, emancipating women, and opposing old rituals. Once the peasants were organized, they showed high motivation, and demonstrated their collective power. Within a year of the Association's founding, the struggle against taxes and donations, rent, and interest reductions was carried out with great vigor.

The peasant movement in Xiaoshan was very vocal, and made strong shockwaves throughout society. The landlords, gentry, and officials of Xiaoshan colluded, and appealed to the authorities of Zhejiang Province, attacking and slandering the peasant movement. The governor of Zhejiang Province ordered a ban on the Peasant Association on the charge of "inciting stubbornness in tenants, and gathering against rent," and gave strict orders to arrest the leading figures.

In mid-December 1921, the officials and landlords of Xiaoshan colluded with Sheng Kaidi – the martial law commander of Shaoxing – to suppress the Peasant Association. On 17 December, Sheng arrested the leader, Li Chenghu, and dissolved the Association by force.

The perverse actions of the reactionary authorities aroused great righteous indignation among the peasants and progressives, who protested against the brutal suppression of the peasant movement by the military and police. The Shanghai edition of *China Daily* published a series of articles, calling the Xiaoshan peasant movement "the vanguard of the class struggle between landlords and tenants" and pointing out that "the country is based on the people, and the people are based on food, so destroying the peasants means shaking the foundation of the country. This is something that the people must not ignore."

Li Chenghu was tortured under arrest, and was not released despite many attempts to free him. He died in prison on 25 January 1922. The Xiaoshan peasants were saddened by his death, and held a service for him where a memorial was erected. Shen Xuanlu wrote an elegiac couplet: "His like cannot be found among the tombs of the Four Mountains. In the history of the Chinese peasant movement, he was the first to rise up."

Although the Party's first attempt to lead a peasant movement failed under the force of the reactionary authorities, it unveiled the prologue of a new type of farmers' uprising.

A much larger peasant movement took place in Guangdong's Hailufeng area, led by Peng Pai, who later became known as the 'King of the Peasant Movement.' This was one of the most widespread and influential peasant movements of the Party's early years.

Peng Pai, who styled himself as 'Hanyu,' was a native of Haifeng in Guangdong Province. He organized an anti-Japanese demonstration in 1916, and left his hometown to study at Guangzhou Guangfu Middle School in 1917. In September 1918 he went to Japan to study at Waseda University. The following year, he joined the Builders' League – a radical youth organization at Waseda University, which focused on peasant issues. This had a great influence on Peng's thinking.

One day in late June 1921, after his return to China, Peng Pai went to a village in Chishanyue in Haifeng County (a 'yue' was an administrative unit in rural Guangdong at that time, equivalent to a town), to spread revolutionary principles among the impoverished peasants. Peng was wearing a white bowler hat, leather shoes, and a white scholar's uniform. Although he greeted the locals with enthusiasm, the peasants – who had long been oppressed by landlords and officials – did not understand, and mistook him for an official who had come to the countryside to collect levies.

"I'm not here to collect levies," Peng explained. "I'm here to make friends with you."

However, when the peasants saw him wearing the sort of neat white uniform that was rarely seen in the countryside, they were unwilling to believe what he said and turned away, saying that they had no time to spare. Others, on seeing him from afar, took a detour to avoid him.

Peng Pai was not discouraged. Having learned a lesson, he took off his "official" clothes, and put on the coarse garb of a peasant instead. He replaced his white cap with a pointed hat. Finally, he took off his leather shoes, and walked back into the countryside barefoot.

In order to get closer to the peasants, Peng Pai went into the fields to help them pull up weeds and turn water. As they pounded rice, he talked with them about family life, and explained the common revolutionary principles in Haifeng dialect. On market days, he gave speeches in crowded places, telling of the suffering of the peasants, exposing the evils of the landlords, and calling on the impoverished farmers to unite and struggle together for a better life. As the peasants listened to Peng's speech, they found it reasonable. The number of people listening to him increased, and the original barriers were gradually removed.

Peng Pai – who had been born into an upper-class family – spent many days touring the countryside on foot, spreading the message. His skin turned black with dirt, his clothes were filthy, and his hair grew long. The landlords, gentry, and ladies laughed at him for his "insanity" and "crazy talk," and his family and friends grew anxious and worried. However, he himself was happy, and felt that he had left the intellectual class.

In the blazing heat of July, Peng Pai went to see the peasants again. He got talking to a young farmer named Zhang Ma'an, who was outspoken and full of energy. Peng befriended him. The more they talked, the more fired up they got. On the night of 29 July, Zhang Ma'an brought his friends Lin Pei, Li Laosi, Li Sixian, and Lin Huan, to Peng's residence, where they were warmly and sincerely welcomed. The six of them talked about how the landlords exploited and oppressed the peasants, and how the peasants should organize themselves for struggle. They decided to take action immediately, and that night the six of them initiated the establishment of the first secret farmers' union in Chishanyue – the 'Six People's Peasant Association.' After a month, the number of members grew to more than thirty.

The Six People's Peasant Association united and guided local farmers to fight against landlords and other feudal forces in the countryside. In order to oppose the landlords' arbitrary rent increases and tenant exchange, they organized a series of 'allied non-farming' activities. In the Haifeng area, where there was a small amount of land and a large population, there were often incidents of peasants competing with each other to rent land from the landlords. The landlords took advantage of this, exploiting the peasants by increasing rent and changing tenancies.

For this reason, Peng Pai encouraged the Six People's Peasant Association to look into countermeasures, stipulating that no members of the Association should compete for land without approval. The landlords had to obtain the consent of the Association before they increased the rent or changed the tenancies of members. If a landlord forcibly took back land, the Association would mobilize the peasants to carry out 'allied non-farming' activities, and avoid renting the landlord's plots. In this way, the landlords dared not increase rent nor change tenancies arbitrarily for fear that the peasants would resist and the land would be abandoned.

The Six People's Peasant Association safeguarded the interests of farmers, and its prestige increased day by day. Local peasants saw with their own eyes that it sincerely wanted to make their lives better, so they gave their trust and loyalty in return. Membership grew. By the end of October, the activities of the Association had expanded to more than 20 villages in the Chishan area. The number of members rose to more than five hundred.

In order to promote the activities of the Six People's Peasant Association, Peng Pai proposed the formal establishment of a Chishanyue branch. On 15 October 1922, the Chishanyue Peasant Association held its founding meeting at the Tianhou Temple in Longshan. Members gathered in front of the temple, and farmers of all ages attended. Teachers and students from Haifeng Middle School and First Primary School also came to give their support. The atmosphere of the founding meeting was warm and positive. Peng Pai presided over the session. He announced the manifesto and articles, which stipulated that farmers should first apply for membership themselves. Only after the key members of the Peasant Association had spoken to them and approved them could they be recognized as members. Every year, members of the Association had to pay dues of 20 cents, and would be given membership cards with the words 'No Work, No Food. Common Will, Joint Cooperation' written on them.

After the establishment of the Chishanyue Peasant Association, Peng Pai traveled to the villages around Haifeng, where he talked directly with the farmers or made speeches in the markets, encouraging people to organize and set up peasant associations to fight for their interests. In the middle of November, the Shouwangyue Peasant Association was established. At that time, there were 3,500 Association members in Chishan and Shouwang. With these two Associations as models, other parts of the country rushed to establish similar unions, and the peasant movement developed rapidly in Haifeng.

One day in November, a new play was being staged in front of Peng's house in Longshepu, and the Peasant Association informed all of the townships to come and watch it. Before the performance, the stage was crowded with spectators. Peng Pai walked onto it with a large stack of land deeds that belonged to him after the division, announcing in a loud voice, "These fields are the fruits of the hard toil of the peasants, who have worked all year long. All of this was taken by the landlord, creating great difficulty for the peasants. We want to completely abolish this unreasonable social system." After that, he read out the land deeds one by one, and then burned them all on the spot. Seeing this, the farmers in the audience were stunned. People couldn't believe their eyes. Then, the stage was filled with people, thundering with joy and resounding with a tidal wave of cheers. The peasants exclaimed, "Mr. Peng would give up everything for the revolution. What do we have to worry about?"[1] The next day, the news of what Peng Pai had done quickly spread to Haifeng and Lufeng.

By the end of 1922, Haifeng County had established peasant associations in 12 counties and 98 townships. Its membership had grown to 100,000 individuals from 20,000 households, accounting for a quarter of the county's total population. By then, the conditions were ripe for the establishment of the General Peasant Association of Haifeng County. On 1 January 1923, the founding meeting was held, with Peng Pai as president. This was the first county-level peasant association in China. At Spring Festival that year, various farming unions came to congratulate the General Peasant Association, and on the 16th of the first month, more than 2,000 peasants asked to join. This led to the climax of the peasant movement in Haifeng. By May 1923, peasant associations had been established in many places across the counties of Haifeng, Lufeng, and Huiyang, with more than 200,000 members.

In September 1923, the Yuebei Peasant and Labor Union was established in the Baiguo area of Hengshan County in Hunan Province, and the struggle it waged raised the first banner of the peasant movement in Hunan. The Union attracted tens of thousands of members that year, but eventually disbanded at the end of the year under the armed suppression of the Hunan warlord Zhao Hengti.

Although most of these new farming associations suffered setbacks, they planted the seeds for later, larger-scale peasant movements. They provided examples for the Chinese Revolution with peasants as the main force, and served as a pioneering model for the flourishing of peasant movements during the Revolution and the Agrarian Revolutionary War.

---

1. Lei, Hui and Zheng, Zuanke. 'Stepping Into "Little Moscow" and Reliving the Passion of Surging Ideals,' *Nanfang Daily*, June 22, 2011.

3

THE VIGOR OF THE YOUTH MOVEMENT

On 23 July 1921, the same day that the First National Congress of the Communist Party of China was held in secret, the Second Congress of the Youth International concluded in Moscow, the capital of Soviet Russia.

At the congress, 23-year-old Zhang Tailei enthusiastically announced the founding of the Chinese Socialist Youth League, explaining its organizational structure and activities. He concluded by stating that "the urgent task is to establish a central organ of close unity" to unify the work of youth leagues throughout the country, to unconditionally accept the guidance of the Communist Party of China, and to strengthen the ties between the Party and league organizations.[1]

The Second Congress of the Youth International stated the basic tasks of the Youth League, emphasizing further changes in the methods of work, direction, and organization, distinguishing between the different elements of the work of the Party and the League, strengthening cooperation and mutual promotion, and drafting a special 'Outline for Working with Colonial Youth' to help guide the youth organizations of these countries in the cause of national liberation. The Congress elected 11 members and four alternate members to form the new Executive Committee of the Youth International, and Zhang Tailei was elected to the Executive Committee, becoming the first representative of the Chinese Youth League to hold this position.[2]

1. *Biography of Zhang Tailei*, p. 82.
2. Ibid., p. 83.

After the Congress, according to the instructions of the Youth International and the decision of the Central Bureau of the Communist Party of China, Zhang Tailei returned to China in the early fall, and took up the historic task of reorganizing and developing the Chinese Socialist Youth League.

However, at this time, the situation of the Youth League in China was very difficult. Its composition was complicated, its ideology was not unified, and organizational activities were almost at a standstill.

What was going on?

Influenced by the patriotic May Fourth Movement, the Communist Party of China saw the youth movement as hugely important during the early days of its founding. In August 1920, at the same time as the early Communist Party organization in Shanghai was established, the Socialist Youth League was also founded in Shanghai to organize and educate the revolutionary youth. The likes of Liu Shaoqi, Luo Yinong, Ren Bishi, and Xiao Jinguang were the earliest group of youth league members in China. Under the impetus of the early organization of the Youth League in Shanghai, branches of the League were established in Beijing, Changsha, Wuhan, Guangzhou, and Tianjin. These branches introduced Marxism to young workers and students, raised their political consciousness, and made certain ideological preparations for the establishment of the Party. At the same time, they absorbed and developed outstanding young workers and students into the Youth League, preparing reserve forces for the establishment of the Party.

However, the early Socialist Youth League was only a group with socialist tendencies, as stated in the document of the First Congress of the League: "At that time, the Chinese Socialist Youth League only had socialist tendencies; it did not define that school of socialism. To this end, the elements were complicated: there were Marxists, anarchists, guild socialists, labor unionists, and inexplicable groups." The complex and diverse composition of the group, and the different individual beliefs made it difficult for the organization to unite tightly, as it often disagreed on conflicting issues. By May 1921, as Chen Duxiu left for Guangzhou, the Youth League leaders who adhered to Marxism went abroad. Yu Xiusong and others went to Moscow, and Shi Cuntong was in Japan. The resulting lack of leadership backbone led to disorganization.

In response to this situation, the First Party Congress in July 1921 looked at the issue of establishing and developing branches of the Socialist Youth League in various regions as a preparatory force for the Party, and clarified the method of absorbing outstanding League members into it. Soon after, a number of outstanding League members were indeed absorbed into the Party, and became the backbone of Party building in various regions.

Shortly after the founding of the Communist Party of China, Zhang Tailei returned to Shanghai. He reported to the Central Bureau of the CPC on the 'Three Great Conferences' of the Comintern and the 'Two Great Conferences' of the Young Communist International, and proposed a preliminary plan to reorganize and develop the League. In order to strengthen leadership, the Provisional Central Bureau of the Socialist Youth League was established.

In November, the Provisional Constitution of the Chinese Socialist Youth League was rewritten, led and organized by Zhang Tailei. Drawing on the experience of the Young Communist International and the Soviet Youth League, and the lessons learned from the establishment of League branches in the past, this constitution began with the ideological establishment of the League, clearly stating that "the Socialist Youth League is a Marxist organization" that "aims to study Marxism, carry out social transformation, and support the rights of the youth." This constitution was recognized and valued by the Central Committee of the Communist Party of China. In order to help the Youth League complete its reorganization and restoration as quickly as possible, the Central Bureau asked local Party organizations to strengthen their leadership, and sent documents about the establishment of the League and its provisional constitution to all localities.

In the same month, as Secretary of the Central Bureau, Chen Duxiu issued the 'Circular of the Central Bureau of the Communist Party of China,' which explicitly demanded that "the National Socialist Youth League must have more than 2,000 members by July next year." It asked local Party organizations to "pay practical attention" to the youth movement and "expedite the reorganization of the Youth League in accordance with the new chapter." In response, local Party organizations selected groups of Party members to start reorganizing and rebuilding the Youth League in accordance with its new constitution.

In January 1922, Chen Duxiu assigned Shi Cuntong to return to Shanghai from Japan to head up the Provisional Central Bureau of the Chinese Socialist Youth League and its Shanghai branch.

On 15 January, the *Herald* – the organ of the Chinese Socialist Youth

League – was founded in Beijing. From the first issue to the third, it was run by the Beijing Youth League, with Deng Zhongxia and Liu Renjing as editors-in-chief. The fourth issue was moved to Shanghai, and was run by the Shanghai Youth League, with Shi Cuntong as editor-in-chief and Cai Hesen and Gao Junyu as editors. In one year and eight months, the *Herald* published 25 issues. Each issue had a four-page spread, with columns such as 'Review,' 'Discussion,' 'Translation,' 'Correspondence,' 'Short Political Commentary,' and 'Essays,' which extensively propagated Marxism and made irreconcilable criticisms of erroneous trends. The *Herald* also translated and published a lot of material from the Youth International and youth movements in various countries, and discussed the construction of the League and youth movements. It had a major influence at the time, and played a publicizing and organizational role in relaunching the work of the Youth League.

After more than six months of work, Socialist Youth League branches everywhere were rapidly restored and developed. By May 1922, 17 branches had been established, in Shanghai, Beijing, Wuchang, Changsha, Guangzhou, Nanjing, Tianjin, Baoding, Tangshan, Tanggu, Anqing, Hangzhou, Chaozhou, Wuzhou, Foshan, Xinhui, and Zhaoqing, with a total of 5,000 members.

With the restoration and rapid development of Youth League branches, the Shanghai Provisional Central Bureau of the Youth League felt that the previous organization and training could not adapt to developments. In order to strengthen the Youth League both ideologically and organizationally, the Central Bureau of the CPC and the Provisional Central League Committee decided to hold the First National Congress of the Chinese Socialist Youth League. A circular was issued to all regions, specifying that the tasks of the congress were "to decide on an official constitution, and organize an official central organ to liaise and unify the national Socialist Youth movement."

On 5 May 1922, the First National Congress of the Chinese Socialist Youth League was held in Guangzhou, attended by 25 representatives from 15 regions, including Cai Hesen, Deng Zhongxia, Zhang Tailei, and Shi Cuntong. Chen Duxiu (Secretary of the Central Bureau of the CPC) and Da Lin (Youth International Representative of the CPC) attended and guided the meeting.

The Congress was held on 5 May because it was the 104th anniversary of Marx's birth, proving that the Chinese Socialist Youth League was a revolutionary organization that believed in Marxism.

The opening ceremony of the First National Congress was attended by all of the representatives from the First National Labor Congress that was being held in Guangzhou, and 1,500 guests from all echelons of Guangdong society. Zhang Tailei came to the podium in high spirits, and delivered his opening speech in a loud voice, followed by a report on the program and the constitution of the League, clearly stating that it was a communist organization. Then, Da Lin addressed the congress and delivered a speech titled 'International Imperialism and China, and the Chinese Socialist Youth League.' Chen Duxiu gave a speech called 'The Two Great Spirits of Marxism,' encouraging young people to study Marxist doctrine and "put it into practical action, to undertake a socialist revolution." More than 10 delegates and guests made speeches, making the conference both compact and grand.

The Congress lasted for six days, from 5 to 10 May. Shi Cuntong gave a report on the status of the Provisional League Central Committee, and delegates from Guangzhou, Beijing, Changsha, and Nanjing reported on the work of the League in their regions.

The Congress accepted the political slogans 'Down with imperialism' and 'Down with warlords' that had been put forward by the Communist Party of China, and analyzed the international and domestic situation since the First World War in the 'Program of the Chinese Socialist Youth League.' It preliminarily expounded the proletariat's ideas about democratic revolution, and put forward three political guidelines for the Chinese revolution at the current stage, such as "eradicating the oppression of both international capital and domestic armed forces" and "fighting for all democratic and liberal rights." It was clearly stated that "the Chinese Socialist Youth League is an organization of the young Chinese proletariat, i.e. an organization that fights for the complete liberation of the working class."[1] The 'Constitution of the Chinese Socialist Youth League' that was adopted at the Congress made clear provisions regarding membership and discipline. It stated, "All young people above the age of 15 and below the age of 28 who recognize the Program and Constitution of the League and are willing to serve the League shall be members of the League."

1. Selected and edited by the Modern History Research Office of the Chinese Academy of Social Sciences and the Party History Research Office of the Chinese Revolutionary Museum. *Before and After the First National Congress of the Communist Party of China, Vol. 2*, People's Publishing House, 1980, p. 31.

The Congress unanimously agreed that the Chinese Socialist Youth League should join the Youth International and become one of its branches. Finally, Gao Junyu, Shi Cuntong, Zhang Tailei, Cai Hesen, and Yu Xiusong were elected as members of the Central Executive Committee of the Youth League, with Shi Cuntong as secretary.[1]

At the same time as the domestic group was established, 18 representatives of work-study students living in France, Belgium, and Germany (including Zhao Shiyan, Zhou Enlai, Li Weihan, Li Fuchun, Wang Ruofei, and Chen Yannian) also held a First Congress on 3 June 1922, in the Bois de Boulogne in the western suburbs of Paris, and formally established the Communist Youth League of China in Europe. They elected Zhao Shiyan as secretary, Zhou Enlai as a member of the publicity committee, and Li Weihan as organizing committee member. They soon learned that the Chinese Communist Party and the Chinese Socialist Youth League had already been established in China, and after contacting the Central Committee of the CPC and the Central Committee of the Youth League, they decided to change their name to the General Branch of the Chinese Socialist Youth League in Europe. Zhao Shiyan, Chen Yannian, and Zhou Enlai served as secretaries in succession. The branch published a monthly magazine called *Youth*, which propagated Marxism and strongly criticized the social reformism and anarchism that were popular at that time.

The formal establishment of the Chinese Socialist Youth League was an important event in the history of the Chinese youth movement. The advanced youth in China now had a fighting organization with unified ideology and actions, and this organization became an important assistant and link for the Party to unite and educate young people.

During this period, under the leadership and guidance of the Communist Party of China and the Socialist Youth League, the Chinese youth movement had a clearer and firmer political direction. The majority of young people accepted the anti-imperialist and anti-feudal democratic revolutionary program put forward by the Communist Party, and accepted the goals of overthrowing imperialism, defeating the warlords, struggling for national liberation, and building a free and independent country. With the support, organization, and

1. *Sunrise in the East: A Chronicle of the Founding of the Communist Party of China*, People's Publishing House, 2011, pp. 386–389.

guidance of the Party and the League, many young people bravely engaged in the fierce struggles of the labor and peasant movements, uniting with the workers and farmers, and raising the youth movement to a new level.

Thereafter, the name of the Youth League underwent several changes.

In 1925, it was renamed the Chinese Communist Youth League.

In November 1935, in order to adapt to the war situation and mobilize young people to participate, the Communist Youth League was reorganized, and the Chinese National Liberation Vanguard, the Youth Salvation Association, and the Anti-Japanese Youth Vanguard were established.

In 1946, the New Democratic Chinese Youth League was established on a trial basis.

In April 1949, the New Democratic Youth League of China was officially established.

In May 1957, its name was changed to the Chinese Communist Youth League, which has been used ever since.[1]

1. *Sunrise in the East: A Chronicle of the Founding of the Communist Party of China*, People's Publishing House, 2011, pp. 254–263.

4

THE EMERGENCE OF THE WOMEN'S MOVEMENT

The beginning of the 20th century saw the rise of a women's movement in China. The influence of the May Fourth Movement and New Culture Movement led to growing calls for equality between the sexes, as well as opposition to feudalism and the suppression of women. Even in the infancy of the Communist Party of China, the complete liberation of women was seen as crucial to the fight against feudalism. As it sought to liberate the people and establish a democracy, it was added to the Party's key agendas. The early leaders of the Party placed great importance on the women's movement, and wrote many articles on the liberation of women. They include Li Dazhao's 'The Modern Feminist Movement,' Chen Duxiu's 'Women's Issues and Socialism,' and Li Da's 'Theory of Women's Liberation.' Mao Zedong also wrote about the plight of women, following a shocking incident in Changsha in which a woman named Zhao Wuzhen cut her own throat in her bridal sedan in protest against an arranged marriage. In nine consecutive articles, including 'Social Evils and Madam Zhao' and 'Not Suicide,' published in Hunan's *Da Gong* newspaper, Mao Zedong lambasted feudal ethics, exposing the dark, cruel and "cannibalistic" nature of the feudal system, and calling on the people to reform society and fight for the liberation of women.

In the early 1900s, Shanghai was a major modern industrial hub with a large population of workers. Cotton mills and tobacco factories were numerous, as were female workers. However, as women were generally poorly-educated in those days, their ideological awareness and comprehension was low, and the women's movement struggled to take off. Early members of the CPC such as

Chen Duxiu and Li Da saw a pressing need for the Party to cultivate a group of female cadres to lead the women's movement, as well as whatever else the revolution called for.

In August 1921, the newly-established CPC restructured the influential China Women's Federation and published the Federation's reform motto, as well as its new charter, in the fifth issue of the fifth volume of the Party magazine *New Youth*. The CPC wrote into the Federation's creed the need for women and men to join hands and participate in all movements initiated by the lower social classes against warlords and plutocrats, as well as all attempts to fight the invasion of foreign imperialists. In October that year, Chen Duxiu and Li Da prepared to establish the Party's first school for female cadres in Shanghai. In November, the Central Bureau of the CPC issued a notice stating that it would be sending out the reform motto and charter of the Women's Federation. It requested that local Party organizations follow the women's movement closely, and promptly reform or build their women's organizations according to the charter.

In Shanghai, where imperialism and northern warlords ruled, the CPC was still a secret organization, and could not openly run a school for female cadres. The school was thus operated in the name of the Shanghai Women's Federation with Li Da's wife, Wang Huiwu, as the secretary, and Huang Zonghan as the president. Huang Zonghan was the wife of Huang Xing – a founding member of the Chinese United League. She was well-respected in society, and knew both Chen Duxiu and Li Da. When Wang Huiwu proposed running the school in the Federation's name, Huang Zonghan thought that it would not only raise the social standing of the China Women's Federation, but also boost the Chinese women's movement. Thus, she readily agreed.

Back then, Li Da and his wife lived in a rented apartment in a *shikumen* at No. 635 Fude Lane on South Chengdu Road. While preparing for the school's opening, Li Da discovered a courtyard behind his apartment that had put up for urgent rental. Aware of the Party's tight budget, Li Da paid the 50 yuan rent with his wages and writing fees. This courtyard became the Shanghai Commoners' (Pingmin) Girls' School. In explaining the name, one of the teachers, Shen Zemin, said, "*pingmin*, meaning 'commoner' is the opposite of *guizu*, meaning 'aristocrat.' In other words, the Shanghai Commoners' Girls' School is where commoners can get an education, and where women are nurtured in the spirit of the common folk."[1]

On 10 and 25 December 1921, the Shanghai Commoners' Girls' School posted student recruitment adverts in *Women's Voices* and the *Republican Daily* in the name of the Shanghai Women's Federation. The adverts clearly and concisely stated, "Our school was founded by women, and its mission is to nurture a class of women who are self-aware but have no means of getting an education, such that they can make a living for themselves and become self-reliant."[2]

On 10 February 1922, the Shanghai Commoners' Girls' School officially opened, with Li Da as the principal and his wife, Wang Huiwu, as a senior class student and his administrative assistant. The school was located at No. 632 Fude Lane on South Chengdu Road (now No. 42 and 44 in Lane 7, North Chengdu Road), in the same building as Li Da's apartment. The school was modest in size – merely a two-storied building comprising two classrooms, a factory, workspaces, and a dormitory. Each classroom had a blackboard and some old study desks.

The school contained a senior class and a junior class. Senior students were at least of a lower secondary school education standard, and studied eight subjects: the Chinese language, mathematics, physics, chemistry, English, sociology, economics, and education studies. Chen Wangdao, Shao Lizi, Zhang Shoubai, and Gao Yuhan taught Chinese language. Shen Yanbing and Shen Zemin taught English. Li Da taught mathematics, Chen Duxiu sociology, Li Xixian economics, Fan Shoukang education studies, and Zhou Changshou chemistry. The junior students had varying levels of education, from complete illiteracy to lower and upper primary school levels. They studied three subjects: the Chinese language, arithmetic, and English. Wang Huiwu taught Chinese, Ke Qingshi taught arithmetic, and Shen Zemin taught English.

The Shanghai Commoners' Girls' School had some of the best teachers in the country, with many of the early CPC members from Shanghai teaching there. The staff were highly educated and accomplished, and used innovative teaching methods tailored to their students' needs. They spread new thought, and kindled revolutionary consciousness through their lessons. For instance,

1. Shen, Zemin. 'This is not a charity!' *Women's Voices*, Issue 6.
2. *Women's Voices*, Issue 5.

to teach the Chinese language, Shao Lizi did not use stories about chaste and virtuous Chinese women, as was the norm in traditional women's schools. Instead, he used newspaper articles, translations of world literary classics, and literary critiques published in magazines – a radical departure from the practice in upper-class women's schools. Meanwhile, Chen Wangdao, who translated and published the Chinese version of *The Communist Manifesto*, encouraged his students to express their emotions in his writing class. English teacher Shen Zemin's teaching materials were the English translations of Guy de Maupassant's novels and Dostoevsky's *Poor Folk*. As a sociology teacher, Chen Duxiu actively promoted the study of the social sciences and the basic principles of Marxism and Leninism to students.

To broaden students' horizons, the school also held weekly two-hour lectures on topics such as women's issues and the women's movement, the link between imperialism and the carving up of land by the warlords, and the reasons why people should oppose imperialism and feudalism. Never before had this been done in a women's school. Chen Duxiu, Li Da, and Yun Daiying were among the many revolutionaries and famous figures who gave lectures at the school, explaining revolutionary principles and rousing students' class consciousness. The likes of Zhang Tailei and Liu Shaoqi also lectured at the school on their return from Soviet Russia, to introduce students to the revolutionary movement and other developments there, further widening their horizons.

The most distinguishing feature of the Shanghai Commoners' Girls' School was its work-study program. The school rules stipulated that senior class fees were two yuan per month, while junior class fees were one yuan per month. Students who joined the school's work units were exempted from paying school fees. This rule played a big part in encouraging many women to enroll in the school and join its workforce.

The Shanghai Commoners' Girls' School's work unit was managed by Wang Huiwu. There were three sub-units within it: sewing, sock knitting, and weaving. Students spent one half of the day working, and the other half studying, paying their school fees and daily expenses with their labor. Additionally, students frequently visited factories to learn more about the lives of the women workers there. They organized literacy classes for these workers, and also participated in and supported workers' strikes. They distributed pamphlets about the revolution on the streets, and headed out to the factories in Yangshupu, Pudong, Xiaoshadu, and Zhabei to promote and spur the launch of fund-raising activities for workers, getting practical training in the process.

Li Da held this work unit in high esteem, writing an article with the specific purpose of voicing his support for the work-study program. In this article, he stressed that students must be diligent and be able to take hardships in their stride, and must never succumb to indolence. They must also exercise strict self-restraint, never relying on others or the school. This innovative approach to running a school not only resolved the problem of a tight operational budget, but also resulted in an organic fusion of theory and practice, blazing a trail in women's education.

The Shanghai Commoners' Girls' School took in around 30 students in all, most of whom were referred by Party members. The age range among these students was huge, with the youngest aged 12, and the oldest aged around thirty. Most of the students in the junior class were women who had dropped out of school many years before. Some of them had wrested themselves from the shackles of family restrictions to seek an education. Others had escaped from feudal marriages. Regardless of their circumstances, they all harbored hopes for the liberation of women, seeking truth and aspiring to revolution.

Wang Jianhong (formerly known as Wang Shufan) was a progressive student from the Hunan Taoyuan Second Women's Normal University. She hailed from Youyang in Chongqing, and was of the Tujia ethnic minority. In 1921, Wang Jianhong interviewed the likes of Chen Duxiu, Li Da, and Wang Huiwu to find out how they were preparing for the opening of the Shanghai Commoners' Girls' School. When she returned to Hunan at the end of the year, Wang spread the word about the school to her classmates, friends, and family. Subsequently, in the spring of 1922, she left Hunan for Shanghai, to enroll in the Shanghai Commoners' Girls' School, along with her good friend and classmate Ding Ling. Accompanying them were Wang Yizhi (a teacher from Hunan Xupu Primary School), Wang Xingyu (Wang Jianhong's aunt), Wang Suqun, and Xue Zhengyuan. While she was at the school, Wang Jianhong juggled work with her studies, even becoming the editor of *Women's Voices* – the official magazine of the China Women's Federation. Her talent and capabilities were recognised by Chen Duxiu and Li Da, and she later became one half of a revolutionary couple with Qu Qiubai.

Ding Ling (known as Jiang Bingzhi at the time) was 18 years old when she enrolled at the Shanghai Commoners' Girls' School. Although it was her first time in Shanghai, she was a very active member of her class, and did well in her studies. It was at the Shanghai Commoners' Girls' School that she was exposed to literary writing. In 1927, she published *Dream Stone* and *Miss Sophie's Diary*, both of which garnered wide attention. In 1930, she joined the League of Left-Wing Writers, and became the editor-in-chief of *Bei Dou* magazine. In 1932, Ding Ling joined the CPC. In May the following year, she was kidnapped by Kuomintang special agents and imprisoned in Nanjing. Prominent Chinese and foreign figures such as Song Qingling, Cai Yuanpei, Lu Xun, and Romain Rolland launched a protest and rescue campaign for her. In 1936, Ding Ling escaped from Nanjing and headed to Shanbei, where she was the first renowned writer to reach a liberated zone, and was warmly welcomed by Mao Zedong, Zhou Enlai, and other left-wing leaders. In 1948, she completed the novel *The Sun Shines Over the Sanggan River*, which later won the Stalin Prize. The novel was translated into many languages and reached an international audience, contributing significantly to the development of contemporary Chinese literature.

Qian Xijun, hailing from Zhuji in Zhejiang Province, was 17 years old when she enrolled at the Shanghai Commoners' Girls' School, in the junior class. She had been a child bride of Zhang Qiuren. Zhang came to abhor the child bride system after joining the revolution, and while he never married Qian Xijun, he was very sympathetic towards her circumstances and cared for her greatly, treating her like a younger sister. He enrolled her at the Shanghai Commoners' Girls' School under the alias 'Zhang Jing.' Henceforth, Qian Xijun was freed from the restrictions imposed by traditional notions of marriage and family, and joined the revolution. At school, she was an active participant in the women's movement alongside her studies. She joined the Socialist Youth League of China in 1924, became a member of the CPC in 1925, and married Mao Zedong's younger brother, Mao Zemin, in 1926. She later joined the Long March, becoming one of the 30 renowned female Red Army soldiers.

Given its tight budget and limited manpower, the Shanghai Commoners' Girls' School struggled to operate, with many of its teachers busy with Party work. When Shanghai University opened, some of students from the Shanghai

Commoners' Girls' School continued their studies there, while others spread across the country for revolutionary work. As such, the school closed at the end of 1922.

The Shanghai Commoners' Girls' School was not only a cradle that nurtured female cadres for the CPC, but was also a trailblazing women's educational establishment. Although it was open for just eight months, it nurtured a batch of renowned female luminaries that included Ding Ling, Qian Xijun, Wang Yizhi, Wang Jianhong, and Qin Dejun, most of whom went on to lead the Party's work in the women's movement. In this is way, the school left an indelible mark and wrote an impressive chapter in the history of education and the women's movement in China.

To spread the word about the women's movement, the Party launched the bimonthly magazine *Women's Voices* on 13 December 1921 whilst preparing for the opening of the Shanghai Commoners' Girls' School. Wang Huiwu and Wang Jianhong were the magazine's editors, while Li Da was the sub-editor. It was the Party's first magazine advocating women's liberation. It openly promoted scientific socialist theories, and pushed for a proletarian women's movement, proposing that "to liberate women is to liberate workers." It called for all women to rise up and "smash all plunder and suppression, so as to gain the right to live and work in a free society."

Party organizations across the country paid close attention to the women's movement, and launched a slew of women's magazines. In Guangzhou, Party organizations launched *Labor and Women*. Deng Yingchao and Li Zhishan from Tianjin started a progressive group called the 'Women's Star Society' to foster unity and boost communication among women. They also launched the magazine *Women's Star*. These magazines were rich in content, diverse in format, and fun and zestful. They exposed how women were being suppressed across the board, and excoriated feudal forces along with the institutions of traditional society. They championed the breaking of old ethics and the fight for equality between the sexes, and encouraged socialization, marriages of choice, and the promotion of the women's movement, whilst exploring the means to liberate women. These women's magazines were well-received by the public, as was the widespread dissemination of new thoughts on the complete liberation of women.

In fronting the women's movement, the CPC deemed it important to address the predicament of female workers. Due to a variety of reasons, the make-up of this group of workers was relatively complex. Most were poorly educated, with a low sense of class consciousness. To advance the women's cause, Party organizations started night schools and clubs, where they used everyday language to introduce female workers to Marxism, thereby raising their proletarian consciousness. The Party organizations also emphasized the education and nurturing of female leaders in the workplace, helping them overcome their weak wills and vulnerability to being exploited by others, and raising their ability to lead the fight for female workers. This boosted the development of the women workers' movement. In April 1922, Party unions rallied 3,000 women workers at the Pudong Rihua Cotton Mill in Shanghai to go on strike. *Women's Voices* encouraged and endorsed the strike, stressing to female workers that "the unions are the focal point around which you should all unite," and that "the capitalists fear the unions the most," effectively rallying women workers of all ranks to support the strike. It was a success, and buoyed the spirits of female workers everywhere.

After a few years of hard work, the women's movement saw rapid progress and made significant breakthroughs, led and guided by the CPC. Chinese women became more aware of the need to fight for their liberation, and their collective identity grew stronger, making them a force to be reckoned with in the fight against imperialism and feudalism. Henceforth, the Chinese women's movement became an important part of the new democratic revolution.

PART 8

Setting the Course:

From the Direct Pursuit of Socialism to a Revolutionary Program of Anti-Imperialism and Anti-Feudalism

Innovation is the inexhaustible driving force for the advancement of history. Combined with national conditions, constant innovation is the soul of a living, breathing nation. In the process of its founding, the Communist Party of China explored a revolutionary path that was in line with China's national conditions, and set a great course for national rejuvenation.

After the Opium War, China gradually morphed from an independent feudal empire into a semi-colonial, semi-feudal society. This transformed society was neither capitalist nor feudal. It was distinct in that while the self-sufficient nature of the feudal era's natural economy had been destroyed, the peasantry continued to be exploited by the landlord class. In practicing comprador capitalism and usury, landlords continued to enjoy significant economic privileges.

Private enterprise had just begun to take off in China, and had a major impact on Chinese politics and culture. However, it did not become the mainstay of the Chinese economy, as it was a weak force that was linked to foreign capital and domestic feudalism. Imperialism controlled not just China's fiscal and economic lifelines, but also its political and military forces. The feudal bureaucrat-landlord class formed the base of China's imperialist rule, and acted for the imperialists. The total or semi-rule of various imperialist powers, along with China's vast territory and long-running internal discord, caused severe imbalances in the development of the nation's economy, politics, and culture.

These distinct factors had a profound impact on modern China's development and revolutionary struggle. In a semi-colonial, semi-feudal China, the conflict between feudal forces and the masses persisted, and was compounded by the conflict between imperialism and the Chinese people. These two sources of conflict became the main battle in Chinese society.

The modern Chinese revolution arose from these conflicts. On the external front, the revolution's mission was to resist imperialistic aggression. Internally, its mission was to overthrow the rule of the feudal landlord class. A bourgeois revolutionary force led by Sun Yat-sen abolished the 2,000-year-old feudal monarchy in the Revolution of 1911. This was a great accomplishment. However, that revolution did not have a clear agenda for fighting the imperialists, and even harbored illusions of 'friendship' and assistance from the imperialists. The absence of a comprehensive framework for a revolution against the imperialistic and feudal forces was the reason China's revolutions failed until the CPC came onto the scene.

Meanwhile, Marxism was taking shape in Europe, where capitalism was well-developed and internal conflicts were starting to surface. How could Marxism be deployed in semi-colonial, semi-feudal China? There was no ready answer. What path should the Chinese revolution take? There was no precedent.

All of this pointed to the need for China (with its unique national context) to forge its own path and take bold and innovative strides in order to rejuvenate itself and narrow its developmental gulf with the West, which had been caused by the backwardness and rigidity of the feudal system in the previous couple of centuries. It was also necessary for China to make up for lost time, step back into the game and play catch-up, and stand as an independent and autonomous society on an equal footing with other nations of the world.

This was precisely why the CPC displayed such immense courage to innovate, along with a steely resolve to break new ground in its founding years. It brought the underlying principles of Marxism into the Chinese revolutionary movement, and underwent a process of bold theorizing and experimentation, moving from a direct implementation of socialism to the establishment of a framework for the revolution against imperialism and feudalism. In doing so, the CPC answered the question of its time. It spurred the Chinese adaption of Marxism, and forged the path towards national rejuvenation with Chinese characteristics.

1

JOINING THE GLOBAL REVOLUTIONARY WAVE

"WORKERS OF THE WORLD, UNITE!" was Marx's clarion call. "Workers and oppressed people around the world, unite!" was Lenin's famous rallying cry, made after studying and expanding Marxist thought.

Founded under the guidance of Marxism-Leninism, the Communist Party of China broke the century-old chains of rigid, inward-looking Chinese thought. With broad perspectives and an open mind, the CPC strode out of China's doorway into the world, setting its eyes on the global arena and forging a revolutionary path that was rooted in China's national context.

In the first two years after the CPC's establishment, the world was in a relatively stable state. On the one hand, the turmoil of the First World War had ended, and the global economic crisis of 1920 had passed. Imperialist countries had suppressed domestic proletarian revolutionary movements and reinforced their autocracies. On the other hand, the newly formed Soviet polities had crushed imperialist military interventions and anti-revolutionary movements in their countries, and were embarking on the path to economic recovery and socialism. Communist parties around the world were growing stronger by the day, and there were ongoing revolutions in colonized and semi-colonized countries.

Thus emerged a temporary equilibrium between the imperialist and revolutionary forces.

As the imperial powers recovered from the war and their domestic situations stabilized, they began to compete intensely over spheres of influence.

The Far East, and especially China, had always been a key battleground for the imperial powers. While Britain and the USA were preoccupied with events elsewhere in the world during the First World War, Japan stepped up the pace in expanding its influence in China, and grew significantly more powerful there. The acknowledgment of its special rights in China at the Paris Peace Conference cemented its position. Meanwhile, the USA's economic prowess had grown exponentially, thanks to its profiteering during the war. In 1919, its overseas investments totaled 13 billion US dollars, making it the country with the largest capital export after the war. As such, conflicts between Japan and the USA in the Far East began to deepen, as did conflicts of interest between Britain and Japan, the USA and France, and Britain and France, in the same region.

To mediate the conflicts between the imperial powers and make readjustments based on positions of strength and the interests of these powers in China and the Pacific, the USA used the guise of upholding international peace to initiate the Washington Naval Conference with Britain's support. The conference was held between 12 November 1921 and 6 February 1922. It involved nine countries, namely the USA, Britain, Japan, France, Italy, Belgium, the Netherlands, Portugal, and China. There were two issues on its agenda, the first of which was to discuss a limitation on naval armaments. The 'Five Power Treaty' was signed after intense negotiations and much infighting. The signatories of the treaty – the USA, Britain, Japan, France, and Italy – agreed to fix the tonnage of ships to be possessed by each of their navies in the ratio of 5: 5: 3: 1.75: 1.75. This effectively eliminated the advantage that the British ships had over the USA, and curbed Japan's hegemony in the Pacific. It also reflected changes in the relative strength of the individual powers.

The second issue discussed at the conference was the problem of the Far East and the Pacific, specifically the China problem. When discussing this, the Chinese government's chief representative made a legitimate request to protect China's national sovereignty. However, this and other issues went unresolved at the conference, as none of the imperial powers were willing to give up their interests in China. Japan was forced to sign the 'Treaty on the Settlement of the Outstanding Case in Shandong and the Annex' with China on 4 February 1922, returning to China some of the sovereign rights of Shandong that it had previously snatched, only because the USA wanted to curb the growing Japanese influence in China and expand its own influence.

The conference also saw the signing of the 'Nine Power Treaty,' with the nine countries agreeing to abide by polices and principles relating to China. The treaty was premised on the 'Open Door Policy' and the 'Principle of Equal Opportunity for All Countries in China,' as proposed by the USA.

The 'Principle of Equal Opportunity' meant that the USA was entitled to all of the same privileges that the other imperial powers enjoyed in China, even if it had come late onto the scene. The 'Open Door Policy' stipulated that none of the imperial powers in China could shut the other powers out of the areas they controlled there. Fundamentally, the USA had made these two proposals because it was a "latecomer" among the imperial powers that had invaded China, and had thus reaped fewer benefits from it. It all boiled down to the USA's desire to have a bigger slice of the pie. Essentially, the 'Nine Power Treaty' formed the basis of the joint rule and control of China by the imperialist powers, curbed Japan's ambition to monopolize China, and prevented Britain and Japan from forming an alliance, all while maintaining the USA's advantage. Such was the blatant carving up of and oppression of China.

The disregard for China's legitimate rights and interests, along with the division of its territory by the imperialist powers, sparked a huge outcry among the Chinese people. Rallies, parades, and school strikes were held in cities such as Shanghai, Hangzhou, Jinan, Beijing, Hankou, and Tianjin to demand that the 'Twenty-One Demands' be retracted, and the integrity of China's territorial sovereignty be protected. Chinese students in the USA also held protests against the imperialists, using China's sovereignty as a bargaining chip.

It was at this point in time that members of the CPC revealed the truth about the Washington Naval Conference to the Chinese people. As Chen Duxiu pointed out:

> "The Far East-related problems discussed at the conference continue to revolve around the distribution and protection of the interests of the imperial powers in the Far East, especially those of the USA and Japan. This is to prevent a war from breaking out among the imperial powers due to conflicting interests, giving the people of small and weak nations a chance to liberate themselves. It is not a case of the imperial powers suddenly showing mercy and being willing to halt their imperialistic economic and political aggressions to help liberate the people of small and weak

> nations! Pity the people of small and weak nations, for under the raids and oppression of the imperial alliance, and before their efforts to transform the world with the similarly oppressed classes and proletariats within the imperial powers succeed, not for a day will they escape the imperialists' brutal rule. To the Chinese people, especially students studying in the USA, I say, 'Wake up!'"

This revelation deepened CPC members' awareness of the international environment in which the Chinese Revolution was taking place, and spurred them to decide on an action plan.

To fight back against the Washington Naval Conference and expose the imperialists' evil intentions to carve up the Far East, the Comintern planned to hold the First Conference of Representatives from Communist Parties and National Revolutionary Organizations of Far Eastern Countries (the Far East Peoples' Conference for short) in Irkutsk, on the very day that the Washington Naval Conference was to be held. However, transport issues and the short notice given meant that many of the delegates would not be able to make it to Irkutsk by November. Thus, the Conference was postponed. The venue was also changed to Moscow, closer to where Lenin and the Comintern leaders were based, lending the event greater political significance and global influence.

The Far East Peoples' Conference was a very important event for the CPC. In the fall of 1921, after it received an invitation to the meeting from the Comintern's Far East Bureau, it immediately sent Bao Huiseng to Guangzhou, Zhou Fohai to the cities along the Yangtze River, and Liu Renjing to the major cities in northern China, to select representatives for the meeting. This was all done discreetly, as requested by the conference organizers. The Comintern representative in China also directly contacted the Kuomintang headquarters in Shanghai to extend an invitation to the meeting.

In a blizzardy Soviet Russia in early 1922, a train from Irkutsk ferrying 178 representatives from China, Korea, Mongolia, and Japan pulled into a crowded train station in Moscow, where a welcoming party crammed the platform. The rousing anthem of the 'Internationale' filled the air as colorful flags fluttered in the wind. Beaming faces in the crowd completed the stunning image of internationalism that greeted the visitors from afar.

The Far East Peoples' Conference was held on 21 January1922, in the

Kremlin's stately Sverdlov Hall. A portrait of Karl Marx hung just above the rostrum, and there were banners draped around the hall with the slogans 'Workers of the World Unite' and 'Liberate the Workers of the East' printed in Chinese, Korean, Mongolian, Japanese, and other languages. There was a stirring atmosphere of camaraderie as the various peoples of the Far East came together for a common struggle.

The Chinese delegation was large, comprising 44 representatives from diverse backgrounds. There were 14 representatives from the CPC, with the remaining delegates coming from the Socialist Youth League of China, the KMT, and the revolutionary groups of women, workers, peasants, and students. This was the first time since its founding that the CPC had sent representatives to a major international meeting.

The CPC's attendance at a key Comintern event was highly significant and symbolic, as it signaled the fact that the Chinese Revolution had become an integral part of the global proletarian revolutionary movement that followed the October Revolution. This global movement had garnered attention and support from revolutionary parties and organizations around the world.

Comintern chair Grigori Yevseyevich Zinoviev announced the opening of the Conference, and nominated Lenin, Trotsky, and Stalin as honorary chairmen. He also presented a report titled 'The State of Global Affairs and the Outcomes of the Washington Naval Conference,' and thereafter passed the 'Resolution on the Outcomes of the Washington Naval Conference and the Far Eastern Situation.' This resolution stressed that for the oppressed people of the Far East to attain freedom and independence, their workers must form an alliance with the proletariats of the developed countries to oppose all imperialists.

As part of the Conference's proceedings, delegates from the various countries presented reports on the state of the revolution and people's movements in their respective nations. CPC representative Zhang Guotao reported on the situation in China, briefing the conference attendees on issues including the circumstances of China's proletariat and farmers, land issues, and the state of student movements and worker strikes. In their reports, the delegates expressly stated that members of the Far Eastern communist parties must first and foremost rise to the challenges of the unfolding revolution and address pressing issues, such as the ties between the communist parties and the various national revolutionary parties within each country.

For this purpose, Georgy Safarov – head of the Comintern's Eastern Bureau – presented a report titled 'The Third International and Far Eastern People's Problem.' On the question of the most important revolutionary task for China, Korea, and other oppressed Far Eastern countries and people, the report cited Lenin's theory on colonialism, and stipulated that the first order of the day for the Far Eastern working class was to liberate all oppressed countries. As for the CPC, its immediate tasks were to free China from the shackles of the foreign powers, overthrow the military governors, reclaim China's territory, and establish a simple, federal-like democratic republic. As for the role of the proletariat and peasants in the struggle for the peoples' liberation, the report emphasized the unique role of the proletariat as "leaders and pillars of strength in the peoples' liberation movement." It specifically noted the imperative of drawing China's largest demographic – the peasants – into the movement, and stressed that the struggle to liberate the people was hopeless if the peasants' revolutionary spirit were not aroused.

Finally, the Conference passed the 'Resolution on the Outcomes of the Washington Naval Conference and the Far Eastern Situation,' and issued the 'Statement on the First Conference of Representatives from Communist Parties and National Revolutionary Organizations of Far Eastern Countries.' The statement exposed the insidious nature of the Washington Naval Conference, expressly pointing out that "the former American, British, and French thieves are fighting over China, with its 400 million-strong population, and enjoying the spoils of their pillage on the blood and tears of the Chinese people." A rallying call was made for all the people of the Far East to "resolutely fight the British, Americans, Japanese, French, and other thieves of the world," and "declare war on the Chinese warlords who exploit China, the Japanese soldiers and bureaucrats, the treacherous American imperialists, and the avaricious British opportunists." The statement also proclaimed, "There shall be no rest until victory is won!" The Chinese delegates' spirits were buoyed by these trenchant words.

Lenin followed the Conference's developments closely, despite having to miss it due to ill health. He was particularly concerned about the cooperation between the KMT and the CPC, which would determine the fate of China's revolution. Despite being unwell, Lenin met CPC representative Zhang Guotao, KMT representative Zhang Qiubai, and Deng Pei, who represented

China's railroad workers. As the trio entered the reception room in Lenin's Kremlin office, hardly able to contain their emotions, Lenin emerged from the adjacent office and shook their hands.

During the amiable conversation that followed, KMT representative Zhang Qiubai consulted Lenin on the challenges facing the Chinese Revolution. Lenin said that he knew little about China's situation, only that Sun Yat-sen was the revolutionary leader. He asked Zhang Qiubai if the KMT and CPC could work together. Zhang Qiubai answered, "Yes – we can definitely work well together." Lenin posed the same question to Zhang Guotao, and asked for more details about the situation in China. Zhang Guotao said that the KMT and CPC could and should work closely in China's national democratic revolution, adding that while problems could arise as they worked together, these could be overcome. He also said that the CPC strove to unite all anti-imperialist revolutionary forces. As he said this, Lenin nodded, satisfied with the answer.

As their meeting drew to a close, Lenin gripped Deng Pei's hands and said, "The railroad workers' movement is crucial. As railroad workers played a key role in the Russian revolution, you too will play an important – even pivotal – role in the Chinese Revolution." Lenin's warm reception, as well as his invaluable advice on the revolutionary movement in China, was crucial in helping the CPC establish the right revolutionary framework, and paved the way for the KMT and the CPC to become revolutionary partners.

After the conference, the energized Chinese delegation toured Moscow, Leningrad, and other Soviet Russian cities, seeing first-hand what a country with the world's first proletarian government looked like. At Smolny – the site of the October Revolution's command center in Moscow, where a memorial had been built to commemorate the underground resistance movement during the Revolution – and on the vibrant city streets, the delegation felt the political enthusiasm and aspirations of a revolutionary people. They also felt the immense joy and deep pride of a people celebrating their revolutionary victory, as well as the warm concern and international camaraderie extended by the Russians to the Chinese. All of this encouraged and inspired the Chinese delegates.

Qu Qiubai, one of the Chinese delegates, recorded what he saw and felt on his trip in his books, *Reflections in Moscow* and *Journey to a New Russia*. Meanwhile, Ke Qingshi wrote and sent a series of write-ups on the wintry landscapes of Siberia and Lake Baikal, the Red Capital Moscow, and the

Winter Palace in Leningrad to newspapers back in China. His detailed and vivid depictions captured the imagination of readers there, and were widely circulated.

The young CPC's debut on the global political stage and its active efforts to integrate the Chinese Revolution with the global proletarian revolution gave it a bigger stage and greater meaning. The warm reception that the CPC received from Lenin, along with the Comintern's sound advice, helped the CPC understand the situation in the Far East after the Washington Naval Conference and recognize the reactionary nature of imperialism. It also helped to set out clearly the nature and mission of China's national democratic revolution. This boosted the emerging CPC's efforts to establish a revolutionary framework, decide on a strategy for a democratic alliance, and build a unified revolutionary front.

2

THE FIRST POLITICAL STATEMENT

In the early 1920s, around the time that the Communist Party of China was founded, the political situation in China was unstable, and the contest between warlords from the various factions had intensified. This was primarily because both imperialistic and domestic feudal forces were propping up the rule of the warlords. Behind every warlord was an imperial power. When the First World War ended, the contest between the imperial powers over China went from direct to indirect conflict in the form of a proxy war waged by the Chinese warlords, who acted as agents representing the interests of the respective imperial powers. Inevitably, as the contest between the imperial powers over China intensified, the conflicts among the Chinese warlords deepened.

After the death of Yuan Shikai, the Anhui warlords, backed by Japan, controlled the central government in Beijing. In July 1920, the Zhili warlords, backed by Britain and the USA, joined forces with the Fengtian warlords and defeated the main force of the Anhui warlords and took control of Beijing. To regain control, Japan threw its weight behind Fengtian warlord Zhang Zuolin to launch a takeover of the central government. During the Washington Naval Conference, the Fengtian troops swarmed into the Shanhai Pass and attempted to vanquish the Zhili troops. In April and May 1922, the first Zhi-Feng war erupted. The Fengtian troops were defeated and had to retreat. Thereafter, the Zhili warlords monopolized central rule in Beijing. They controlled almost all of the provinces in northern and central China, and set their eyes on expanding their influence southwards. China's political scene plunged into a state of unending internal conflict and widespread war.

The contests and scuffles between the warlords spelled disaster for the Chinese people. The country's finances were heavily strained, and people's lives became harder. The situation was even worse in the war zones, where people barely survived. Under such circumstances, Chinese political groups and their representatives had different views on China's future.

The Zhili warlords, who held onto central power, proposed unifying China by force. Using military force to achieve political aims was a common practice of the Beiyang warlords, as they sought to eliminate their rivals and establish autocracy. Yuan Shikai and Duan Qirui were among the major warlords who had risen to power on the back of military expeditions. After the Zhili warlords had gained control of the central government, Wu Peifu proposed unifying China by force at a military conference in Luoyang. He planned to tap into the imperialists' support and launch a military expedition northward to eliminate Fengtian warlord Zhang Zuolin and his company. He also conspired to join forces with the company of Chen Jiongming of the Guangdong Army to oppose Sun Yat-sen's southern government, and rallied other warlords, including Sun Chuanfang and Yang Sen, to invade provinces such as Fujian, Hunan, and Sichuan in an attempt to unify China.

Local warlords and politicians mooted the idea of a federation of autonomous provinces for China, with the Hunan warlords the first to propose this. In 1920, Tan Yankai – Commander-in-Chief of the Hunan Army – came up with the slogan 'Hunan people to govern Hunan' after expelling the warlord Zhang Jingyao. In November, Tan publicized his proposition through telegrams, in the hope of countering the Zhili faction's proposition of unification by force. In 1921, the Sichuan warlord Liu Xiang sent telegrams proclaiming "complete autonomy for Sichuan." In April, Guizhou warlord Lu Tao sent telegrams proposing "a shift from individual provincial autonomy to a federation of autonomous provinces." After his defeat in the Zhi-Feng war, the Fengtian warlord Zhang Zuolin announced autonomy for Liaoning, Jilin, and Heilongjiang. Soon after, warlords from other provinces either declared autonomous rule for their province or proposed federal rule. Organizations for autonomous movements sprang up everywhere. One such organization was the Joint Office for Autonomous Rule, set up by 15 provinces, including Beijing, Jiangsu, and Anhui. Another was the Association of Autonomous Rule for all provincial representatives in Shanghai. Although these organizations wielded significant societal influence, in reality, the movement for a federation of autonomous provinces was merely an expedient measure for the warlords to combat the consolidation of the central warlords' forces and protect their individual interests.

The bourgeois reformists proposed forming a 'government of good people.' In May 1922, the likes of Hu Shi, Liang Shuming, and Wang Chonghui put out the article 'Our Political Proposition' in the magazine *The Endeavour*. In it, they proposed that China would be saved if Chinese elites came forward to form a 'government of good people.' Backed by the Zhili warlord Wu Peifu, in September that same year, Wang Chonghui, Luo Wengan, Tang Erhe, and others (so-called 'good people' with no political affiliations) formed such a government, with Wang Chonghui as Premier. In reality, power still rested in the hands of the Zhili warlords, who used the puppet government to boost their political standing. This 'government of good people' did not do any real good, and was dissolved after just three months. The harsh reality was that the idea of a 'government of good people' was merely a delusion on the part of a group of bourgeois reformists who were dissatisfied with the current state of affairs but unsupportive of a revolution, as well as liberals and the petty bourgeoisie from the upper stratum of the feudal class. A 'government of good people' simply could not work with scuffles between warlords constantly breaking out and the economic and political crisis in China deepening by the day.

Another proposition from the bourgeois reformists was to 'save China through constitutionalism'. Some reformists dreamed of applying the Western world's model of government to China, transforming and saving it by drawing up a constitution. This view was widely discussed and promoted in magazines such as *The Eastern Miscellany*. Among other things, it was proposed that the constitution should stipulate that the system of military governors, inspector-generals, and the like be abolished, a nationwide tally of military strength and troop distribution be conducted, and a cap be placed on the annual national military budget. The constitution should also ensure the independence of the education system and its funding, promote equality between the sexes, improve people's material situations, and alleviate poverty. Under the autocratic rule of the warlords, the proposition of 'saving China through constitutionalism' was akin to making a deal with the devil, and was an impossible dream of the bourgeois reformists.

Meanwhile, the Kuomintang led by Sun Yat-sen persisted with its stand for a democratic revolution, but failed to propose a revolutionary framework that could rally the people. In November 1920, after the Guangxi warlord forces had been expelled from Guangdong by the Guangdong Army, Sun Yat-sen returned to Guangzhou from Shanghai and relaunched the Constitutional Protection Movement. He was appointed Extraordinary President of the Republic of China at an extraordinary parliamentary session held in Guangdong in April 1921. Sun had planned to tap into Chen Jiongming's military forces to launch the Northern Expedition from Guangdong and unify China. Alas, while Chen Jiongming appeared to stand with the KMT and support Sun Yat-sen's work, even proclaiming to be a socialist, in reality he was working for the imperialists and conspiring with the Zhili warlords. In June 1922, Chen openly staged an armed rebellion, exposing his reactionary colors as an imperialist lackey. Sun Yat-sen was forced to leave Guangzhou, and the second Constitutional Protection Movement and Northern Expedition had to be aborted.

Where was China heading? What kind of future lay in store for its people? These were questions that made Chinese patriots feel troubled, lost, and anxious.

As they built the CPC, Party members began to link the tenets of Marxism to the Chinese revolutionary cause. They actively pondered and searched for a revolutionary framework that suited the Chinese context, using Lenin's theory of colonialism as a guide.

In November 1920, Chen Duxiu led the drafting of the *Manifesto of the Communist Party of China,* in which it was stated, "The communists' goal is to recreate society according to the ideals of communism. However, in order to realize our vision of an ideal society, the first step is to abolish the existing capitalist system, which can only be done by forcefully defeating the capitalist countries." On this, Mao Zedong later commented, "To mention only the socialist revolution without mentioning the anti-imperialist and anti-feudal democratic revolution is an empty dream. But it is basically correct as a program of socialist revolution. However, state ownership of land does not work. The peaceful transition of national capital is unexpected. Even more unexpected is that the revolution did not take the form of a general strike but instead took the form of a people's liberation war led by the CPC – a peasants' war, essentially."

After the official founding of the CPC, its members immediately dived into efforts to overthrow the grisly rule of the reactionary classes and realize socialism. Alas, they soon realized that in a semi-colonial, semi-feudal China, the most pressing task was not going to be an immediate socialist revolution.

At the First National Congress of the Communist Party of China, it was suggested that in principle, the framework of overthrowing bourgeois rule and putting the proletariat in power, stamping out private means of production, and eventually realizing socialism and communism was absolutely right. However, it did not suit China's conditions at the time, because the majority of its modern industries were controlled by foreign capital. Hence, whether it was the rising wave of workers' strikes in Shanghai, Changsha, and Hong Kong, or labor movements in other cities, conflicts with the imperialists were inevitable. Even economic movements to improve workers' lives easily turned into political movements against the imperialists and the warlord government. At the same time, the imperial forces and feudal warlords were always in cahoots, going all out to sabotage public movements, and even resorting to military force to suppress them.

Through these real-world struggles, members of the CPC realized that if the Chinese revolution did not begin by opposing imperialist invasions and warlord rule, China would not gain independence, its people would not be liberated, and it would be impossible to realize socialist and communist ideals. The CPC and the Chinese bourgeois democrats had some similar revolutionary goals, which made cooperation possible. The better understanding of the fundamental problems of the Chinese Revolution that was achieved through these real-world struggles spurred the CPC to concretize the realistic revolutionary goals and strategies needed to realize socialist ideals. With guidance from Lenin and the Comintern during this critical period, the CPC became more certain of the direction that the Chinese Revolution should take. It continued to come up with new revolutionary slogans, and searched actively for a revolutionary framework that suited China's national context.

In May 1922, the Secretariat of the Chinese Labor Union held the First National Labor Conference in Guangzhou, where slogans such as 'Down with Imperialism,' 'Down with the Warlords,' and 'There are many enemies before us, amongst them global imperialism and the local warlords' were first heard. That same month, the Socialist Youth League of China held its First National Congress in Guangzhou, where it proposed to "abolish the military regime and lift China from the oppression of global imperialism." The slogans from these two meetings indicated that the Party recognized that at this point of the revolution, the enemy was not the bourgeoisie but global imperialism and the local feudal warlords. This signaled a turning point in the Party's understanding of the democratic revolution.

As the domestic situation evolved, the Central Committee of the CPC recognized that as an emerging proletarian party in a time of political turbulence and multifarious ideologies, it needed to announce its proposition on the situation in China so as to clarify its stand, make itself known to the Chinese people, and show them the path to revolution.

At that time, Shanghai Party members suggested that the Central Committee of the CPC announce the Party's proposition on the situation in China and clarify its stand as soon as possible, instead of waiting for the Second National Congress to be held. They nominated Chen Duxiu for the drafting of the document, and gave their unanimous approval after a round of discussions and amendments by the Central Bureau. Then, they had someone deliver the document to Beijing for Li Dazhao and the Beijing Party's scrutiny. They unanimously approved it.

On 15 June 1922, the Central Committee of the CPC published the famous 'Communist Party of China's Proposition on China's Situation.' This was the first time that the CPC had publicized its proposition on the weighty issue of the Chinese Revolution. It also marked the start of the Party's use of Marxism-Leninism to analyze the state of Chinese society and resolve the problems of the Chinese Revolution.

The document analyzed China's current political situation and the nature of its society. It fully affirmed the importance of the Xinhai Revolution in the struggle against imperialism and feudalism. It also pointed out that because the bourgeois democratic faction had repeatedly yielded to the old feudal forces, the fruits of the revolution had fallen into the hands of the warlords. Consequently, under the dual oppression of global imperialists and local warlords, China had become a semi-independent feudal country. The document also included analyses and critiques of the various political propositions that had been put forth, such as 'unification by force,' 'a federation of autonomous provinces,' 'a government of good people,' and 'saving China through constitutionalism.' The document clearly stated that these propositions could not turn China's situation around, and reminded workers, peasants, students, and the petty bourgeoisie to "beware of the bourgeois scholars and politicians' compromised pseudo-rhetoric of peace," and to recognize that "the warlord regime is the source of China's domestic and international troubles, as well as the source of the people's suffering." It stressed that "the only way to defeat the warlords is to build a democratic political system."

'The Communist Party of China's Proposition on China's Situation' also clarified the CPC's revolutionary goals and strategies, and proposed the underlying principles of the revolutionary framework. It helped the Party complete the historic task of setting the revolutionary framework at its Second National Congress, and laid the foundation for the Party's politics and ideology.

The CPC's revolutionary view stood out amongst the multifarious political propositions of the time thanks to its boldness and distinctiveness. The fact that the Party announced its political proposition when society was suffering from the autocratic rule of the warlords and bullying from the imperialists demonstrated a great deal of revolutionary courage and a strong sense of mission. The Party's political view provided crucial instructions for a Chinese revolution that had just stepped into a new democratic phase, and helped the people ascertain the way forward in the revolutionary struggle.

3

ESTABLISHING THE GOALS OF THE CHINESE REVOLUTION

"WHO ARE OUR ENEMIES? WHO are our friends? This is the most important question for the revolution."

Thus reads the very first sentence from the first chapter ('An Analysis of the Classes in Chinese Society') in the first volume of the *Selected Works of Mao Zedong*, and it truly hits the nail on the head.

It seems simple enough: For the revolution to succeed, allies and enemies have to be identified, and a correct, clear, and realistic revolutionary framework has to be drawn up.

However, before the founding of the Communist Party of China, one of the key reasons that the Chinese Revolution could not succeed was the failure to identify the targets of the revolution and unite true allies against true enemies. In addition, not one social class nor political party had openly declared imperialism and the feudal warlords as the two biggest enemies of the Chinese Revolution. It was not until the Second National Congress of the CPC that an anti-imperialist, anti-feudal democratic revolutionary framework was clearly proposed, correctly answering the question of the times.

On 16 July 1922, in the sweltering heat of summer, 12 passionate intellectuals dressed as businessmen hurried to No. 625 Fude Lane on South Chengdu Road (now No. 30, Lane 7, North Chengdu Road) in the British Concession of Shanghai. This was the location of Li Da's house – a two-story wood-and-brick structure with a study and bedroom upstairs and a small reception room downstairs. The Second National Congress of the Communist Party of China was held in this very reception room. Li Da's wife, Wang Huiwu, stood at the doorway cradling their child, keeping a lookout for suspicious passersby.[1]

There was a change in the location of the CPC's Second National Congress because Li Hanjun's brother's mansion at No. 106 Wangzhi Road, and Chen Duxiu's house at No. 2 Old Yuyang Lane, both in the French Concession of Shanghai, had been raided by district police in July 1921 and October 1921 respectively. Hence, Li Da's house at No. 625 Fude Lane became an important liaison point as it was unknown to the authorities. It was a short distance from the Li Mansion on Wangzhi Road, and melded perfectly into the rows of identical *shikumen*-style houses with their green and red brick walls. Each house had its own front and back door, allowing guests to enter secretly and leave safely. This, and the fact that it was hard to tell the houses apart, made the location relatively safe.

This was precisely why secret agents were unsuccessful as they scoured the streets and alleys of Shanghai in the suffocating heat, trying to find hints of activity linked to the "scourge" of communism. What was doubly frustrating for these agents was the fact that the CPC's Second National Congress was being held secretly, right under their nose, without them knowing.

The Congress was held from 16 to 23 July 1922. Those who attended were not elected representatives. They had either been nominated by the Central Committee of the CPC or chosen as representatives after internal discussions. As well as members of the Central Committee, the attendees included Party members who had returned from the First Conference of Representatives from Communist Parties and National Revolutionary Organizations of Far Eastern Countries (the Far East Peoples' Conference for short) in Moscow. There were 12 representatives from provincial and district CPC organizations, and they represented the 195 CPC members nationwide.

More stringent measures were taken to ensure the secrecy of the Congress, after the first had been raided by French secret agents. The decision was made to reduce the number of full-scale meetings and hold mostly small gatherings instead. Each meeting was held in a different place. Hence, there were only

1. Zhang, Junfeng. *Beginnings: A Factual Recount of the Founding of the Communist Party of China Part II*, 2011, Jiangsu People's Publishing House, p. 612.

three full-scale meetings held during the eight days of the Congress, and meeting venues were changed three times, making it a highly nerve-racking and secretive affair. The measures taken did ensure secrecy, but they also caused CPC members to lose contact with one other. In a cave dwelling in northern Shaanxi, Mao Zedong told the American journalist Edgar Snow, "I wanted to attend the Second National Congress in Shanghai but couldn't, because I had forgotten where it was being held, and wasn't able find any of my comrades." Because the meeting venues kept changing, Mao Zedong was unable to attend the Second National Congress of the CPC, regrettably missing out on a piece of Chinese history.

The first full-scale meeting of the Congress was conducted by the CPC Central Bureau's general secretary Chen Duxiu, who had been elected at the First National Congress. First on the meeting agenda was a report from the Central Bureau, with Chen Duxiu briefing the representatives on Party work over the past year as well as the progress of labor movements across the country.

In his report, Chen Duxiu expounded on the Party's framework and strategies for China's democratic revolution. He pointed out that as a Chinese proletarian political party, the CPC's ultimate goal was to start a proletarian revolution in China and establish a dictatorship of workers and peasants in line with the principles of communism. However, it was impossible to achieve this goal at that time, given the current social, political, and economic realities in China. What was most important now was to start a democratic revolution. To this end, the CPC had no choice but to help the bourgeoisie overthrow the oppressive imperialists and autocratic feudal warlords so as to build a truly democratic republic. Once the democratic revolution had succeeded, the socialist revolution could begin. After Chen Duxiu's report, Zhang Guotao briefed the representatives on the Far East Peoples' Conference and the First National Labor Conference. He also relayed the Comintern's instructions to the representatives. Thereafter, Shi Cuntong – General Secretary of the Socialist Youth League of China – reported on the League's First National Congress. The Congress representatives discussed these reports and briefings, approved the Central Bureau's work report, and affirmed the Central Committee's proposition on the situation in China.

The second full-scale meeting of the Congress revolved around the seven working principles of the democratic revolution that were to be written into the Congress manifesto. The representatives nominated Chen Duxiu, Zhang Guotao, and Cai Hesen as members of the manifesto team. The team then nominated Chen Duxiu for the job of drafting the manifesto. Chen spent two days drafting it, discussing it, and making amendments with Zhang Guotao and Cai Hesen, before finally completing it for the approval of the Congress representatives.

The third full-scale meeting of the Congress was held on 23 July. To analyze the state of global affairs and China's politico-economic situation, representatives drew on Lenin's theory of colonialism and semi-colonialism, as well as takeaways from the Far East Peoples' Conference. They discussed the Party's mission, approved the 'Manifesto of the Communist Party of China's Second National Congress' and the 'Constitution of the Communist Party of China,' and passed nine resolutions. The representatives also decided to publish the *Weekly Guide* as the Party magazine to promote CPC policies. Finally, they elected Chen Duxiu, Zhang Guotao, Cai Hesen, Deng Zhongxia, and Gao Junyu as members of the Central Executive Committee, with Chen Duxiu assuming the post of Committee President. Cai Hesen and Zhang Guotao were separately placed in charge of the Party's publicity and organization work. With this, the Second National Congress of the Communist Party of China fulfilled its planned agenda and drew to a successful close.

The focus and most important contribution of the CPC's Second National Congress was the proposal of the democratic revolutionary framework, laid out in the historically significant 'Manifesto of the Communist Party of China's Second National Congress.'

The manifesto analyzed the international environment after the First World War and Russia's October Revolution. It looked at the invasion of capitalism and the imperialist powers into China, and how Chinese society had become semi-colonial and semi-feudal. It exposed the invasive nature of imperialism, and informed the people that "the advancement of capitalism in Europe and the USA happened mostly through pillaging Africa and Asia, and turning these regions into mega markets and huge plunder sites." The manifesto also revealed the distinct circumstances of the Chinese Revolution, namely that global imperialists had invaded and plundered China through military, political, economic, and cultural means, causing it to gradually lose its territorial integrity and political independence, and impairing its economic development. The nature of Chinese society had changed, and "China had in fact become a joint colony for all the imperialists, with the Chinese people like meat dangling from the jaws of the avaricious imperialists."

The manifesto revealed the true nature of the Washington Naval Conference, and exposed the hypocrisy and deceit of the imperialists. It told those who still harbored illusions that while the imperialists claimed to be advocates of self-determination and equality for all people, "the Chinese people, having suffered from decades of oppression, know only too well what the imperialists mean by 'equality' and 'self-determination.' They also know only too well that equality and self-determination can only be attained after the capitalist imperialists have been defeated." More accurately, there had been clear and firm objections to Japanese imperialism from around the time of the May Fourth Movement. However, many people still harbored illusions about British and American imperialism, failing to see their invasiveness due to a veil of hypocrisy and deceit. In the early years of the Party's founding, it was impossible to change people's limited understanding of imperialism. It was through the Far East Peoples' Conference and the Second National Congress that the Party was enlightened on the nature of imperialism.

The manifesto also made an in-depth analysis of China's politico-economic situation, and pinpointed the two factors behind Chinese society's semi-colonial and semi-feudal nature. It noted that, with the imperial powers directing China's politics and economy, all of its important political and economic decisions were subject to manipulation by these powers, resulting in the semi-colonial nature of Chinese society. Meanwhile, family farming and cottage industries continued to form the basis of China's economy, and industrial development had a long way to go. With its economy still in a semi-primitive phase, China continued to be ruled by a feudal autocracy of warlords and bureaucrats, resulting in the semi-feudal nature of its society. This autocracy represented the imperialists' interests abroad, and the feudal landlords' interests on home soil. As the manifesto stated, the facts proved that it was capitalist imperialism and the feudal warlord-bureaucrats that had caused the greatest suffering to the Chinese people (i.e. the bourgeoisie, workers, and peasants). Thus, a democratic revolution that opposed these two forces was of great significance. The manifesto went on to say that a truly unified nationalist state could never be established, and domestic peace would never be achieved, unless the oppressive rule of the warlords and global imperialism was brought down.

The manifesto marked out the Party's goals under the current circumstances as ending civil strife, defeating the warlords, establishing domestic peace, overthrowing the oppression of global imperialists, achieving total independence for the Chinese people, and unifying China as a true democratic republic. This effectively set the framework for that stage of the Party's anti-imperialist, anti-feudal democratic revolution. That is to say, it formed the Party's basic revolutionary framework. The manifesto also clarified that the Party's overall goal was to "mobilize the proletariat in a class struggle in order to abolish the system of private ownership and establish a worker-peasant dictatorship, before gradually transforming China into a communist society."

The manifesto stayed true to the overall Party goal set at the First National Congress. This goal determined the Party's overarching revolutionary framework, which, in conjunction with its basic framework, correctly linked the overall revolutionary goal to the revolutionary mission at hand. The two frameworks fused the communist movement and the national democratic revolution, taking a Chinese approach (one that was different from that of the Western capitalist countries and was instead rooted in China's national context), and launching an anti-imperialist, anti-feudal new democratic revolution before progressing to a socialist revolution. This theoretical proposition revealed the fundamental conflicts of Chinese society, and reflected the objective conditions of the Chinese Revolution. It pointed China's new democratic revolution in the only direction that was correct.

The revolutionary framework proposed at the Second National Congress revealed the basic conflicts of Chinese society, and reflected the objective conditions of the Chinese Revolution. It clarified that in its current stage, the Chinese Revolution should take the form of a democratic revolution. Its targets were imperialism and feudalism, and its revolutionary force comprised the workers, the peasants, the petty bourgeoisie, and the national bourgeoisie. The strategy employed in the revolution was to organize all of the classes into a united front. The mission and goal were to overthrow the warlords and the oppressive imperialists to attain independence for the Chinese people and unify China. The future of the revolution was realizing socialism and ultimately communism.

These clear insights carved out the direction of China's new democratic revolution, and played a key role in the development of the Chinese Revolution and the CPC.

From deciding to initiate a socialist revolution at the First National Congress to ascertaining the need to start with a democratic revolution before progressing to a socialist revolution at the Second National Congress, there was a major shift in the Party's strategic direction. It also signaled the success of the Party's innovative efforts to realistically marry the tenets of Marxism with the Chinese Revolution, and marked significant progress for the Party in the Sinification of Marxism.

Within just a year of its founding, the Communist Party of China drew on its advanced thoughts and theories and, with the political courage to break new ground, rooted itself in China's national context. For the very first time, it proposed a clear national framework for an anti-imperialist, anti-feudal democratic revolution. Like a torch beaming through the fog, the CPC cleared away the people's ideological confusion and shone the way forward on China's revolutionary path.

Epilogue

THE WHEELS OF HISTORY ROLL forward. The tide of the times is vast and turbulent.

Since its birth, the Communist Party of China has gone through a difficult but glorious 100 years. Looking back, the Chinese communists' original intention and founding mission was to work for the happiness of the Chinese people and the rejuvenation of the Chinese nation. From then until now, the CPC has taken up its historic responsibility, uniting and leading people from all national ethnic groups to strive onward. Chinese communists have written a magnificent epic that has spanned the nation, accomplishing major changes. They have created a Chinese miracle that has attracted global attention, ushering in the possibility of achieving the great rejuvenation of the Chinese nation.

If we take the founding of the Communist Party of China in 1921 as a dividing line and go back 100 years, we see that in 1821 (the first year of the Qing Dynasty's Daoguang era) the ambitious new emperor tried to restore the decaying feudal empire by strictly banning the opium trade. However, the Opium War of 1840 shattered his illusion. During the 100 years from 1821 to the founding of the Party in 1921, the Chinese nation was at the mercy of others. The Chinese people were oppressed, and in deep distress. Chinese society was impoverished and weak, with internal and external worries. It fell into misery due to frequent wars, and was gradually reduced to a semi-colonial, semi-feudal society.

Following the founding of the Communist Party of China in 1921, China underwent radical changes after a century of hard struggle. The CPC grew from a small secret organization of a few dozen people to the world's largest party with more than 90 million members. The Chinese nation has made a historic leap from decline and poverty to rising up, growing rich, and becoming strong. It is now closer to the goal of great rejuvenation than at any other time in history.

In the century before and after 1921, the fate and development of the Chinese nation were very different. Before, China was sinking. The nation was downtrodden and humiliated, and all of its efforts to save itself ended in failure. In the 100 years after 1921, China rose up. It became independent and strong, and the people were liberated. The struggle, although difficult and convoluted, took great strides towards rejuvenation. The contrast is sharp.

History and reality eloquently illustrate the fact that the great rejuvenation of the Chinese nation is closely linked to the appropriate leadership of the Communist Party of China. Without the CPC, there would be no People's Republic of China. Without its strong leadership, the rejuvenation of the Chinese nation would not be possible.

The revival of the Chinese nation is a historical process in which a nation rises from prosperity to decline, and then re-emerges from decline onto the world stage – a historical process of entering modern civilization and being among the ranks of modernization.

The 100-year history of struggle from 1921 to 2021 tells us that the greatest opportunity for revival is the trend of global progress. If we grasp this trend, we will seize an opportunity. Innovation is the force behind the pursuit of rejuvenation. The desire to constantly innovate runs in the blood of the nation.

Rejuvenation can be achieved by taking bold and significant steps when focusing on development. This is the 'master key' to achieving it. To quote a famous Chinese saying, "while the enemy may have erected a wall of iron, we can succeed by climbing right over it."

Entering a new era, the great rejuvenation of the Chinese nation has ushered in new historical opportunities and unparalleled challenges. In the face of the unprecedented global changes of a century, the Party's Central Committee with General Secretary Xi Jinping at its core has provided new directions, new solutions, and new choices to solve a series of major issues such as China's development, national rejuvenation and the world economy, and global governance. The influence and attractiveness of China's development philosophy, path, and model have been significantly enhanced. China is playing an increasingly important role as a builder of world peace, a contributor to global development, and a defender of the international order, approaching the center of the world stage as never before.

Entering the new era, the Party has put forward a series of new ideas and strategies with great political courage and strong responsibility. It has introduced a series of major policies, launched a series of major initiatives, and promoted a series of major tasks, solving many long-standing problems, and carrying out many major events that had not been attempted before. The Party and the State have made unprecedented achievements, and have undergone historic changes.

In the new era, the Communist Party of China led by General Secretary Xi Jinping has responded to the development of the times, and has systematically answered the major issues of the day in terms of the combination of theory and practice: what kind of socialism with Chinese characteristics ought we uphold and develop in the new era, and how? General Secretary Xi has deepened his understanding of the laws of the Communist Party, socialist construction, and human social development with a new vision, and founded Xi Jinping Thought on socialism with Chinese characteristics in the new era, leading the Chinese nation to great rejuvenation.

All that has passed is a prologue.

Today, socialist China has reached the historical intersection of its 'Two Centenary Goals.' Standing at the coordinates of the past and the future, we firmly believe that the great Communist Party of China will continue to be dynamic and powerful. It will unite and lead the Chinese people to build a modern and powerful socialist country that is rich, strong, democratic, civilized, cohesive, and attractive, and will strive to write a new chapter in the great rejuvenation of the Chinese nation.

Index

ABOUT THE AUTHORS

Shao Weizheng is a renowned Party history expert and an authoritative scholar on the history of the founding of the Communist Party of China. He has proved the date of the CPC's First National Congress and the number of attendees, solving two long-standing problems in Party history, and producing far-reaching effects in China and abroad. Shao is the author of the first history of the founding of the CPC in China, and the editor of *Sunrise in the East – A Chronicle of the Founding of the Communist Party of China*, which is listed as recommended reading for Party members by the Central Propaganda Department's Theory Bureau and the Central Organization Department's Cadre Education Bureau. Shao was editor-in-chief of *Party History for Youth*, which was selected for the 2020 Popular Theory Readings Publishing Project. He lectures on CCTV's Lecture Room, '100 Stories of Party History', and is the most senior presenter of the CCTV program, Lecture Room.

Liu Xiaobao is an Associate Professor at the National Defense University, and has participated in the writing of books such as *Party History for Youth* and *The Red Boat Reflects the Original Intention.*